In the Zone:
The Twilight World
of Rod Serling

In the Zone:
The Twilight World
of Rod Serling

Peter Wolfe

Bowling Green State University Popular Press
Bowling Green, OH 43403

Copyright © 1997 Bowling Green State University Popular Press

Library of Congress Cataloging-in-Publication Data
Wolfe, Peter, 1933-
    In the zone : the twilight world of Rod Serling / Peter Wolfe.
      p. cm.
    Includes bibliographical references and index.
    ISBN 0-87972-729-2 (clothbound). -- ISBN 0-87972-730-6 (pbk.)
    1. Twilight zone (Television program). 2. Serling, Rod, 1924-
--Criticism and interpretation. I. Title.
PN 1992.77.T87W66   1996
791.45'72--dc21
                                      96-47540
                                          CIP

Cover design by Gary Dumm

To

My Two

(the way it should be)

Cheekmaster J. Cheekmonger

and

Meetie Q. Meetno

—the walk

—the place

—the food

Contents

Acknowledgments

The author thanks those whose time and care, expertise and energy, went into the preparation of this book: Brenda Jaeger, who typed and edited the final draft; Philip Wolfe, who supplied important details of technical production regarding matters like lighting, camera positioning, and miking; Roland Champagne, who helped fill in the cultural background; Lucinda Williams and Judy Moresi, who located important out-of-print material; Ron Simon of New York's Museum of Television and Radio, who provided access to the Museum's Serling tapes; Arlen Schumer, who shared his expertise in Serling and the *Zone*; Martin Sage, Jane Williamson, and Costa Haddad, who helped organize a grant that sped the book's production.

The combined help of the following people amounts to a major contribution: Beverly Bateman, Phil Van Zandt, Harry Rivers, Bob Brazil, John Strebler, Pat Balaban, Edie Ball, Deborah Cardwell, Jim Colquhoun, and John H. Stevens.

Introduction

The main body of this work consists of a thematic, artistic, and technical analysis of *The Twilight Zone*, a television anthology first shown on CBS from the fall of 1959 to the late spring of 1964. Justifying the analysis is the truth that *The Twilight Zone* was the best art-directed show in TV history and one of the most influential. The show's founder, main scriptwriter, and artistic director, Rod Serling, if not a household name today, remains one of the very few TV personalities of his time whose name, voice, and face are known to many Americans born after 1950. And why shouldn't they be? He won six Emmys and served for two years as president of the National Academy of Television Arts and Sciences. What's more, these honors were deserved. In the early 1950s, he gave up his job as a radio scriptwriter in Cincinnati to write TV plays. The change forced him to learn how to write for the eye rather than the ear in order to exploit TV's capacity for intimacy. He mastered this difficult art so well that he made a brilliant career of it. And even though that career sometimes lagged, this author of more than 200 teleplays (Sander 225) set the standard by which his counterparts gauged themselves. But he was more than a conscientious writer of first-rate plays. Of the four hottest young scriptwriters of TV's so-called Golden Age (Gore Vidal, Reginald Rose, and Paddy Chayevsky were the others), only Serling continued writing for the small screen rather than caving in to the lure of the movies.

But his decision to devote himself wholeheartedly to TV sometimes rankled. The reasons for his discontent lay mostly within him. A look at the life and psyche of this complex, conflictive man suggests that he often subverted his joy. Serling qualifies as TV's last angry man (to invoke the subtitle of Gordon F. Sander's excellent 1992 biography) partly because of his feuds with those sponsors and studio chiefs who favored lightweight formula programming over his more serious, challenging teleplays. Much of his wrath turned inward, as well. Becoming the most honored writer in video history failed to quiet the demons of this truculent man-child of five-feet-four-and-a-half inches who smoked four packs of cigarettes a day.

Perhaps, like some of his protagonists, he never knew what he wanted, this hot-tempered dynamo with a nostalgic streak. An ethnic

1

Jew, he married a Protestant blueblood and later became a Unitarian. Though haunted by the combat duty he saw as a paratrooper in the Philippines, he always wore a bracelet bearing the insignia of the Army Air Corps. Deeply insecure, he always wanted to be the center of attention. And he would go to extremes to gain his goal. To his intimates' dismay, he never outgrew a schoolboyish penchant for supermacho antics and the telling of smutty jokes.

On the credit side, this sometimes difficult colleague and friend compels our admiration as a writer. He tests our assumptions about humanity both by asking us how to live well and by searching for the best human life. Moreover, he does this important work without overstepping the bounds of reason and artistic probability. His most famous character, Mountain McClintock of "Requiem for a Heavyweight" (aired 10/56), has to quit the ring. Nor can he get a college degree. But this washed-up fighter has other options. For instance, his warmth, patience, and training can help youngsters acquire athletic skills in a day camp or youth center. A life change won't be any easier for him than for any number of *Twilight Zone* heroes, though. Serling portrays good people who want to lead good, decent lives but sometimes err when the demands of being good overwhelm them. The struggle can take different forms. For instance a *Twilight Zone* play will portray the agonies of military command, the penalties entailed by getting one's wish, or the grip of the dead upon the living. Also prompting health and vitality is Serling's love of the neglected and the discarded—buildings and neighborhoods as well as people.

Irradiating all is a fund of patience and common sense this neglectful husband and father might have drawn from to improve his own life. His belief in the second chance, for instance, both helps lighten our burdens and makes the world a more forgiving place. Just as valuable is his view of life as an organic continuum. The lives we lead are the ones we have been building; they stem directly from our taste in food, clothes, and music, our jobs, and our household routines. Consistent with the faces we wear and the dreams we dream, they're what we deserve. They constitute a reality as binding as our lymph glands and our digestive tracts. People in the zone who deny their defining realities, say, by colonizing another planet or by changing identities, always come to grief. The explanation for their woes lies close at hand: the place we run to always turns out to be worse than the place we fled.

This excellent advice reached a large audience. When *The Twilight Zone* debuted in October 1959, nine out of every ten American homes had TVs, many of which were tuned to CBS at 8:00 p.m.(ET) every Friday. Most of the show's viewers snapped off their sets at 8:30 feeling that the teleplay they had just witnessed had somehow either jostled or thickened their worlds.

Without having met Serling, I felt in 1975, when he died, like many of these viewers; I had lost, if not a friend, then someone who spoke to my inner self. At times, usually while thinking about *The Twilight Zone,* I still find myself trying to believe that he was less unpleasant than is believed, as we do with family nuisances whom we love. My efforts may be misguided. His struggles with himself had one happy outcome—the sensibility that produced *Twilight Zone* scripts still admired today, like "The Sixteen-Millimeter Shrine" (10/59) and "On Thursday We Leave for Home" (5/63). The internal cost of writing scripts like these is conveyed in part by Serling's early death at 50. The cost is still being tallied by his survivors. For them, the account can never be squared. Yet, it can't be written off as a loss. If we accept Freud's notion of the artist as a battlefield, we can then view the inner conflicts that may have killed Serling prematurely as the polarities that energized his art. For this field of creative energy we must be grateful. Nor would we be alone in expressing our gratitude. A true pro, Serling would have approved of it. How warmly we can probably guess. The tolerance and good will he always tried to extend to others might well have led him to say what the hell and join us in confirming his career a success.

1

Probing Vertically

The *Twilight Zone* episode called "Static" (aired 3/61) opens with some boarding house residents staring at a TV set. They're watching a western. Charles Beaumont, author of "Static" made the teleplay a western for at least two reasons. Westerns dominated television; the Nielsen ratings had *Gunsmoke* (CBS) and *The Rifleman* (ABC) at the top of the popularity charts for August 1959 (Barnouw 213-14). Shows like *The Rifleman,* along with *Cheyenne, Death Valley Days,* and *Davy Crockett,* shunned serious adult issues in favor of entertaining audiences with tales of action and adventure. The chase on horseback being witnessed in "Static" harks to this escapism. It's also used to counterpoint the deeper interactions probed by the radio performers of Beaumont's and Rod Serling's youth, like Major Bowes, Fred Allen, and Tommy Dorsey, particularly Dorsey's rendition of the Washington-Bassman song, "I'm Getting Sentimental Over You," which is both heard and danced to in Beaumont's telescript.

This counterpoint invokes another. Though Serling, the guiding force of *The Twilight Zone*, had a nostalgic streak, he also welcomed advances in the media. A TV anthology series like *Have Gun, Will Travel* proved that the western could deal with moral complexity and maturity. Rather than taking an elitist stance, the easterner Serling adopted the same standpoint as that of the Richard Boone series. The frontier drama, "The Grave" (10/61), treats hidden guilt. Serling's "Showdown with Rance McGrew" uses the format of the popular TV western just as insightfully. As its punning title suggests, this February 1962 teleplay both criticizes the sagebrush-flavored pap served to passive TV watchers of the day and, more surprisingly, includes a hidden manifesto: Serling's overturning of the clichés infesting many of the day's TV dramas of the Old West reflects a resolve to treat his materials honestly. This resolve declared itself in "Jess-Belle," a hour-long episode that aired in February 1963, the same month that *The Beverly Hillbillies* topped the Nielsen survey as television's most popular program (Barnouw 314). Rather than patronizing rustics, like *The Beverly Hillbillies* or *Green Acres,* Earl Hamner Jr.'s "Jess-Belle" uses them to investi-

5

gate questions like community bonding, sexual love, and demonic possession.

Avoiding the easy way out helped *The Twilight Zone* imbue the hour format elsewhere with sophistication and depth. Inspired by the millions who watched Lt. Col. John Glenn's February 1962 orbit around the earth, Richard Matheson adapted his short story "Death Ship" for *Twilight Zone*. The February 1963 teleplay shows three spacemen trapped in a cycle that will stop them from returning home to earth. Serling's "The Parallel" (3/63) hews more closely to the Glenn prototype. It shows an astronaut orbiting the earth and then supposedly touching down 46 miles from liftoff, where he discovers a universe parallel to our own.

The astronaut's strange discovery inspired Serling. Perhaps the first writer to understand television's artistic potential, he always warmed to such challenges. In April 1960, the Serling-written "Big Tall Wish" had appeared on *The Twilight Zone*, not only starring the black actor Ivan Dixon but also featuring a black-dominated cast, a breakthrough so bold it may have been unprecedented. Other acts of boldness followed. "The Rip van Winkle Caper" (4/61) and "The Long Morrow" (1/64) addressed the question of suspended animation. Five years before Stanley Kubrick's *2001: A Space Odyssey,* "Uncle Simon" (11/63) described some of the dangers of artificial intelligence, a topic depicted in "From Agnes—With Love" (2/64). Some of the ideas depicted on *The Twilight Zone* remain alive. Although the treatment differs greatly, the reversing of time's forward flow, portrayed in both "Valley of the Shadow" (1/63) and "A Short Drink from a Certain Fountain" (12/63), anticipates Martin Amis's 1991 novel *Time's Arrow;* the freezing of time in an urban setting in "A Kind of Stopwatch" (10/63) causes some of the same surprises found in Nicholson Baker's *The Fermata* (1994).

Adult problems first mooted by TV talk-show hosts and group-therapy leaders in the 1980s also got air time on *The Twilight Zone*. One of these consisted of the problems faced by older adults. Like the August 1953 *Kraft Television Theater* production of Serling's "Old MacDonald Had a Curve," *The Twilight Zone*'s "Kick the Can" (2/62) describes elders who want their juniors to take them as seriously as they take themselves. The play shows, among other things, that, in the right hands, fantasy transcends escapism. Underscoring Ernest Truex's brilliant performance as elderly Charles Whitley, Serling explains, in his epilogue, or closing narration, that "childhood, maturity, and old age are curiously intertwined and not separate" (qtd. in Zicree 262). He speaks home. All of us would gain from enacting aspects of childhood, middle age, and maturity every day; a balanced, healthy life rests most firmly on a regimen that includes play, or exercise, work, and rest. In "Kick the Can," a brilliant refutation of sociogenic aging, the elders who romp like youngsters are scorned and resented by peers who lack both the nerve and the imagination to follow their lead.

Should some restraint be observed? Naturally. It takes Professor Ellis Fowler of "The Changing of the Guard" (6/62) both time and heartache to realize that after 51 years in the classroom, he should have retired long before his headmaster orders him to; during an interview with the headmaster, Fowler lets on that he hasn't opened his mail for two weeks. Harmon Gordon of "A Short Drink," by trying to vibrate as keenly as a wife 40 years his junior, burns so much of his sagging energy that he forfeits the joys of maturity. Serling's conservative, common-sense attitude toward the elderly, stated in his monologue and enacted in his December 1963 script, allows for drama. Both "The Incredible World of Horace Ford" (4/63) and "Long-Distance Call" (3/61) disclose the stresses caused by adults of different generations living in the same space. These stresses can metastasize, "Call" and "Young Man's Fancy" (5/62) portraying the tremendous force that a dead mother or grandmother can exert from the grave. Do the two dead women want their descendants with them? we wonder. The life that those descendants would have to forfeit to effect such a union calls into question the nature of love. Is love always tainted by selfishness? If it ignores responsibility to the beloved does it stop being love?

The Twilight Zone looks squarely at such tough questions, even though the half-hour format of most of the shows (and the best shows, at that) rules out a comprehensive treatment. "The Purple Testament" (2/60), which unfolds during combat in the Philippines, deals with paranormal powers and altered states of mind. In it, Lt. William Fitzgerald acquires a fearful potency: any soldier who appears to him with his face glowing and haloed will soon die in battle. In "Mute" (1/63), a child taught by her parents to communicate telepathically loses the power when she's orphaned but without learning, in the meantime, how to talk. A disorder getting still more attention today than *The Twilight Zone* explores is that of alcoholism. Works like "A World of Difference" (3/60), "The Encounter" (5/64), and "Spur of the Moment" (2/64), show drink shattering people's jobs, homes, and self-worth.

The Twilight Zone's final episode, "The Bewitchin' Pool" (6/64), depicts a shattering of a different sort—that perpetrated by Serling's generation of achievers. These parents of our own baby boomers, i.e., those Americans born between 1946 and 1964, having survived the storms of both the Depression and World War II, carried a heavy load of insecurity into adulthood. As a result, many of them, riveting upon the tangible, became materialistic and status obsessed. This perversion of tradition, especially those values centering on the family, gains expression through Gloria and Gil Sharewood's California mansion and adjoining swimming pool. Whereas Aunt T, guiding spirit of a "backwoods paradise" (Zicree 398), extols the dignity of work to the Sharewood children, Gloria and Gil turn work into a battleground: she accuses him of burying himself in his job, and he derides her resolve to re-enter the work force. Rather than choosing between them, when they announce that they're divorcing, their two kids dive into the family's swimming pool and, through a dislocation of the space-time continuum, resurface in the pond adjoining Aunt T's community of children. As a teleplay, "The Bewitchin' Pool" is one of the lamest in the *Twilight Zone* canon. But, as the apostrophe before the adjective in its title suggests, the work does voice a preference for earthiness and decency over the freeway glitz dividing people both from each other and themselves.

I

The Twilight Zone usually serves serious warnings without compromising its entertainment value. The show is as enjoyable as it is provocative. The fun takes different forms. Figures like Shakespeare, Lincoln, and, in another story, his assassin, John Wilkes Booth, play major roles. Elsewhere, our own century supplies the figures of Hitler and Khrushchev. Such turns have kept the term "the twilight zone" in common usage even though the vehicle that introduced it left the air in 1964. James Edward Parker has noted the term's unique persistence: "The Twilight Zone's unique format and imaginative writing have made the show title a household term used to describe some place and situation that is strange and unusual" (2). The term occurs everywhere, coming from the mouth of prizefighter Archie Moore, Secretary of State Dean Rusk, or a character in Tony Kushner's *Angels in America* (New York: Theater Communications Group, 1993, 94-95). In the film *The Naked Gun 2 1/2: The Smell of Fear* (1991), directed by David Zucker, Lloyd Bochner repeats a line said to him in the March 1962 *Twilight Zone* episode "To Serve Man." The *Twilight Zone* legacy takes many forms. First recorded in 1980, Bernard Hermann's song, "The Twilight Zone," has become a staple in the repertory of one of America's outstanding vocal groups, the Manhattan Transfer. *Rod Serling's The Twilight Zone Magazine* ran as a monthly from April 1981 to June 1989 even though its eponym had died in 1975. Chucky, the demonic red-headed doll who performs a series of murders in the film *Child's Play* (1988) and its sequels, probably owes his life to the angelic-looking Talky Tina of "Living Doll" (11/63).

Talky Tina has resonated in the popular imagination because of the way her words reach their hearers. These hearers include us. To witness statements like "My name is Talking Tina and I'm going to kill you" coming from a sweet, high-pitched voice and a frozen baby doll's smile is to know the uncanny. It also means knowing an economy of means associated with *The Twilight Zone*, a strategy developed to offset the constraints imposed by the half-hour format (which translates to 23 or 24 minutes of playing time) most of the shows were fitted to. Animating this economy is excellence in writing, directing, and acting. Much of it inheres in knowing what to leave out and how to control the viewer's response to what's left in. For instance, we may wonder how Christian Horn of "A Hundred Yards over the Rim" (4/61) leaps forward 114 years in time by stepping over the brow of a hill. But no explanation is given because explanations, being static, usually slow dramatic pace. Similarly, the aging John and May Holt of "The Trade-Ins "(4/62) go to the New Life Corporation to rejuvenate their bodies and spirits. Instead of questioning the technology that causes the rejuvenation, the Holts accept it.

If much of the grip of *The Twilight Zone* stems from a deadpan acceptance of the outlandish, much takes root, as well, in memorable phrasing. Five Serling-written episodes clinch the point. Though remembered mostly as a TV personality, Serling wrote rich, provocative prose. A character in "Third from the Sun" (1/60) conveys Serling's phrase-making skill by saying "have some cards" rather than "play cards" while looking for ways to fill in time before embarking on an illicit rocket launch. The arresting phrase, "have some cards," evokes the same singularity set forth by the episode's title. Speech is also richly evocative in "A Stop at Willoughby" (5/60). The imperative barked by a tyrannical advertising executive, "This is a push business! A push-push-push business! Push and drive! All the way!" shows Gart Williams, his gentle, introspective junior colleague, to whom it's addressed, that the pressures of his job will crush him. What suits him better is the small-town ease of America in 1888, a milieu where "a man can slow down to a walk and live his life full measure." This phrase, uttered by a train conductor, and the executive's dog-eat-dog imperative define, between them, the boundaries of Williams's world and the limits of his hopes. What's more, they do this important work more economically than would pages of brooding analysis or even dramatic interchange.

Without trying to reduce a rich, complex teleplay to a phrase, Serling nonetheless imbues "Dust" (1/61) with a line of dialogue that lodges immediately in our hearts and keeps resonating there long after we have switched off our televisions. The words "Pay heed to the magic!" are spoken by the desperate father of a youth about to be hanged for murder. Old Gallegos, the youth's father, claims that the dust he bought from a dishonest peddler who scooped it off the desert will save his son's life. The magic he refers to in his desperation subsumes both human and divine love. This desperation also galvanizes the magic. The snapping of the rope when the trap on which Luis is standing is sprung insures the youth's survival. It also evokes the continuity between sacred and profane love. In a stroke reminiscent of Graham Greene, God has interceded and, against all probability, snapped a thick coil of fresh rope. Both the physical and emotional climate in which the miracle occurs lend force to the enjoinder "Pay heed to the magic!" Everything has been brightened, blessed, and redeemed. Divine mercy has superseded man's justice, symbolized in the play (as in "Execution" [4/60] and "I Am the Night—Color Me Black" [3/64]) by the locals whose savagery has drawn them to the "necktie party." Their frustration expresses Serling's belief that God can manifest Himself in the most ugly, squalid settings, like the depressed, baking frontier outpost where "Dust" takes place.

The landscape of "A Hundred Yards Over the Rim" (4/61) is also parched and bitter. But this harshness is as redeemable as that of "Dust." This potential for spiritual uplift surfaces quickly in Christian Horn, leader of a convoy of migrants from Ohio already worn and whipped by the rigors of their overland march to California. When one of Horn's fellow pilgrims announces his resolve to return home from what is now New Mexico, he's answered in language quick and sharp: "If you try to go the 1500 miles back to St. Louis, I guarantee you'll leave your bones bleached on some desert, or lose your scalps, or freeze on a mountain pass." This warning foreshadows the truth that Christian Horn, like John Bunyan's Christian in *Pilgrim's Progress,* is a suffering wayfarer whose faith leads him to the promised land. Though weak and malnourished, Horn relies increasingly on his tie with God to help him endure the long, hard westward pull. This tie, never far from his consciousness, declares itself most dramatically in the following statement, made to the owners of a roadside diner into whose time frame, 1961, he has just slid: "I may be crazy, or the world may be turned upside down. But I know I've been put here for a reason." Both Chris's words and the events leading from them create a religious drama as vital as 23 or 24 minutes of playing time will allow. While preserving God's mystery, the teleplay invokes the interdependence of people, the unity swathing all creation, and, by extending the life of Chris's sick son into the twentieth century, the might of God's benevolence.

The most trenchant truths in *The Twilight Zone* usually come from people ripped from the safety of their daily routines. A man in "Jess-

Belle" (2/63) made promises to his lady love with a face "hot as blood."
In a show aired the previous month, "The Thirty-Fathom Grave," Chief
Bosun's Mate Bell reveals that longstanding guilt has eaten away his
peace and security. Like Serling's "The Rack," performed in April 1955
for ABC's *United States Steel Hour,* and the *Twilight Zone* play "The
Last Flight" (2/60), "Grave" probes the ambiguities rising from combat
cowardice. Strange tapping noises coming from the sea floor near
Guadalcanal are heard on the destroyer on which Chief Bell is now serving. The noises come from a submarine sunk 20 years before by Japanese fire. The dizziness overtaking Bell leads to the disclosure that he, the
only survivor of the attack that sank the sub, may have betrayed his shipmates by deserting his post. Now these dead shipmates want him to join
them inside the sub's rusting hull. "They're calling muster on me!" Bell
shouts before diving into the sea, where he later drowns. Nor can the
rescue teams that follow him into the Pacific find his body. The mystery
of unity has reasserted itself. Memorable in their own right, Bell's last
words tie in with the motif of the second chance (Zicree 46), prominent
in Serling's most famous teleplay, "Requiem for a Heavyweight," produced on CBS's *Playhouse 90* in October 1956. The motif recurs in the
Twilight Zone scripts "The Last Flight" and "In His Image" (1/63). Bell's
anguished last cry chimes with the *Twilight Zone* sensibility ("Last
Flight" was written by Richard Matheson, and "In His Image" by
Charles Beaumont). It proves that no self-doubter who believes himself
unworthy of a second chance will get one.

But even more striking than the language of *The Twilight Zone* are
the show's visual images, television depending chiefly upon the camera
for its richness and impact. Regardless of the images the *Twilight Zone*
fan cherishes, many of them convey the photographic skill distinguish-
ing the series. One can single out the glowing, spinning horses on a
carousel bearing Martin Sloan in "Walking Distance" (10/59) jump-cut-
ting to a 45-rpm record blaring rock-and-roll music in an ice-cream
parlor. The forward flow of time asserts its relentlessness again at the
climax of "Long Live Walter Jameson" (3/60), where the title character
ages and then crumbles to dust. An effect just as eerie and perhaps more
moving comes in "The Eye of the Beholder" (11/60); the disfigured rub-
bery-looking faces of the medical staff of a hospital exude pity for beautiful Janet Tyler as she leaves her room after the final attempt to make
her look like everybody else has failed. Another distraught woman,
Marsha White, is seen through a pane of pebbled glass in "The After
Hours" (6/60), and the grief of a whole population finds expression in
the paint running down a canvas on "the hottest day in history" in "The
Midnight Sun" (11/61).

The power generated by a visual image often depends upon the skill of the actor or actors who help form the image. In this regard, the casting of *The Twilight Zone* reflects both technical skill and an uncanny foresight. Many of the *Twilight Zone* episodes included young actors with more promise than reputation. A youthful Doug McClure appears in "Mr. Denton on Doomsday" (10/59). Another early show, "Judgment Night" (12/59) has in its cast both Patrick MacNee, who would costar opposite Diana Rigg in the next decade in *The Avengers,* and James Franciscus, the title figure in the TV anthology *Mr. Novak.* "Mirror Image" (2/60) includes a young Martin Milner, known today for his acting in *Route 66* (1960-64) and *Adam 12* (1968-75). And in Leonard Nimoy of "A Quality of Mercy" (12/61), Greg Morris of "The 7th Is Made Up of Phantoms" (12/63), and Martin Landau of both "Denton" and "The Jeopardy Room" (4/64), *The Twilight Zone* trained three young actors who would later win friends as regulars in the series *Mission Impossible.* In this vein, *The Twilight Zone* used child actress Ann Jillian of "Mute" (1/63), who later played adult roles on television (Zicree 308). Mirroring this phenomenon is the appearance in *The Twilight Zone* of former child stars Roddy McDowell ("People Are Alike All Over" [3/60]), Mickey Rooney ("Last Night of a Jockey" [10/63]), and Jackie Cooper ("Caesar and Me" [4/64]) in adult roles.

The range of actors who played in *The Twilight Zone* reflects both the imagination and the diligence of the show's casting department. From the London stage came Gladys Cooper and Donald Pleasance. Buster Keaton's turn in "Once Upon a Time" (12/61) wins charm from the restoration of devices from Keaton's heyday, the silent film era, like the use of cards to replace dialogue, a clunking piano supplying background music, and a camera that shot 16 frames a second rather than the customary 24 in the scenes from the teleplay that occur in 1890. The fun created by such professionalism casts a wide net. Presumably, actors enjoyed performing in *The Twilight Zone.* Gladys Cooper and the younger Gail Kobe appeared three times, as did Russian actor Vladimir Sokoloff—each time as a Latino (in "Dust" [1/61], "The Mirror" [10/61], and "The Gift" [4/62]). A handful of male actors, John Anderson, Cyril Delevanti, Jack Klugman, and Burgess Meredith, put in four appearances. One actor, Vaughn Taylor, appeared five times. But the record for *Twilight Zone* appearances belongs to bit player Jay Overholts, who can be found in "Where Is Everybody?" (10/59) and "One for the Angels" (10/59) from the show's first season; "A Thing about Machines"(10/60), "The Odyssey of Flight 33" (2/61), "Twenty-Two" (2/61), and "Static" (3/61) from the second; and "The Jungle" (12/61) and "Showdown with Rance McGrew" (2/62) from the third.

But as amusing as such trivia are, they shouldn't mislead us into applying quantitative judgments to *The Twilight Zone*. Called by Arlen Schumer in a multimedia talk given in Chicago in June 1991 "the greatest art-directed television show," *The Twilight Zone* always stressed quality. Thus its directors and producers could inspire the best energies of the talent and technicians associated with it. Though Agnes Moorehead lives in posterity as Citizen Kane's mother, she also won the hearts of many video views for her tour de force acting in the one-person *Twilight Zone* play, "The Invaders" (1/61). Other great performances include those of Donald Pleasance in "The Changing of the Guard" (6/62), Robert Duvall in "Miniature" (2/63), Pat Hingle in "The Incredible World of Horace Ford" (4/63), and James Whitmore in "On Thursday We Leave for Home" (5/63). One of the series' most shining moments, Art Carney's drunken speech in "Night of the Meek "(12/60), about the need to make Christmas something finer and nobler than department-store commercialism, would have either crumbled or sunk into a bog of sentimentalism delivered by a lesser actor. But Carney's timing, vocal control, and sensitivity to his character, all augmented by the close-up camera shots of the joins in his false beard, make the speech vivid and penetrating.

As is implied by Schumer's praise of the art direction of *The Twilight Zone*, the show has the breadth and the flexibility to accommodate the clean, raw vivacity of actors like Richard Conte or Steve Cochran, the charm and sophistication of Wilfrid Hyde-White or Cecil Kellaway, and the silent-film antics of Buster Keaton. The Serling sensibility that unified the series also included in its scope the use of different production techniques. "Kick the Can" (2/62) opens with a wide-angle shot of a retirement home. When the action moves indoors, the camera tracks to various residents, or inmates, of the home, all of whom look weak, vague, and joyless. The first elder who shows any pep, played by Ernest Truex, also displays a trace of guilt as he descends the stairs, presumably to leave the home forever. This emotional counterpoint carries into the next scene. The car that Charles Whitley, the Truex character, climbs into remains motionless. This extended image of immobility exerts added pressure by being seen against a hillside swarming with children.

The rhythm created by such moments turns the mind to poetry and music. And the place the rhythm suffuses is known as the twilight zone. Serling's practice of ending most of his prologues and epilogues with references to the zone impinges upon elements of programming and formatting that blur the term's meaning. Curiously, little is lost as a result, since the blurring of normal guidelines and definitions gives the term its savor. Savor it has. Twilight or dusk was the poet William Wordsworth's favorite time of day because its softening of daytime clarity muffled the contours of objects in a way that brought out vital hidden truths about them. These truths stir the imagination, which is good, because the imagination can perceive their worth more accurately than either the noonlit faculty of reason or the blackness of night. Serling, too, valued the soft, gray twilight as a realm unto itself. It hasn't yet taken on the romance or terror of night while having also left behind the pragmatism of day. In its velvet grip, differences vanish, and shapes merge in strange, intriguing combinations. The eye can't be trusted. Serling called the zone "that shadowy area of the almost-but-not-quite; the unbelievable told in terms that can be believed" (Naha 35). Fact undergirds the Zone. The believable can't be dislodged: the gray-lit zone flows from the realm our workaday selves inhabit; in fact, it's part of that realm.

When *The Twilight Zone* was dropped by CBS in 1964 after five seasons, Serling rejected ABC's offer to buy it because ABC wanted to turn it into a series of ghost stories. This format would have been limiting. The twilight zone can reorder the appearance-reality dualism. It can also make us rethink the borderline dividing shadow from substance. Serling's prologue to "The Incredible World of Horace Ford" (4/63) called it "a special province, uncharted and unmapped, a country of both shadow and substance." In the zone, mannequins ("The After Hours") and robots ("Uncle Simon") can function like people, and the casual acceptance of the fantastic (e.g., time travel in "No Time Like the Past") takes on added force thanks to provocative camera techniques. But all of this is anchored in the dailiness of daily living. Hectic Edward Hall of Charles Beaumont's "Perchance to Dream" (11/59) tells a psychiatrist, "The mind is everything." Serling agrees with Hall up to a point, since truth in the twilight zone comes more often in delirium, hallucination, or nightmare than in fact. What's more, much of the impact of the series' best episodes, like "The Sixteen-Millimeter Shrine" (10/59) or "Shadow Play" (5/61), trades on the elusiveness of the line dividing body and mind.

But the line keeps beckoning us. One of Serling's prologues calls the twilight zone the "dimension of the imagination," while another refers to it as "a wondrous land whose boundaries are that of the imagination." The link with English romantic poetry has returned to view. The person who enters the zone is mentally active. Rather than merely observing, he/she records, transforms, and creates. Whereas some find the zone sinister and forbidding, others benefit from knowing this "middle ground" (Zicree 17, 121). Though jobless, broke, and alcoholic, Joey Crown of "A Passage for Trumpet" (5/60) uses the revelation that life offers many small joys to reject the death he had invited by throwing himself in the path of a moving car. The motif recurs in "Passage on the Lady Anne" (5/63), during which a couple decides to rebuild their troubled marriage rather than divorcing; because it fends off death, love deserves our best efforts, the Ransomes discover. Preservation isn't always the issue. Though Erich Streator of "Living Doll" (11/63) dies because of the "unwelcome addition" of Talky Tina into his home, he might have benefited from it. Referring to the doll, Serling says of Streator in his prologue that, "without her he'd never enter the twilight zone." He needed the lesson he learned there, even if he had to pay for it with his life; families are built on love. His failure to survive, let alone profit from, this lesson is his own fault. Like Chief Bell of "The Thirty-Fathom Grave" (1/63), he's a self-blamer who'd rather cling to his low self-esteem (he believes that he's sterile) than risk the imponderables of love. Perhaps Serling blesses his entry into the zone because people like him spoil life for those close to him.

A milder punishment awaits Roger Shackleforth of "The Chaser" (5/60). "Madly, passionately, illogically, miserably, all-consumingly" in love with a woman indifferent to him, he gives the woman a love potion he had bought for a dollar. The potion works all too well. Leila's indifference gives way to a devotion so sticky and suffocating that Roger pays $1000 for some undetectable poison he later tips into her champagne. Her announcement that she's pregnant, though, makes him drop the glass containing the poison. He can't go through with the murder. But his act of mercy or cowardice brings the recognition that he's now shackled to Leila forever. Serling pities him, calling him, in the show's epilogue, "a lover boy who should have never entered the twilight zone."

On what evidence does he base his opinion? Roger erred by opting for the quick fix. The harm he causes by denying reality is symbolized at the outset by the impatient people lined up behind him while he tries again and again to telephone an indifferent Leila. Had he not bought the love potion right after ringing Leila, he might have found a more suitable mate. Now he's chained to a slavishly attentive one. His plight is emblematic. The outcome of a journey into the twilight zone always refers to daily living. The laws that limit all of us will snap back into place. Just as Keats's glimpse of eternity in the "Nightingale" ode ends with a return to the prose of everyday, so must wayfarers in the twilight zone rejoin the common tide, if they can. Entering the zone is an imaginative act. Once there, people find themselves immediately tested. The epilogue to "Once Upon a Time" (12/61) endorses the imperative "Stay in your own back yard." George P. Hanley of "I Dream of Genie" (3/63) finds that happiness can't come from money, power, or fame. It's an impulse from within. Nor will time travel make it happen, as the main figures of "Walking Distance" (10/59)," A Stop at Willoughby" (5/60), and "No Time Like the Past" (3/63) learn. Serling has a Tolstoyan contempt for single causes. Life to him is process; largely, we get the faces and the lives we're meant to get, and these realities usually stem from events and attitudes that have been in place for decades. The title figure of "The Trouble with Templeton" (12/60) revisits the past, but only to learn that his false impression of it has stopped him from living at full stretch.

As an unfolding continuum, life must admit change. Otherwise, stagnation will undermine it. In order to adapt, we have to extend limits, take risks, and make new demands on ourselves. These challenges discomfit us. Like Keats, when Serling takes us into the unknown, he makes us wonder if we're leaving our humanity behind or facing it for the first time. But the loss of logic and reason imposed by the zone both promotes self-awareness and intensifies self-being in some of the series' best shows, like "Nervous Man in a Four-Dollar Room" (10/60) and "The Obsolete Man" (6/61). The enhancement can bring pain. Experiments like the one devised by the founders of a community devoted to telepathic interaction as a way of life in "Mute" (1/63) cause confusion and grief. But they also promote progress. That the road to progress is littered with regrets and psychological scars defines one of many ambiguities *The Twilight Zone* invokes. Can humanity advance without first enduring great hardship?

II

Unfortunately, network executives and sponsors shied away from such questions. By the mid-1950s, said Raymond Williams, television had replaced movies as "the major dramatic institution" (57). Helping to effect this change were teleplays like Paddy Chayevsky's "Marty" (1953), Reginald Rose's "Twelve Angry Men" (1954), and Gore Vidal's "Visit to a Small Planet" (1955). Serling's "Patterns" (1955) was such a hit that it became the first live TV play to be repeated on the small screen (about six weeks after its initial appearance, on the *Kraft Television Theater*). Academics noted the groundswell of popularity caused by these works. Marshall McLuhan and his University of Toronto colleagues, Harold Innis and Eric A. Havelock, traced cultural progress itself to changes in modes of communication. In McLuhan's famous credo, the medium is the message, lies the claim that statements matter less than how they are stated. Such credos generated others that would shape a new democratic world of telecommunications. In the 1960s, communications became a subject in university courses taught by historians, anthropologists, and sociologists. But the networks hewed to their own agenda. The TV studio executives of the time saw themselves primarily as promoters of their advertisers' products. Entertainment was a second criterion, with public service lagging behind as a distant third.

The most popular TV sitcoms of the late 1950s, when *The Twilight Zone* debuted, like *I Love Lucy, Leave It to Beaver,* and *Father Knows Best,* were bland glorifications of home and family both suburban in setting and conformist in social outlook. Serling was fascinated by the power of these shows to win such a huge following. In 1957, he called television "a medium that . . . could play to an audience greater than a Broadway play reached in one solid year of SRO crowds. With this kind of potential . . . television was something to be reckoned with" ("About Writing for Television" 10-11). But the reckoning called for special skills. Television is both an art and a popular industry. Whereas the stage dramatist writes for an audience measuring in the hundreds, the TV playwright has to please millions. His very career depends on the ability to win mass appeal. Serling took the teledrama, a subgenre Chayevsky called "the most perishable item known to man" ("About Writing for Television" 6), and infused it with production values that integrated mass culture with the elite. What's more, he did it again and again; "Patterns," "Requiem for a Heavyweight," and a least a dozen *Twilight Zone* episodes ranking with the best original drama in TV history. This accomplishment deserves our acclaim. Serling was the first writer to understand the artistic potential of television. Perhaps only Graham Greene and John le Carré in fiction and the Beatles, with their concept albums, in music demolished the stylistic prejudices that once divided the highbrow from the popular and the vernacular.

To Serling, a good TV play could overcome the handicaps imposed by a 30-minute time frame that had to be segmented for commercial breaks. What enabled television to fuse the virtues of film, live theater, and radio drama and then raise them to a new level was television's intimacy. "Remember that television is an intimate medium," he said at an interview held at the Famous Writers School. "It is most meaningful and most effective when you keep in mind that the closer you get to people and the more vertical you probe, the better your drama" (Quinn 230). TV suited itself well to the vertical probe. Good makeup, a counterpoint of well-judged camera angles, and superior lighting gave the TV close-up advantages over its cinematic counterpart. Although the actor may be speaking directly into the camera in both media, he touches the TV viewer more intimately. First, the small screen makes greater demands on our attention, encouraging us to invest more of ourselves in the show we're watching. Next, watching the show in the comfort of our living rooms not only helps focus our attention but also sets up a tension between the familiar and the new, a tension that a script incorporating fantasy, science fiction, or film noir techniques can use to its advantage.

This insight and resolve created clashes with the executive branch. "You argue, you fight, you try to protect what you have written," Serling told Mike Wallace in 1961. "But you're battling networks, advertising agencies, sponsors, and pressure groups. I've been forced to make concessions . . . in every television play I've written" (286). Obviously he didn't make enough of them to please his chiefs. Even though actors coveted the chance to appear in *The Twilight Zone* (Sander 169), complaints came from the show's paymasters. Sponsors grumbled about the controversial issues raised by the series and threatened to withdraw their support. Colgate-Palmolive-Peet and the Liggett and Myers Tobacco Company, makers of Chesterfield cigarettes, *did* drop their sponsorship of *The Twilight Zone* during the show's two opening seasons. Other problems surfaced. Low ratings caused the show's cancellation in 1962, and, when *Twilight Zone* returned late the next season, it expanded to an hour-long format, an arrangement that clashed with most of its artistic premises. The discord was noted and smoothed. During the last year of its five-year run, the show went back to 30 minutes (Schumer, *Visions* 155 n.2). But by this time, changes had occurred in upper-level artistic staffing, like the resignation of Buck Houghton, the show's producer. Serling himself left *The Twilight Zone* to teach a course in playwrighting at his alma mater, Antioch College, "because of fatigue, physical and mental" ("Education: Those Who Can" 108). But his leave of absence didn't restore his old form. Although he knew that *The Twilight Zone* had sagged artistically after its second (1960-61) season, he couldn't revive it. Joel Engel rightly calls *The Twilight Zone*'s fifth and final season "its least creative and most awkward" (235).

Even in its sad last innings, *The Twilight Zone* continued to be identified with Serling, its driving force and unifying sensibility. Of its 156 episodes, 92 came from Serling (with 59 more from either Beaumont or Matheson) (Engel 217). Among the joys the show retained over its five-year run despite changes dictated by sponsors and network executives were the prologue and epilogue framing the action. The format of the epilogue stayed the same during the run of the show. Though spoken by Serling, it was done as a voiceover, unaccompanied by Serling's face. This formatting showed fine artistic judgment, sustaining the mood evoked by the foregoing action rather than breaking it by intruding Serling's face. The mood, in fact, would be extended further, producer Buck Houghton running the credits at program's end against a graphic depicting one of the program's leading motifs alongside appropriate background music. This strategy reflects careful planning. Obviously, *The*

Twilight Zone's producers wanted to involve the audience. The involvement included re-siting or confirming the audience's impression of what it had just watched. The prominence given to the image against which the credits ran could alert the audience to the image's importance and force it to rethink the image's place in the preceding drama.

What won the show its most enduring fame, though, were Serling's prologues, not his epilogues or what followed them. This fame, reflecting one of the notable charms of the show, stands firmly. Ironically, it also rests upon an afterthought or concession on the part of CBS. Hard as it is to imagine *The Twilight Zone* without the imprint of Rod Serling's voice and face upon it, Serling became the show's host only because Orson Welles, to whom the job was first offered, declined. Heretofore a writer and not a performer, Serling took up his new task with some hesitation—which vanished quickly. CBS President Frank Stanton said perceptively of him, "He was the only writer I had every met who looked like his work" (Sander 159). Not only looked, but also talked and acted, we may add: Engel has referred to his "chopped, teeth-clenching voice" (185), and Bob Greene, reviewing Engel's 1989 Serling biography, speaks of a "clipped, dramatic inflection that is still widely imitated today, 30 years after the first broadcast" (16C).

Why this appeal? Sander attributes it in part to Serling himself, noting his man's "huge eyebrows, dark, Jewish good looks, [and] intense demeanor" (159). This smoldering intensity, together with his nasal baritone voice, did help make him, in Arlen Schumer's apt words, "the only true star of *The Twilight Zone*" (1991). But there was more. Rather than walking onto the set (and into a wall sketch of his profile, like Alfred Hitchcock), Serling would be facing the viewer as soon as the camera picked him up. This technique served him (and the show) well. Underscoring the intimacy that he saw as one of television's chief assets was his earnestness. Avoiding irony and playfulness, he would speak sincerely. He was the person you saw, with no two ways about it. His was a voice, a face, and a posture that inspired trust—but not complete trust. Though he wasn't holding back, neither was he telling the whole story. But why should he have? Rather than saying too much, he preferred to draw us into the coming action and, through the candor of his narration, induce an intriguing counterpoint for the sudden twists that often closed the shows.

Further intimacy comes from his standing on the set where the opening scene unfolds, often not speaking till a minute or two into the action (sometimes longer in a 60-minute work like "The Thirty-Fathom Grave"). This tactic sharpens dramatic structure; the whip-pan that shows him on the set with actors already established in their roles increases his involvement with them and the trials awaiting them. The range of settings into which these trials intrude endows this warmth with metaphysical resonance; like Walt Whitman (who supplies the title of the May 1962 teleplay "I Sing the Body Electric"), he's willing to put himself on the same footing as the needy and the afflicted. Even when he disapproves of a character, like the "twisted fanatic" Oliver Crangle of "Four O'Clock "(4/62), his very presence in Crangle's apartment denotes both respect for Crangle's right to believe what he wants and sympathy for him during his coming ordeal. Ordeals don't jag his straight-from-the-shoulder style. He speaks his prologue from 1863 Virginia in "Still Valley" (11/61), from a Philippine jungle on the last day of World War II in "A Quality of Mercy" (12/61), and, wearing a snow-flecked overcoat on a February night, from the edge of a forest clearing near which a spacecraft just landed in "Will the Real Martian Please Stand Up" (5/61).

Serling stays in one place during most of his prologues in order to focus the viewer's attention on his words rather than his person. But he can move from time to time to impart flexibility of tone together with thematic foreshadowing. First seen standing before a grandfather clock that will play a key part in what follows, he moves across the set of a furnished home to look out of a window at a couple preparing to enter the home in "Young Man's Fancy" (5/62). "The Last Rites of Jess Myrtlebank" (2/62) shows him opening a barn door from the inside, walking through the doorway, and then addressing us as if we were outdoors, facing the barn. In "Five Characters in Search of an Exit" (12/61), he addresses us from the curving lip of the large cylinder which holds the characters. Curiously, when Herbert Hirschman and Bert Granet became coproducers of *The Twilight Zone* for the show's fourth season, they did away with the useful convention of the on-set host, posing Serling in front of a plain gray background to speak his prologues. But perhaps complaints are out of order. This change, harebrained as it was, did not reverse the gains caused by the one that occurred after the end of the series' first (1959-60) season, during which Serling spoke his prologues off camera.

Most of the shows, in the first season and after, would start in the same way. A slow down-pan from a clear, starlit night would dissolve into a long, or establishing, shot to situate the viewer, i.e., Düsseldorf for "Mute" or the Ozarks for "Jess Myrtlebank." Then the camera would close in to provide, first, a mid-range shot and then a close-up. Final say on camera positioning, as with most other aspects of the series, belonged to Rodman Edward Serling (1925-75). As the series' creator, 40 percent owner, main writer, and executive producer, Serling also had total autonomy in the area of script control. As indicated by "Cavender Is Coming," a May 1962 teleplay he wrote for Carol Burnett, this autonomy included casting.

But who was he? Born and raised Jewish in Binghamton, New York, he enlisted in the army the day after his 1943 high school graduation. After serving as a combat paratrooper in the Philippines, he enrolled at Antioch College in Ohio, where he met and made a hypergamous marriage to highborn fellow student Carol Kramer. He was graduated in 1950 and took a job writing advertisements at WLW, a Cincinnati radio station. Some of his spare time he spent freelancing and working on a weekly dramatic show for a different local station. Encouraged by his progress, he moved to Connecticut with Carol in 1954 in order to be closer to New York, seat of the country's radio and TV market. His success as a TV writer was meteoric. The next year saw the production of "Patterns" on NBC. Besides being honored as the first live teleplay to be repeated on a major network, "Patterns" won an Emmy. Other accolades followed. "Requiem for a Heavyweight" (1956) won Serling a second Emmy. By the time *The Twilight Zone* debuted in October 1959, he had won a third (for "The Comedian") along with a Peabody Award for Television Writing, and he had his work performed on the prestigious *Playhouse 90* and *Lux Video Theater.*

What is the mainspring of the creativity that gave rise to this wild success? The appearance of the word *ghost* or *ghosts* in the titles of three of the eight tales comprising the Serling anthology, *Into the Twilight Zone: A New Collection of Startling Explorations in the Realm of the Supernatural,* suggests a preoccupation with the paranormal that does, in fact, run through his work. Yet the work also has an in-your-face crunchiness. Several of the teleplays center on boxing ("Requiem," "The Big Tall Wish" [4/60], "Steel" [10/63]), and a number unfold in a climate of war or revolution. In these works, either an armed conflict is taking place ("Purple Testament" [2/60], "Mirror" [10/61], "Still Valley" [11/61]), or, having recently ended, is still emitting shock waves that could be lethal ("Rack" [4/55], "Two" [9/61], "Passersby" [10/61], "Death's-Head Revisited" [11/61], "Old Man in the Cave" [11/63]). Other thematic strains in the work that probably stemmed from firsthand experience include a fondness for small-town America ("A Stop at Willoughby" [5/60]), an affinity for film-noir techniques ("A Passage for Trumpet" [5/60]), and, from growing up in the Depression, an awareness of the hardships of poverty ("The Man in the Bottle" [10/60]).

These themes account for much of the intellectual and emotional drive of the programs. But they've not defined the sensibility animating the drive. In fact, few writers of our day resist critical categories as much as Serling. Taking a grim view, S.T. Joshi calls him "a singularly complex, even tormented, individual" (22) whose "vision of human life is dark, pessimistic, cynical, and even misanthropic" (23). An assenting James Wolcott shows this grimness infusing some of the teleplays, in contrast to the friendly sparkle and warmth exuded by the sitcoms of the day:

> The Twilight Zone was the dark negative of the sunny snapshots of suburbia shown on sitcoms like Ozzie and Harriet and Leave It to Beaver. . . . It presented worst-case scenarios of what might happen if the launch buttons were pushed: neighbors beat on the door of bomb shelters closed to outsiders; Norman Rockwell villages become ghost towns. . . . Other planets offered no refuge, as astronauts found themselves wriggling in air, tweezered between giant fingers. (98)

While not denying this grimness, other viewers have subordinated it to a didacticism they find in Serling. Peter R. Ermshwiller's reference to "Serling's knack for entertainment with a message'" (50) posits in his man a wish to be taken seriously. Though Serling's critics haven't charged him with preferring moral instruction to emotional drive or psychological bite, they do find a trace of calculation and conventionality tinting the work. "Generally, Serling incorporates his middle-class audience's attitudes and stereotypes in his scripts" (378), said Quinn in 1966, and Ziegler concurred with him 19 years later by calling Serling's art "basically conservative" and "constructive." (34).

The "normalizing vision" Ziegler ascribes to Serling (34) declares itself in the grief suffered by The Twilight Zone's overreachers ("Dead Man's Shoes" [1/62]), its materialists ("The Rip van Winkle Caper" [4/61]), and its sadists ("Death's-Head Revisited" [11/61]). The moralistic bias accounting for this grief could well stem from Serling's twin experiences of coming to consciousness during the Depression and into manhood during the war. Wrongdoing is particularly dangerous during times of hardship, and it calls for hard punishment; ranks need to close, not fragment, to help the commonweal. The fascism portrayed in "Eye of the Beholder" (11/60), "He's Alive" (1/63), and "Number Twelve Looks Just like You" (1/64) indicates, too, Serling's awareness that panaceas proposed to end strife often aggravate it. As a social thinker, Serling belongs in a centrist tradition that puts its faith in the American puritan ethic of hard work, fair play, and respect for one's fellows; the title figure of "The Brain Center at Whipple's" (5/64) merits our scorn for replacing trained, diligent craftsmen with machines.

This forthrightness sparked in Serling's psyche a flair for upward mobility. He married above his social station, won money and prestige through his writing, and bolted Judaism for the Unitarian Church. And why shouldn't talent, diligence, and a little luck raise him above his origins? Life's greatest rewards are not material, and his record shows that, besides deserving them, he also had the sensibility to enjoy them. Artistically, this attitude, which Serling espoused, bodied forth a set of values that encouraged J.E. Parker to study him as a video moralist. But others have taken a different slant. Robert Quinn, less impressed with Serling's moral conscience than Parker, stresses his subject's preoccupation with tone and mood. According to Quinn, Serling's elevation to the artistic directorship of *The Twilight Zone* brought a shift from a gritty realistic style to one governed by a fascination with the occult (27). Schumer locates Serling's imaginative core elsewhere (1991). Citing the influence of the surrealist André Breton, he calls Serling "a pop American surrealist." Schumer did well to include the word, American, in his label. Breton's belief that paradox, contradiction, and even nonsense can disclose truths beyond the reach of rationalism floods *The Twilight Zone*. Scripts like "King Nine Will Not Return" (9/60), "Twenty-Two" (2/61), and Charles Beaumont's "Shadow Play" (5/61) all portray nightmare as a path to the truth. In "Nightmare at 20,000 Feet" (10/63), neurosis begets insights that save lives. Because they have not yet been trained to prize reason, children see more deeply than adults in "Long-Distance Call" (3/61) and "The Gift" (4/62).

But the adult world of accountability usually reinstates itself at the end of a *Twilight Zone* episode, Serling's pay-as-you-earn morality disclaiming the primacy of the irrational. Though built around an almost deadpan acceptance of the fantastic, "The Old Man in the Cave" (11/63) describes the importance of keeping faith during times of woe, while "The Masks" (3/64) deals with the pitfalls of selfishness. Also germane is Serling's sympathy with older adults. Born in 1890, the same year as Serling's father, 69-year-old Lew Bookman of "One for the Angels" (10/59) represents the hard work, sacrifice, and dedication that helped develop the country. Serling's calling Bookman in his prologue "a nondescript, commonplace little man" voices his gratitude for this legacy. America owes more of her greatness to the obscure many than to her famous public figures. Grounded in reality, *The Twilight Zone* transcends fantasy, horror, and science fiction. Lacking autonomy, these genres serve *The Twilight Zone* mostly as plotting devices. They also stand near the edge of the world in order to comment on it. They tell us, in the spirit of Breton, that life contains many more possibilities than are usually thought to exist. A character may believe him/herself the first or last member of our race. Motifs like the mystical cult of the state or the remaking of society along scientific lines may destroy justice, human rights, and individuality itself. The treatment of these motifs in a work like "Third from the Sun" (1/60) shows *The Twilight Zone* using science fiction to provide an escape, but only a temporary one. After taking us from our familiar routines, the script sheds new light upon these routines and then invites us to re-enter them with a new sense of purpose. What looked like a refuge from reality has turned out to be a springboard that vaults us back into it.

Both the drypoint sharpness of the imagery and the straightforward acting in "Third from the Sun" and "Person or Persons Unknown" (3/62) contrast admirably with the weirdness of the action being developed. This Magritte-like tension (noted by Schumer in his 1991 *Twilight Zone* lecture) reworks the argument that reason is just one way to know and experience the world. Endorsing the argument, the series calls upon non-linear, nonrational forms of awareness to expand our consciousness, to scare us a little, and to push us past the limits imposed on us by Newtonian physics. The belief that the universe contains other forms of awareness than ours either frees or threatens us. In either event, we're riveted. Many of us have fallen under the program's spell, which Serling always intended. Good acting, sets neither too cluttered nor too bare, and provocative music join hands in the best *Twilight Zone* episodes with inventive black-and-white photography to charm and excite the public, not the dilettante or the connoisseur.

2

Tracking the Zone

Perhaps a key to Serling's artistic motivation lies in the undistinguished "Showdown with Rance McGrew." Rightly called by Marc Zicree "dated, tedious, and silly" (269), this February 1962 script is one of several in the *Twilight Zone* canon whose triviality distracts from the value of the revelations they make. Joshi says of "Showdown" that "the whole story gives the impression of being a parody of itself, and perhaps a parody of the entire . . . series" (26). Self-reflexive the story is, but perhaps it's also more of a veiled position paper or credo than it is a parody. Through its title figure, "a three-thousand-buck-a-week phony baloney" who stars in a TV series about the Old West, Serling is signaling his intent to resist heightening or degrading his material for the sake of audience appeal. If Rance is tasteless or even rancid, his creator won't follow suit. The show's inventive beginning shows that creator's grasp of the benefits of incongruity. The down-panning camera settles on a western frontier town. Against a background of melodramatic music, two cowboys are gazing down a long, treeless street, where the odd horse languishes alongside a hitching post. The men are discussing a would-be shooting victim—who appears presently. Rance, wearing sunglasses, drives up in an open king-size convertible, which is blaring rock-and-roll music and sporting a set of huge steer horns on its grill.

We're not in the Old West, but on a Hollywood film set, where a TV western is being made. Rance, the star, is more than an hour late. Unrepentant, he proceeds to inconvenience and annoy his coworkers with his ineptitude, unfitness, and prima donna ways. Then the film set suddenly becomes an actual frontier saloon. Jesse James walks in. He has been looking for Rance; the film that Rance is making includes a scene in which Jesse shoots him in the back. Jesse protests; the frontiersman's code of honor ruled out such cowardice. Demanding redress, he challenges Rance to a duel. Nor can Rance hide behind the claim that he's just an actor in a TV play. This claim, in fact, heightens Jesse's demands for justice. His demands make sense. Though Rance can't ride a horse, fire a pistol, or fight with his fists, he has been earning a fortune defeating every bushwhacker, rustler, and fast gun who comes into his town. And now he wants to enhance that crackling image at the expense of Jesse's honor and reputation.

The action peaks with the showdown adumbrated by both the play's title and its first scene. After begging Jesse to spare him, Rance returns to the shooting set of the play-in-progress. The real-life Jesse returns with him, but as his agent; time travel can carry a person forward in time as well as back. It carries Jesse for a good reason. He will make sure that Rance treats his subject matter more honestly than heretofore. Ironically, though the childish, egotistical Rance will suffer more knocks and look less heroic than he did, his setbacks will make him more vulnerable and likable. This realism will improve his show, ridding it of the wooden acting style and hackneyed prose characterizing the genre. It will also make Rance more like a real person and thus easier to identify with. The probability that this new approach to his materials will improve his acting, too, attests further to Serling's belief that honesty helps everybody.

But Serling knows, too, of honesty's difficulties and dangers. A companion piece of sorts to "Showdown" is "A World of His Own" (7/60). Advisedly, "World" ran at the very end of the series' first season. Even though Serling did not write the script, he must have appreciated the dovetailing of its theme with its placement at season's end. The script (by Richard Matheson) turns on a problem facing all fiction writers—the reality of characters. John Fowles spoke to this problem in chapter 13 of *The French Lieutenant's Woman*, where he pronounced that storytellers must let their characters obey their impulses, even when those impulses clash with the authorial intent, or the work in which the characters appear will suffer. The main character of "World of His Own," Gregory West, "one of America's most noted playwrights," has learned this lesson. Just as he can create a character by describing her into a tape recorder, he can also uncreate her by burning the strip of tape on which the description appears.

I

This strange power invokes issues addressed by some of the king-pin writers of our century. Mary, who has just poured West a martini, complains, in the play's opening scene, about his practice of dematerializing her, particularly when his wife Victoria is close by. Not only does she love West; claiming a true existence of her own, she also wants a permanent place in his life. West demurs. As in Oscar Wilde and Pirandello, the picture that threatens to splinter the surrounding frame threatens the artist's welfare, too. West enjoys the status quo. A god surrogate as in James Joyce, he can control lives. He also understands the dynamism of art; without an audience to witness them, his plays, rich and provocative as they may be, run to waste; they can't play to empty houses and hope to survive. Thus he has Victoria open the door for Mary after recreating Mary for Victoria's benefit. The circuit swathing artist, artifact, and audience has completed itself, all the more effectively because of the audience's, i.e., Victoria's, active participation.

Her activity has solidified his power. Like a god, he defies normal categories. Mary's very existence makes us ask if he's a common philanderer or a creative genius entitled to bend society's laws and codes. The question invokes a caution, dramatized by Victoria's accidentally erasing herself by throwing a strip of her husband's Dictaphone tape into the fireplace. In line with its author's conservatism, the Serling script "What You Need" (12/59) already made the point that any special talent must be used sparingly lest it recoil upon its user. By showing up at the end of "World" in Greg West's studio, Rod Serling, who, like West often dictated his plays, implicates himself in the issue. West's act of uncreating him in the play's final event harks back to Frankenstein, a work that haunts the genre of science fiction. Like the charred film strip bearing West's description of Serling, Mary Shelley's monster shows that our creations can undo us. The point can be extended. The calamities erupting in towns with names like Homeville ("No Time Like the Past" [3/63]) or Centerville ("Stopover in a Quiet Town" [4/64]) imply that the processes of self-destruction and self-creation are joined; whatever nourishes us carries a stinger in its tail. We're less likely to be jabbed by it, though, if we relax our grip on the things that define us. By bestowing too much importance on things of value, we mute their blessings and bring out their drawbacks.

The theatrical climate in which "World" takes place calls forth another warning—that life is a stage. Despite our convictions that we enjoy a free-standing reality, we may be merely acting out someone else's script. Bob and Millie Frazier of "Stopover" discover that they may be condemned to live forever as pets in a model village owned by a gigantic child. After landing on an asteroid, Peter Craig of "The Little People" (3/62) arrogates godlike powers to himself upon learning that the asteroid is peopled by ant-size creatures. But then he's inadvertently killed by a spaceman so huge that Craig looks antlike to *him*. And will another spaceman, many times larger than Craig's killer touch down on the asteroid and destroy *him*? The question invites itself because pride, like Craig's, exacts heavy penalties in the twilight zone, a lesson that Serling, like Joyce before him, applies more strictly to the visionary than to anyone else.

Though not original, even with Joyce, the lesson counts with us, developed, as it is, by characters, images, and verbal exchanges that are freshly perceived and artfully integrated. Andrew Sarris put Serling's didacticism at the heart of his achievement: "With a touch of the crusader and the crank in his makeup, Serling turned out to be that most valuable of entertainers, the one who tries to lift up the populace rather than talk down to it. If it did nothing else in its six [*sic*] years, *The Twilight Zone* helped jar the complacency of the mass audience" (47). Rarely does Serling explain or offer collective solutions (exceptions to this policy being the epilogues of "Walking Distance" [10/59] and "He's Alive" [1/63]). By withholding direct commentary, he both keeps his ideas from hardening into polemic and engages the viewer's imagination. His restraint has served him well. The handful of ideas underlying his scripts don't suffice for the reformer but, owing to their deft handling, prove ample for the artist. An artist Serling is. For instance, he will set works like "The Passersby" (10/61) and "Still Valley" (11/61) in the Civil War both to reinforce his character portraits and to lend weight to the action.

Like the United States of a century before, *The Twilight Zone* lacked geographical stability and political cohesion. The unrest provoked by this shakiness transformed the Civil War mood into a mirror of Serling's own day. Now unrest and anxiety always cry out for organization and discipline; otherwise, they will boil into mob rule, as in "The Monsters Are Due on Maple Street" (3/60). Yet those who impose these civilizing virtues often abuse them, showing that in *The Twilight Zone* every coin has at least two sides. "The Obsolete Man" (6/61), "Death Ship" (2/63), and "On Thursday We Leave for Home" (5/63) link wrongdoing to rank, hierarchy, and privilege. But politics, though important, matters less than people in *The Twilight Zone*—as should be the case in a just government. The human factor controls technique, as well. Works centering on interplanetary travel like "Third from the Sun" (1/60) and "The Parallel" (3/63) aren't science fiction in the ordinary sense. Their methods are realistic, and the horrors they unearth are natural rather than fantastic. They uncoil from human motives, not from machines or their mad inventors. In 1975, F. Jeffrey Armstrong noted the "special emphasis" Serling placed on "character psychology and motivation" (286). His insight is well judged. Serling excels as both a writer of dialogue and portrayer of people because he shows them as they are to themselves and not as extensions of an observer. But their reality is fragile. When they define themselves by scientific systems, for instance, they bring themselves to grief. The title figure of "The Brain Center at Whipple's" (5/64) automates his factory so thoroughly that he puts himself out of work. Nuclear fallout causes widespread environmental pollution in "The Old Man in the Cave" (11/63). "Two" (9/61) and "Probe 7—Over and Out"

(11/63) extend nuclear holocaust beyond problems caused by toxic fall-out. In both works, the world has been depopulated. But the man and woman who begin each teleplay as foes leave the set together at the end. All of our attempts to destroy each other run afoul of the life pulse.

The monster in "Pickman's Model," an adaptation of an H. P. Love-craft story that aired on *Rod Serling's Night Gallery* (12/71), wore a rubber suit adorned with fur, fangs, and scales. This garishness has no counterpart in *The Twilight Zone*. The science fiction adapted by *The Twilight Zone* wears its gimmickry lightly in order to look at matters like survival. Mostly, its special effects, rather than existing in their own right, enrich character with intelligence and sympathy. The opening shot of "No Time Like the Past" (3/63), for instance, foreshadows brilliantly the play's central idea, that science in the form of time travel cannot change the past, even if the time traveler knows what needs changing. Facing away from the camera, Paul Driscoll is bent over a video screen and surrounded by an elaborate instrument panel consisting of buttons, dials, and flashing lights. To his rear—and closer to the viewer—are two iron retaining rails, a foot or so apart. So dominated is he by technology that he can't expect anything good from it. His expectations are met. Stopping in Hitler's Germany, Hiroshima 1945, and the *Lusitania* just before its torpedoing in 1915, the time-traveling Driscoll finally goes to Homeville, Indiana, of 1881, where his attraction to a local woman tempts him to stay. The aborted romance of Driscoll and Abigail Sloan restores Serling to the turf where he feels most comfortable—and where *The Twilight Zone* provides its warmest insights. Like "The Fever" (1/60), "A Most Unusual Camera" (12/60), and "What's in the Box" (3/64), "No Time" focuses on closely observed, small domestic dramas that spin out of control.

The only one of the series' three maritime dramas whose main characters profit from the second chance given to them, the hour-long "Passage on the Lady Anne" (5/63) uses its added length to lend its treatment of marital crisis subtlety and impact. First, Charles Beaumont's script gains a great deal from visual shorthand. An impatient Allan Ransome, waiting to be served in a travel agency, is first seen looking at his watch. Then he lights a cigarette without offering one to his wife, an omission he will repeat. We soon see why. The Ransomes have come to the travel agency because Eileen has convinced Allan that the only way to save their foundering six-year marriage is to take a cruise together. Grum-blingly, he gives in. Finally situated in their lavish stateroom, Eileen removes her coat and moves around, exulting in the old-world charm and elegance. Her cold, withdrawn husband keeps his coat on during this sequence and lingers on the edges of the camera eye.

Deft camera work continues to yoke character and idea. In the next sequence, Eileen leads the way across the ship's deck and up a ladder, which she and Allan climb to improve their view of the receding land during the ship's departure, an event she suggested witnessing, to begin with. Much of the contrast between her enthusiasm and good will and Allan's crankiness reaches us visually. During a talk with some fellow passengers, Allan is standing in shadows, sometimes in profile, whereas Eileen appears above him, looking in our direction. Later, when she's seen in profile, he's facing away from the camera. This juxtaposition, as effective as it is, occurs but once, the production crew of "Passage" exercising good restraint. The technique of showing Eileen from the front most of the way dominates because the actress playing her, the attractive Joyce van Patten, has a full face. Character, graphic art, and idea run in the same groove through the final scene. Here, Eileen and Allan, both of whom have resolved to rebuild their marriage, are looking straight into the camera.

Marc Scott Zicree also locates Serling's creative urge in "a primary concern for people and their problems" and, further, in "some search for an emotional truth, some attempt to make a statement on the human condition" (7). Serling's attitude here is one of acceptance, the familiar and the homey stirring his imagination. Most of "Will the Real Martian Please Stand Up" (5/61) takes place in a rural Adirondack diner; "Mirror Image" (2/60) unfolds, too, in Serling's home state of New York in a setting as drab and commonplace as could be wished, a bus station; the main setting for "Nick of Time" (11/60) is a diner in small-town Ohio, where he attended college. Other examples come to mind. The venue for "I Am the Night—Color Me Black (3/64) is a "small inconsequential village." Yet the obscure can be the seedbed of important truths; Pedott of "What You Need" (12/59) and his fellow street peddler, "nondescript commonplace" Lew Bookman of "One for the Angels" (10/59) both enact miracles. Marsha White, performing "a most prosaic, ordinary, run-of-the-mill errand" in "The After Hours" (6/60), makes a shocking self-discovery. The desert sand that saves a young man's life in "Dust" (1/61) helps explain her revelation. Life at its most drab and ordinary is a miracle to Serling. But it obeys fixed laws. The eponym of "Mr. Dingle the Strong" (2/61) will always be Luther the loser despite the physical and mental exploits he performs after being empowered by space aliens.

These exploits impress Serling less than does the steadily lived life they interrupt—the plod of daily living. Other *Twilight Zone* dramatists concur with this view. Matheson's "The Last Flight" (2/60), the first non-Serling script in the series, contains one fantastic element, that of time travel. Counterpointing this wrenching of reality is the play's "utter straightforwardness" (Zicree 59) of presentation; in its sets, camera work, and acting, the play is simple and plain, director William Claxton ignoring technical dazzle in favor of using story and character to hold our interest. Dazzle is usually suppressed in the zone. For instance, if nothing is gaudy in "Last Flight" or Jerry McNeely's "Self-Improvement of Salvadore Ross" (1/64), nothing is visually exciting, either. All this is deliberate. Serling wanted the *Twilight Zone* episodes to look as unedited and blatantly daily as his subjects. He always prized accuracy of detail together with directness in reporting. His instinct for the difference between literary and true passion also taught him the virtues of consistent plotting, honest motivation, and lifelike dialogue as vehicles through which to develop character. Yes, high-contrast lighting, changes in camera angles, or jump cuts between scenes will create an air of surreality. But his visual wit is rarely self-indulgent. More functional than decorative, it captures a state of mind or builds a mood. The acting performances the wit supports, moreover, have the ambience of real life rather than of theater, ranging from desperate Richard Conte of "Perchance to Dream" (11/59) to drawling, backwoods James Best of "The Last Rites of Jess Myrtlebank" (2/62).

Various literary conventions enrich *The Twilight Zone*, like the Gothic. "The Howling Man" (11/60) and "The Lateness of the Hour" (12/60). Both open in heavy storms, and most of the action in both works occurs in large stone buildings remote from civilization in which a prisoner is being kept. The expectations set forth by a convention can also be reversed. Anne Henderson of Matheson's "Spur of the Moment" (2/64) marries her girlhood sweetheart in defiance of her parents' wish to pair her off with a well-groomed young careerist. But if youthful impulse prevails over adult prudence, as it does in countless love stories, its victory can sour. Seen 25 years after their elopement, Anne and David Mitchell are both alcoholic wrecks, living in her family mansion, which has gone to ruin because of David's having squandered the family's money. *The Twilight Zone* will also reverse the gloomy expectations put forth by a genre, or convention, to bring cheer. Serling's "Passage for Trumpet" (5/60), for example, unfolds in an atmosphere redolent of the pessimism of film noir, an atmosphere conveyed by cheap rooms, dark alleys, and wet city streets seen at night and prowled by low types. Yet the pessimism evoked by these lower-depths trappings is brightened. At the end, the hero gets a second chance to redeem his nasty, bitten-up life. Tone and idea clash elsewhere. Challenging the peace and innocence foreshadowed by its title, Beaumont's "A Nice Place to Visit" (4/60) begins with a burglary. Neither the burglary nor the downbeat film noir settings in the play's opening scenes provoke the redemption the title led us to expect. The production staff of *The Twilight Zone* worked hard at opening scenes. Edward Hall, the Richard Conte character of "Perchance to Dream," rivets us straightaway when he calls himself "the tiredest man in the world" and then tells a psychiatrist that he hasn't slept for 87 hours because if he nods off, he'll have a nightmare that will stop his weak heart.

Incongruity and irony galvanize other episodes. Robots prove loving and gentle in "The Lonely" (11/59) and "I Sing the Body Electric" (5/62). The death that takes an elderly recluse in "Nothing in the Dark" (1/62) materializes as a handsome young man (played by an apple-cheeked Robert Redford). Appearance also belies reality in "I Shot an Arrow into the Air" (1/60), the villain of which has chiseled Ivy League good looks as opposed to the generic middle-class features of his benevolent commander. Surfaces continue to deceive: the devil worshiper in "Still Valley" (11/61) is a benign-looking elder with a soothing, resonant voice. The most notorious wrecker in the series is one Anthony Farrant of "It's a Good Life" (11/61), a six-year-old with average little-boy good looks, including a pair of guileless blue eyes. Anthony is the worst kind of tyrant. He knows everything; he leaves nothing to chance; he brings out the worst in people, turning them into simpering, cringing conformists. Even when they're out of his sight, his family and neighbors praise whatever he does, lest he "wish them into the cornfield," a place from which they never return. Though less important than Anthony, angelic-looking Susan, his senior by a few years, spices the plot of "Caesar and Me" (4/64). Obsessed by her aunt's boarder, the jobless ventriloquist Jonathan West, she eavesdrops on him, insults him, searches his room, and phones the police to explain his guilt in a robbery he committed the night before.

Why? Her malice adds little to the action. But it does contribute eerily to the tale's mood. Perhaps West stands for the father who may have deserted her. Displacement is a major trope of the tale: West is an Irish immigrant, and he and Susan both live in a boarding house. What's more, Susan wears a wedding ring, indicating a desire for male company other than that of a father. Frustrated desire has warped her. In the closing scenes, she's carrying a dart gun shaped like a rod, which she fires at West. Not satisfied with reporting him to the police, she must also kill him, using a phallic weapon to remind him of his impotence and incompetence. Her intimate talk with his dummy, Little Caesar, at the end shows that she has displaced West. But the rough justice that will make her Caesar's next victim fails to satisfy. The likable but unavailing West never defends himself against her. Could he have sought her out? His passiveness makes us wonder if he has courted her to assuage his guilt over having left a child of his own in Ireland.

Less of a psychological critic's playground than "Caesar and Me" is the more conventionally written "Midnight Sun." Like "Caesar," though, most of the interest it generates occurs to the side of the main action and expresses itself through an extravagant character. The November 1961 teleplay describes a city plagued by out-migration to the north, power cuts, and rampant looting, as the earth, having left its orbit, is moving closer to the sun every day. The midsummer madness caused by the fierce heat spares nobody. Norma, a young artist, feels the force of this lesson when a desperate-looking man bursts into her apartment and gulps the precious water kept in her refrigerator. But surprisingly the intruder is more pathetic than his victim. He's haunted by the recent death of his wife, an artist like Norma, and his own artistic sensibility, alive to the wrong he has inflicted on his wife's alter ego, fills him with self-contempt. Just before leaving Norma, he asks her forgiveness. We have learned everything about him and nothing. Though never spoken of again, this nameless sufferer helps develop one of the play's leading ideas—the corrosive effect of hardship upon human ambiguity—while preserving his mystery.

In Serling, the play's author, a primordially American exuberance and innocence hold sway over the impression he can give of being a slick cosmopolite who knows all the angles. Neither sexual promise nor sexual menace has a place in his work. The mock-heroic hyper-vividness of scenes from his best work depicts commonplace yearnings—for security, justice, and the joys of the past. He hews to the values of the neighborhood, not the state. We watch *The Twilight Zone*, not for wisdom but for reassurance. Free of dogma and creed, it imparts a sense of the oneness of existence. Earl Hamner Jr.'s "A Piano in the House" (2/62) glimpses the secret selves we all harbor—the graceful dancer hiding inside obesity and the middle-aged brat who hides his fear of others behind a facade of cynicism. And just as the same person both wins and loses in "Judgment Night" (12/59) and "A Quality of Mercy" (12/61), so does the May-December marriage of "A Short Drink from a Certain Fountain" (12/63) imply the basic unity of people. The unhappiness of the Gordons' marriage is unsettling. But perhaps mid-twentieth century America had not yet attained the awareness to make such a marriage work. With grace and invention, *The Twilight Zone* uses ordinary incidents, like a marital spat, to invoke an abiding truth or suggest a new direction. This artistry transcends social and intellectual categories. *The Twilight Zone* strips character, setting, and community down to an essence as bare as the underlying rhythms of nature. The insights conveyed by this stripping-down can encroach upon myth. The hidden currents that govern lives, relationships, and whole communities flow through the zone. These currents beckon us because we recognize a sameness between the characters they support and ourselves.

II

Women help bring about this recognition. But their centricity in the zone has been ignored. In 1966, Robert Samuel Quinn said that Serling puts his female characters in "generally passive relationships" in which they love their husbands "as one loves an overlord" (289). Agreeing with Quinn, Joel Engel, addressing in 1989 an audience more attuned to women's potentialities and freedoms, said, "Throughout his career, Rod Serling rarely wrote convincingly or insightfully about women" (17). A look at "Perchance to Dream" supports Engel's argument. Though written by Beaumont, this November 1959 script belongs to *The Twilight Zone*'s first season (it was the ninth show to appear), a time when Serling's high hopes for the series must have honed his attentiveness to all aspects of the show's production, from scripting to lighting and makeup. The only woman in the cast of "Perchance" fits the archetype, from H. Rider Haggard, of she-who-must-be-obeyed. Played by Suzanne Lloyd, this mana figure splits in two, doubling her power base. When she's not the capable, efficient psychiatric receptionist-secretary, she's playing the beautiful, destructive temptress Maya (a sign of her power comes in the way adjectives and compound nouns pile up in descriptions of her). Invading the dreams of the harried heart patient Edward Hall, she lures him onto a roller coaster ride and then commands him to jump. Jump to his death Hall does. But the composite Maya/Miss Thomas role gives feminists little to cheer about. Far from enhancing her, her dual existence flattens her into a literary cliché, bleeding her of humanity.

The long list of submissive, subservient women in *The Twilight Zone* canon offers feminists just as little joy. Both Horace Ford's mother and wife in "The Incredible World" (4/63) suffer quietly and patiently at the hands of pouting, headstrong Horace, their source of financial support. Another monument, or monster, of compliance is Jessica Connelly, Alan Talbot's fiancée of Beaumont's "In His Image" (1/63). Like the mother and wife in "The Incredible World," Jessica overlooks her man's petulance; she puts up with his surly evasiveness; she's always glad to help him. She agreed to marry him after knowing him only four days, and since that time she has watched him upset or offend everyone he speaks to in our company. She has also put up with his shouting at her, and she complies with his bizarre order that she leave him near a dark country road late at night. Why? How could she expect her compliance to tone down such antics? Phyllis Britt also shows great loyalty and patience dealing with her churl of a man in Martin M. Goldsmith's "What's in the Box" (3/64). She holds dinner until his arrival home from work, even though he's very late, and at meal's end she cleans up, unfazed by his sour ingratitude. After hearing him call her a "stupid cow" and a "bird brain," she helps him from the floor and calls a doctor when he passes out. Yes, she does throw a lamp at him and hits him on the head with a glass box—but only after learning that he has been deceiving her with another woman. As patient as she is, though, she's not patient enough. For protesting Joe's infidelity, this loyal wife of 27 years gets punched out of her living-room window.

Perhaps *The Twilight Zone*'s greatest paragon of female devotion is Flora Gibbs of "The Fever" (2/60). Here is Serling's description of Flora in the short-story version of his teleplay: "She was quiet voiced though talkative, long, if unconsciously, suffering and had led a life devoted to the care and feeding of Franklin Gibbs, the placating of his sullen moods, his finicky appetite, and his uncontrollable rage at any change in the routine of their daily lives" (72-73). The description, from *Stories from the Twilight Zone,* carries into the teleplay. But it doesn't say everything. If Flora sinks her feelings to please her husband, she also knows more about personal relationships than Franklin does. When the two of them win a free trip to Las Vegas, it's not she but her rigid, cantankerous husband who becomes obsessed by a one-armed bandit. Not only does he give the machine all his money; he also hears it calling his name and then sees it stalking him. In *Le Rire,* or *Laughter* (1900), Henri Bergson saw comedy springing from a likeness that develops in a work of art (like Charlie Chaplin's *Modern Times* [1936]) between people and machines; people whose looks and actions are mechanical provoke laughter. *The Twilight Zone* gives a different picture. The machines that take away 13,000 jobs in "The Brain Center at Whipple's" (5/64) and the one-armed bandit that Franklin Gibbs imagines into life both graze tragedy. They also remind us that men, not women, are the ones dominated by machines in *The Twilight Zone,* suggesting both that women live life more fully than men and that they define themselves through relationships rather than through achievements. Operating from a broader human base, they are more content, too, than their men to be on a level with life. Seeing things in broader perspective, they confront the unforeseen more confidently; nor do they need external sanctions. Don Carter of "Nick of Time" (11/60) keeps putting pennies into a fortune-telling machine called the Mystic Seer. His statement, "Every answer seems to fit," shows him to be a moral vacuum through which the interference of gullibility has rushed. His moral balance must be very fragile if it's so easily upset. Even when he asks the Seer if it's a "stupid piece of junk," he's told, "It all depends on your point of view." Finally, his wife, Pat, persuades him that he's sacrificing his independence and intelligence to chance. But as the Carters are leaving the diner where they found the Seer, they cross paths with an older couple. The woman looks whipped and weary, as her frantic escort, having forgotten her, hurries to ask the machine about his future.

What the two couples from "Nick of Time" share with Flora and Franklin Gibbs of "The Fever" is that in all three cases the men show poor judgment, low self-confidence, and a lack of restraint. This pattern runs through the canon. As has been seen, a wife goes to great lengths to save a marriage her husband put at risk in "Passage on the Lady Anne" (5/63); then a husband breaks a promise to his bride in "Young Man's Fancy" (5/62). A man in "The New Exhibit" (4/63) literally brings his work home with him, and the work, five life-size wax figures, leaves no room for his wife. His life collapses quickly. The job of keeping bread on the table and love in the heart usually falls to women in *The Twilight Zone*. Their means-oriented approach to life helps them meet the challenge. They can also trust their intuition. In "Jess-Belle" (2/63), the eponym's mother knows that Jess has been bewitched by Granny Hart; after the bewitchment occurs, Ellwyn Glover knows that her fiancé Billy-Ben Turner has fallen under Jess's spell; Granny Hart later knows that Bill-Ben will visit her on his wedding night.

With all these intuitive gifts on display, one asks why *The Twilight Zone*'s scriptwriters didn't give women more prominence in the series than they did. Works like "Still Valley" (11/61), "A Quality of Mercy" (12/61), "The Little People" (3/62), and "The Thirty-Fathom Grave" (1/63) have all-male casts. Also, much of the memorable acting in the series comes from men. Already cited on this score have been Robert Duvall and James Whitmore among others. An explanation for this imbalance stems from the truth that most of the meatiest parts for TV drama during the run of *The Twilight Zone* (1959-64) were written for men, the western being the form taken most often by the era's weekly video anthologies. The few choice parts given to women put them in the orbit of the family, examples of this trend being Lucille Ball and Donna Reed.

The Twilight Zone, though, took women more seriously than has been credited. Counterweighting Mickey Rooney's one-man "Last Night of a Jockey" (10/63) is Agnes Moorehead's one-woman "The Invaders" (1/61). And if a slew of *Twilight Zone* episodes are acted entirely by men, "Night Call "(2/64) has an all-female cast. The series also includes some excellent acting by women. Inger Stevens's performances in "The

Hitch-Hiker" (1/60) and "The Lateness of the Hour" (12/60) showed more subtlety and depth than her role as the title figure in the sitcom *The Farmer's Daughter.* Accordingly, Anne Francis brought more acting skills to her sharp, lived-in performances in "The After Hours" (6/60) and "Jess-Belle" (2/63) than she did to the series *Honey West,* where she played a female James Bond. Finally, Ida Lupino's aging Hollywood actress, Barbara Jean Trenton, in Serling's "Sixteen-Millimeter Shrine" (10/59) has a passion equal to that of any of the series' performances by male actors. Lupino, incidentally, is also the lone woman director in the series, sustaining with insight and tact the tension between Cajun primitivism and urban chic in Serling's eerie "The Masks" (3/64). The tension maintained between outlandishness and believability in "Caesar and Me" (4/64) reminds us that the work was the only *Twilight Zone* episode written by a woman, Adela T. Strassfield (Zicree 418). Though Serling waited till the second half of *The Twilight Zone*'s last season to air scripts both written and directed by women, he nonetheless did it.

A feminist he should never be called. But his including in his series a woman writer and director makes him a rarity for his time. He was one of the first in his field to help resourceful, imaginative women clear hurdles heretofore unclearable. This development, along with the strength, gentleness, and intelligence written into female roles throughout the life of the series, clinches the belief, held by two generations of TV watchers, that *The Twilight Zone* was far ahead of its time. Yet it also belonged to its time. Success in a medium that addresses a mass audience consists of giving that audience a sense of its own value. Without appearing forced or literary, Serling showed his viewers how close the literalness of their workaday lives stood to the surreal. Viewers today still find the affinity compelling. Like most great artists, Rod Serling created, in *The Twilight Zone*, the imaginative climate in which he could best perform.

3

Strains from the Golden Age

"Our society is a man-eat-man thing on every level," said Serling in a 1958 *Time* magazine interview ("Tale of a Script" 36). Urbanization and technology have come to dominate the planet, skewing our desires and antipathies. Mild introspects like Henry Bemis of "Time Enough at Last" (11/59) and Gart Williams of "A Stop at Willoughby" (5/60) will be crushed by their society's rugged individualist ethic. Neither at work nor at home can either man escape the prod to get ahead. Both men must suffer. And their pain lances our hearts. Serling's treatment of the theme of the sensitive soul forced to step to the rhythms of a materialist, mechanized society conveys an unpretentious air of honesty and truth. The candor flows from artistic intent. Serling is less interested in what happened, the event per se, than he is in why his people react morally and emotionally as they do.

Haunting the motivation behind most of what goes on in *The Twilight Zone* is a longing for the innocence and serenity of our pre-urban past. As Carol Serling pointed out in 1987, her late husband always equated this drowsy content with his home town of Binghamton: " I think he had a not-so-totally realistic memory of his childhood in Binghamton. . . . Oh . . . his hometown was a great love. That's why whenever he had an opportunity, he'd go back to Binghamton, and sometimes just drive around on the street, and kind of relive his boyhood" (qtd. in Rosenbaum 49). Works like "Willoughby" and "Walking Distance" (10/59) give this nostalgia the form of summer nights featuring merry-go-rounds, band concerts, and cotton candy. Harking to the remembered Binghamton of Serling's youth, this earthly paradise, says Engel, is both "a place without problems" (101) and "a kind of geographical womb to crawl back into" (13). Serling's reference in the epilogue of "Static" (3/61) to that "strange and wonderful time machine called a radio," underscoring the play's running tribute to radio's charm and emotional impact, also conveys a nostalgia redolent of his longing for the slow-pouring ease of bygone Binghamton summers. As Carol Serling said, this nostalgia stayed with him. When asked in 1975, a few months before his death, to pick an era he would enjoy living in, Serling answered, "Victorian times. Small town. Bandstands. Summer. That kind of thing. Without disease. I think that's what I would crave, a simpler form of existence" (qtd. in Breville 69).

But how long would the craving last? If Serling was wistful and nostalgic, a side of him also sought hard work, competition, and the fast track. This self-division showed itself as early as "Patterns" (1955), which played on television more than four years before *The Twilight Zone*'s debut. Aging Andy Sloane, vice-president of Ramsie and Company, is an early example of the archetypal figure in Serling of the obsolete man. Because Sloane's energy and thus his productiveness have waned, his chief has hired the younger Fred Staples to replace him. This ruthlessness offends Staples. Though ambitious, he recoils from the idea of profiting at the expense of his frayed older colleague, a man who has given Ramsie and Company decades of loyalty and talent. But Staples finds his morality challenged by the offer of a vice-presidency in the large, thriving New York firm where he and Sloane work. He can, moreover, pluck the coveted prize, one that would normally come within his reach only after five or ten more years of toil, without lifting a finger. But rather than taking refuge in moral innocence, he attacks Ramsie for forcing Sloane's retirement.

Staples's crisis ends in a cheat. After an intense last-act debate with the corrosively efficient Ramsie, Staples accepts the promotion offered to him. But he also serves notice that he'll stick to his ethics. As vice-president of the firm, he'll be his chief's loyal opposition. But for how long? we ask. CEOs prize loyalty over brilliance in their top aides, whose main duty consists of making those CEOs look good. Staples's Ohio background is a shorthand for his decency, grainy honesty, and down-to-earthness. But has the man-eat-man ethic ruling Madison Avenue already started to erode these Midwestern values? Staples is last seen with his wife, Fran, not his boss, suggesting that he rates home and family over work. But the two are at his office, rather than at home, and he's sending her away with the news that he has to work late. The curtain falls with him holding the stage by himself.

Serling's intent is clear. Yes, the strong man must bear the burden of his aloneness. Staples has the self-confidence to know that Fran will remain true to both him and his dream despite his heavy work load. He knows, too, that being alone for long spells, though stressful, will focus his mind and boost his productivity. But the play's title calls his sacrifice into question. Fran, "lovely, sweet, uncomplicated, full of warmth and affection" (Reach 63) as a college girl, has grown sour, strident, and greedy. By taking on the worst features of the pattern of the rising young executive's wife, she'll goad her husband into working longer and harder. And what will this stepping up of his work routine bring him? Has it already started to take shape? Specifically, how much longer will it take Fred Staples to play Andy Sloane to Ramsie or Ramsie's son? Serling's belief in the deadening effects of repetition, borne out in *Twilight Zone* episodes "Death Ship" (2/63) and "The Bewitchin' Pool" (6/64), implies that Staples is already trapped; every day he toils at Ramsie and Company and, certainly, every overtime hour he logs in deepens the groove of the cycle he walked into when he left Ohio.

I

Both Staples's job and the psychological cost it entails disclose again in Serling the self-division that rules out easy answers. Though drawn emotionally to the tranquillity of the Victorian age, he knows that the Victorian age is over. What's more, he understands that it wasn't tranquil for everybody. Jeremy Wickwire, the robot-caretaker of Happy Glades, a remote asteroid in Charles Beaumont's "Elegy" (2/60), has given the place the look of a turn-of-the-century town because that particular milieu probably eclipsed all others in providing an abundance of creature comforts. But sharks lurk below the surface of Happy Glades, hungry and waiting. The charming, debonair Wickwire poisons the three astronauts whom chance brought his way. Richard Matheson's "Once Upon a Time" (12/61) and Serling's "Mr. Garrity and the Graves" (5/64) serve the same warning. Life in both Harmony, New York, setting for the Matheson script, and Happiness, Arizona, is raw and primitive. It can even unleash danger; all but one of the people buried in the graveyard of Happiness died violently. Then Woodrow Mulligan complains of the high cost of living in rural New York in 1890. Mulligan, played by Buster Keaton, finds more to moan about. He's nearly run down by a horse and then, twice, by a bicycle. But mid-twentieth century America riles him, too. Rollo (played distractingly by Stanley Adams sounding like Sydney Greenstreet) accompanies Mulligan on his time trip from Harmony of 1962. The allure of the past fades quickly. Soon after going back 71 years in time, Rollo starts missing the spring mattresses, airfoam pillows, and electric blankets of his own time. But he shouldn't feel cheated. Dramatizing the idea that every era has its drawbacks as well as its assets, Mulligan slams into someone on a bicycle within moments of re-entering the Harmony of 1961; immediately, he and his victim begin speaking in unison.

The phrase from Serling's prologue to Montgomery Pittman's "Two" (9/61), "man's battles against himself," sets forth the truth, enacted often in the zone, that conditions throughout history resemble each other more closely than we might have imagined. The monsters are already in place in Serling's "The Monsters Are Due on Maple Street" (3/60) in the form of friendly, financially secure white homeowners. All it takes to bring out their demons is an electrical outage. Like the conflictive Serling—a stubborn hot-tempered dynamo with a nostalgic streak who never outgrew an adolescent penchant for supermacho antics—many of the zone's inhabitants struggle more with themselves than with others. Their struggles express an important truth: the social criticism developed in *The Twilight Zone* matters less than the insights the show gives into individual behavior. But what can the private individual expect? If mid-century America takes much of its identity from Mr. Misrell's description of his New York advertising firm in Willoughby, "It's a push, push, push business," then competition and confrontation will both run high. People will stumble over each other and themselves grabbing at prizes, while they invoke the Emersonian creed of self-reliance to justify their greed. Yet greed alone doesn't take their measure. In arrogating money and status to themselves, these denizens of the zone expend great chunks of new-world energy. Profusely outward bound, they define themselves in action.

A bored Walter Bedeker of Serling's "Escape Clause" (11/59) says of the immortality he has traded his soul for, "Immortality—what's the good of it when there aren't any kicks? Any excitement at all?" Bill Feathersmith of Serling's "Of Late I Think of Cliffordville" (4/63) also makes a pact with the devil. But instead of asking for eternal life, he opts for the rough-and-tumble of commerce. "Getting it was the kick, not having it," this robber baron says within hours of making the biggest coup of his career. At age 75, he's still searching for new heights to scale. His earlier *Twilight Zone* counterpart, Rocky Valentine of Charles Beaumont's "A Nice Place to Visit" (4/60), needn't bargain with the devil. He's already in hell. But it's not the hell he had envisioned. He eats sumptuously, and he keeps winning at roulette and poker, often in the company of beautiful, adoring women. This "scared, angry little man" finally discovers that hell means having all your wishes granted. His discovery shocks him. The extrusion of chance from gambling robs his conquests of value; victory only brings joy in the presence of defeat.

The belief that we need challenges floods *The Twilight Zone*. Gart Williams of "Willoughby" yearns for a modus vivendi "where a man can slow down to a walk and live his life full measure." Can this dual goal be achieved so long as our veins run with blood and not water? That Williams dies pursuing this goal reflects his creator Serling's doubts. To slow down to a walk is either to stagnate or to bring on the demons. Rather than fending for herself, Barbara Polk of Serling's "Uncle Simon" (11/63) ministers to a hated uncle for 25 years in order to inherit his money. Simon Polk's death changes nothing for her. Though Polk leaves her his fortune, the control he exerts from the grave negates its value. She remains the victim of her own passiveness. E. Jack Neuman's *Twilight Zone* script "The Trouble with Templeton" (12/60) offers its own plea for decisive action. The aging actor, Booth Templeton, prefers idealizing the past to coping with the present. Only when he admits that his beloved ex-wife, the avatar of his days of joy, cheated on him can he give his acting career the sense of purpose it deserves. Another who flees into the past in order to dodge the challenges of today is the title figure of Reginald's Rose's "Incredible World of Horace Ford" (4/63). Horace, like Booth Templeton, receives some unwanted but helpful shock treatment. Revisiting his allegedly blissful childhood, he's mocked and mauled by some boys he remembers as his friends. "In reality, his childhood was a terrible time," says Zicree of the revelation accompanying Horace's knocks and lumps, adding, "Now, finally, he is able to put it [his ugly childhood] behind him" (337).

The ugly needs to be scuttled in order to live more fully, regardless of whether its roots lie in our personal or our collective past. The many *Twilight Zone* scripts set in earlier times make us wonder, when did the loss of American innocence that Serling prized so much take place? Did it happen with the Cold War, which spelled out the failure of the American-led West to democratize the globe? With Japan's attack on Pearl Harbor, which showed us our vulnerability to the outside world? With the Spanish-American War, which built our appetite for imperialism? Or back with the fratricide of the Civil War? Serling's flair for both historical and wartime settings implies a suspicion that our cherished national innocence never existed. Signs of a smallpox outbreak greet Bill Feathersmith's re-entry into the Cliffordville, Indiana of 1910. Paul Driscoll of "No Time Like the Past" (3/63) causes the very disaster he had tried to prevent. Plays like "No Time," "Cliffordville," and "Back There" (1/61) have nostalgic titles chosen to clash with the horrors they unleash. All three Serling plays contain a caveat, as well. Though the past tempts us, it must be left alone. All we can accomplish by reliving it is to inflict harm on ourselves, as Martin Sloan of "Walking Distance" learns when he comes back from the world of his 11-year-old self with a limp. The problems Hector Poole foists on himself by his newfound ability to read minds in "A Penny for Your Thoughts" (2/61) prove that our finite limitations can be a blessing.

Trying to ignore or transcend these limitations always backfires. The attempt to right an old wrong ("One More Pallbearer" [1/62]), to defy the natural flow of time ("Queen of the Nile" [3/64]), or to assume multiple identities ("The Four of Us Are Dying" [1/60]) causes grief and calamity. Old Ben in "The Fugitive" (3/62) performs miracles. Though questioned about it, his reluctance to heal the crippled leg of his little neighbor Jenny proves to be supremely wise. Accepting what is given teaches us how to cope. Place names like Harmony, New York, and Happiness, Arizona, may be less ironical than they sound. Though neither refers to an earthly paradise, each implies the superiority of the given over the imaginary or the ideal. The restoration of the status quo in both "The Man in the Bottle" (10/60) and "Mr. Garrity and the Graves" (5/64) pleases everybody after it becomes clear that miracles create more havoc than joy.

One reason why miracles or special gifts of any kind should be used sparingly, if at all, inheres in the tension generated between people and their environments. Whereas an environment, physical or social, a complex of immutable data, resists change, individual reality is changeable. A giant becomes a mite in "The Little People" (3/62); by drinking youth serum, a man of 70 in "A Short Drink from a Certain Fountain" (12/63) dwindles into babyhood; an eager lover and his passive beloved switch places in "The Chaser" (5/60). Most of the transformations in *The Twilight Zone* stem from overreachers, a natural enough breed in a country ruled by the push to get ahead. Perhaps posterity will judge *The Twilight Zone*'s most enduring legacy to consist of the advice to want what we get after we have gotten it. Money and power offer little. Though hotly coveted and competed for, these prizes don't ennoble or refine anybody. When Hecate the night janitor and Feathersmith the tycoon reverse places in "Cliffordville," Hecate taunts his ex-boss in the same way that ex-boss had taunted *him*. And why does the taunting take place at all? Serling wants us to ask. Why are these two possessors of a $36 million business empire drinking alone in their offices rather than celebrating with friends? They probably have no friends to celebrate with. Power, fame, and money prove just as empty to George P. Hanley of "I Dream of Genie" (3/63), a weaker script from *The Twilight Zone*'s worrisome fourth season. Like Henry Corwin, the drunken department-store Santa Claus in "Night of the Meek" (12/60), Hanley finds his vocation in giving. The end of the play has him garbed as a genie who grants people three wishes.

Hanley understands that besides observing its own rhythm and flow, life takes shape from realities long in place. Any attempt to jar these realities confirms their force. The murderer Joe Caswell in Serling's "Execution" (4/60) vanishes from the scaffold where he's to be hanged in 1880. But he doesn't escape death, which occurs in 1960 New York, to which a time-scientist had called him. He deserves to die, as a convicted murderer, and no displacement of time can save him. His death will benefit the rest of us, life being happier and safer without vicious murderers like him in our midst. This conservative attitude also helps sufferers in the Serling-written "Passage for Trumpet" (5/60), "Man in the Bottle" (10/60), and "Trade-Ins" (4/62) savor those fugitive gleams that brighten the murkiest of lives.

Always sensitive to the dangers of majority rule, Serling will stand up for the nonconformist in order to disclaim what he sees as a national tendency to force people into accepted social patterns. "Mr. Bevis" (6/60) expresses the "tightly wound . . . extremely intense" (Sander 217) Serling's warning to himself to relax and learn self-acceptance. But the teleplay also confirms Serling's faith in the value of kindness and warmth. The whimsicality of James B. W. Bevis has cost him his job (for the eleventh time in the past 18 months) and gotten him evicted from his apartment. His guardian angel lifts his burdens, paying his debts, buying him a new car, and allowing him to relive the day of his eviction and firing. Though Bevis accepts this largesse, he also finds his spirit shackled. He can no longer indulge the little eccentricities—the loud, ill-matching clothes, the zither playing, the model ship building—that made life so joyful for him. Yes, he has grown more reliable, and he works more effectively than before, a sign of which is the raise his boss gives him. This model citizen also pays his rent on time. But the neighborhood kids won't play football with him any more, and the pushcart vendor on his street has stopped giving him free apples. Being respectable gnaws at him as much as it did Twain's Huck Finn. He returns to his former poverty, unemployment, and near homelessness. Though deprived, he can at least enjoy life. No Marxist, Serling endorses his decision in the play's prologue: "Without him, without his warmth, without his kindness, the world would be a considerably poorer place, albeit perhaps a little saner."

But what price sanity? Whereas Serling values Bevis's spontaneity and verve, he also knows that any firm staffed with Bevises will fold in a matter of weeks, if not sooner. This "most prolific writer in TV history" (Sander 225) drew on his respect for work routine to meet deadline after unreasonable deadline in a trade more stressful than most. It was probably a surfeit of stress that inspired him to write not only "Bevis" but also "Cavender Is Coming" two years later. The rigidity of characters like Ramos Clemente of "The Mirror" (10/61) and Oliver Crangle of "Four O'Clock" (4/62) taught him the deadliness of taking himself too seriously. Perhaps "Bevis" and "Cavender" (5/62) both fail artistically because Serling didn't distance himself enough from the warnings they voiced; these works exaggerated in order to correct an exaggeration in the opposite direction.

Unfortunately, this second exaggeration pertained to his personal life and his career, whereas the first one lived safely in the aesthetic sphere. An artistically apt mirroring relationship between the two realms couldn't be wrought in the four or five days Serling usually allotted to the writing of a 54-minute teleplay. In both its impetus and its structure, "Cavender" is a companion piece to "Bevis," even though the title of the later work tries to hide this embarrassing truth. Like Bevis, Agnes Grep, the main figure of Cavender, is a sweet-tempered oddball who can't hold a job. As with Bevis, too, her guardian angel (Cavender) lifts her into the ranks of respectability, a clime she rejects because of its coldness and vanity. Cavender, after restoring her to her grubby rooming-house routine, calls her "the richest woman I know." Serling would support this verdict. The life Agnes chooses, tumbledown as it is, chimes with a value system that years of trial-and-error have installed. Consistent with her idiosyncrasies and self-expectations, it suits her.

Serling wouldn't recommend it to, say, serious, inquiring Jana Loren of "The Lateness of the Hour" (12/60) or the driven Christopher Horn of "A Hundred Years Over the Rim" (4/61). But these earlier figures could profit from Agnes's sense of fun. Sour, misanthropic Archibald Beechcroft of Serling's "The Mind and the Matter" (5/61) repopulates the world with doubles of himself. In less than half a day, he's bored stiff. If ordinary people irritated him, at least they were independent centers of significance, capable of generating surprise, and not mere copies of one another. Beechcroft quickly learns the pitfalls of the Godgame. He's also nearly ready to accept the verdict, from Serling's epilogue, "with all its faults it may well be that this is the best of all possible worlds."

But Serling knows that the last word on this topic can't be said. Showing both taste and judgment, he refrains from expanding on the topic. A great deal of nature is mysterious and incomprehensible; nature's laws aren't for us to figure out. Both simple and complex, familiar and strange, they can nevertheless be lived—and sometimes lived around. Serling believes in the possibilities of the ordinary. Something new, wide, and bright will open out before his zone-dwellers just when they seem trapped. Mousy, grubby Jackie Rhoades of "Nervous Man in a Four-Dollar Room" (10/60) must choose between two lethal alternatives. He can refuse to kill a tavern owner who has crossed the mob Rhoades sometimes works for and be murdered himself, since he rejected the contract. Or he can accept the contract, knowing full well that, strictly a small-timer, he'll bungle the job and either go to jail or get killed as a result. Jackie spends the hours prior to the deadline set by his paymaster looking into the mirror, where he sees a better, finer version of himself than the furtive, bitten-up stooge he has dwindled into.

This mirror image represents both a new direction for him and an embodiment of the realm, so intriguing to the English playwright and scholar of time, J. B. Priestley, of what might have been. A dollop or two of self-confidence might have pushed Jackie into taking a few more risks in the form of applying for a good job or inviting a pretty woman out on a date. But fear has always stopped him. Now, at age 34, instead of living with his family in a comfortable home, he's stuck in a cheap, cramped room. The Angel Gabriel in "A Passage for Trumpet" (5/60) told another urban loser, "Take what you get, and you live with it." Jackie/John Rhoades can either live or die. The choice is his. But his immediate challenge consists, first, of recognizing his latent strengths. Only then can he act on them, infusing them into his daily routine.

"Stay in your own back yard," Serling tells us in the epilogue to "Once Upon a Time" (12/61). But before setting down stakes, we have to look into our private pasts, assess the value systems we have evolved, and then judge our potential for growth. Though Jackie Rhoades may never get a white-collar job or make enough money to own a good suburban home, his mirror meeting with himself will insure him a richer existence than the mean, grubby one he has been living. The happiest people in *The Twilight Zone* are those who have accepted the place they have made for themselves. Professor Ellis Fowler of "The Changing of the Guard" (6/62) can enjoy retirement once he sees that his 51 years in the classroom were laced with distinction. For the elderly Castles of "Man in the Bottle "(10/60), happiness comes from returning to the threadbare life they had made for themselves and realizing how rich it was.

Serling's message, a spinoff of the self-help books of the 1950s by Norman Vincent Peale and others, has started to cloy. Redeeming it in part are the nifty dialogue, the twist ending, and the psychological insight of the teleplay in which it usually appears. "Cavender Is Coming" puts forth the comforting idea that material hardship can be ignored. The play shows two bunglers pooling their energies and thereby lifting each other to a higher level—all because their hearts are right. One of these bunglers, as in "Mr. Bevis," is an angel. The acts of magic he performs, like those in "The Man in the Bottle" and "I Dream of Genie," bring more worry than joy, or even relief. But the predictability of "Bevis" and "Cavender," the flatness of the people, and the forced humor drain Serling's upbeat message of conviction. Genies and guardian angels don't exist, these blemishes remind us, even to show us that life is an organic continuum whose laws are intrinsic rather than imposed.

II

Twilight Zone scripts that advise us to savor the status quo join hands with those like "The Fever" (1/60) and "The Shelter" (9/61), which both show how vulnerable the status quo is to attack. This vulnerability can be justified. Several times Serling declares his belief that human nature is nasty and that nastiness is self-defeating. Once again, the belief comes across most vividly in an artistic flop. A space alien who calls himself Williams crash-lands his rocket in Mexico in "The Gift" (4/62). He has come to Earth to give humanity the formula for a cancer-curing vaccine. But before presenting his gift, he's killed by some local soldiers. The challenge of the unknown has defeated them. But how do they differ from us, if at all? What we don't understand we fear; what we fear we hate; what we hate we want to smash. Misled by emotions heated by mob psychology, Serling's Mexicans not only kill their visitor; they also burn the document that contains his cancer-cure formula. "The Invaders" (1/61) varies the theme. This time, the visitors are human, and they have landed their craft on a remote asteroid inhabited by one woman. They shoot her and then slash both her leg and her hand with a knife they had filched from her. Only at the end does it come out that these predators are conducting a mission for the U.S. Air Force.

Serling had used space travel in, among other scripts, "People Are Alike All Over" (3/60). An astronaut who crash-lands on Mars is both surprised and pleased to find his human-looking hosts friendly, caring, and intelligent. He soon discovers, though, that his only access from the comfortable, well-furnished house they have put him in to the outside world is a row of vertical iron bars. He's a zoo exhibit. Along with this jarring finale, the play's title invokes the brutality displayed in "The Shelter" and "The Monsters Are Due on Maple Street" (3/60), two works set in New York State. Evil has asserted its force with shocking speed, its perpetrators convinced that they've done no real harm and that they're no worse than their neighbors. To counter the argument that Sam Conrad's captors in "People" are just Martians, one can point out that, like the treacherous Kanamits in "To Serve Man" (3/62), they both look human and pervert human values in order to lower the guard of their human victim.

"Elegy" (2/60), though written by Beaumont, combines Serling's belief in man's wickedness with his fascination for space travel. Again, space travel releases the vice normally held in check by our daily routines. The play opens well. Contrasting with its nostalgic title is the first image shown on the TV screen—a speeding rocket. Then the mood shifts again. The rocket has landed on as asteroid bearing many of the signs of Serling's boyhood Binghamton, that is, peaceful small-town

America in the early years of the century. The astronauts see a tractor, a barn, and a haystack. Then some gracious estates and an auditorium in which a beauty contest is being held come into view. But our astronauts can't be back on Earth. They've journeyed 600 million miles, the sky above them reveals two suns, and all the people they see are both speechless and frozen. The corpse-like associations put forth by this silent immobility has thematic import. In the subtext of "Elegy" lies a warning served often in *The Twilight Zone*, that our longing for the past is a temptation that must be resisted. The old-world charm and peace of Happy Glades conceals dangers. In a 1991 speech delivered to the Rod Serling Memorial Foundation, Arlen Schumer contrasted the promise evoked by our pre-urban past and the deadliness of trying to merge with it. In "A Stop at Willoughby" (5/60), says Schumer, "The protagonist's wish for a return to the past and its easier way of life ends in death."

But "Elegy" has more to say about this death drift. Chubby, avuncular Jeremy Wickwire, the caretaker of Happy Glades, disarms the three visiting astronauts with his gracious manners and his rich, plummy voice. In cultivated tones, he explains to his poisoning victims that they have to die because their survival would destroy Happy Glades. Man is inherently warlike; any place inhabited by humans will forfeit peace. Beaumont's late teleplay "Valley of the Shadow" (1/63), a superior work, adds force and depth to this argument in a way consistent with the ontology enacted elsewhere in *The Twilight Zone*. The people in Peaceful Valley, the town that journalist Philip Redfield blunders into, are kinder, nobler, and wiser than ordinary earthlings. Their compromising of their security at the end to free Redfield after he tries to kill three of their leaders bespeaks their superiority. But is this clarity wasted? Have they overrated Redfield to their own detriment?

He has told his captors that he will explain their doings once he gets home to Albuquerque. But who would believe him? This ignoramus looks at a road map showing a fork in a road, declares that he's lost, and heads in the direction opposite from that indicated by a road sign. He has already driven his car till the gas gauge reads empty. Stupidly, he throws his road map out of the car, surprising his dog, whom he quickly promises a steak probably to soothe his conscience for littering the environment. Arriving in Peaceful Valley doesn't sharpen his mind. He leaves his dog alone in his convertible car for minutes at a time, even after it bolts to chase a cat. Earlier, when he had gone looking for the dog, he left his car door open on the driver's side—the side closest to the road, where it stands the greatest risk of being sheared off by a passing vehicle. Will his dog survive his master's blunders long enough to get his promised steak? Later, that master leaves the dog alone with a stranger before letting him run free in an unfenced yard. Finally, when another stranger calls Redfield by name, he doesn't act surprised.

His thickwittedness has disrupted the life of the town so much that he becomes the threatening shadow of the play's title. Then why do the town's leading citizens send him back to Albuquerque? Perhaps they believe him too dull to harm them. But they could have another reason—those secrets in their possession that will both improve and prolong human life. Though Redfield claims that these men must share their secrets with the outside world, he's ignored—at least for now. They'll only publish when the world is completely at peace. Vindicating their reluctance, Redfield shoots them and then steals the secrets. But the pages containing the secrets are blank. This blankness, no joke, holds the lesson of Redfield's Peaceful Valley sojourn. The stolen book of blank pages is the only one extant. Having outgrown their need for assurances, the residents of Peaceful Valley now carry the book's message in their hearts. The value of the blank pages staring up a Redfield stems from the challenge they pose; their blankness redirects our quest for peace and happiness back to ourselves. Redemption must come from within. Whether it can strike roots in the dull, thick hide of Redfield is one of the biggest questions posed in *The Twilight Zone* canon. Everything he has done in our presence argues against it. Yet the decision of his captors to free him—particularly after he shoots them—sets in motion a magnanimity they see him rising to.

This test, rather than violating Redfield's deepest instincts, will force him to cope with them. Whether he has the coping power can't be known. More apparent is the path that his Peaceful Valley interlude has cleared for him. Trouble erupts most often in the twilight zone when people flout the controls by which life is usually regulated and sustained. Reasoning from Matheson's "Nick of Time" (11/60), Robert E. Ziegler says, "Paradoxically, the need they [the impatient and the self-doubting] feel to escape the constraints of logic will cause them to subject themselves to an even greater sense of enslavement" (34). Walter Jameson's immortality, bought from an alchemist 2000 years ago, in "Long Live Walter Jameson" (3/60), shows how a boon that violates the natural course of events will become a burden and a curse. Though Jameson wants to die, he lacks the courage to kill himself.

One of the legendary *Twilight Zone* episodes, "Walter Jameson" counterpoints the homey with the fantastic. Enhancing the work's merit is another fugue-like effect—the tension between the straightforward morality of its main plot and the ambiguity lacing its subtext. After claiming to be 44 years old, historian Walter Jameson admits to Professor Sam Kittridge, a chemist in the college where both men teach, that his real age is closer to 2000. Kittridge, Jameson's prospective father-in-law, hears this news from a double remove. First, he wants to protect his daughter Susanna from marrying a man who never ages; three decades from now, as an old woman, she'll have a husband who both looks and acts years her junior, a husband who will also survive her. Mortality has invaded the 70-year-old Kittridge's heart. Speaking as a sick, perhaps even dying, man, Kittridge covets the very quality—immortality—that he wants to shield his daughter from. Looming over his moral crisis is the near certainty that Susanna will find his disclosures about Jameson so fantastic that she will laugh at them. Jameson, meanwhile, is suffering his own crisis. Though he wants to marry Susanna, his knowledge that he will outgrow his love for her also makes him want either to break the engagement or, better, to kill himself. His painful dialogue with her father has shown him that, by staying alive, he'll only keep hurting the people who love him.

One of these people pays him a surprise visit, "a hideously withered old woman" (Zicree 93) who identifies herself as his discarded wife, Laurette. The encounter between Laurette Bowen and the man she calls Tommy creates some wonderful visual irony, the vigorous middle-aged professor and his fragile, wrinkled visitor bickering as husband and wife. This irony focuses our attention for the play's finale. Laurette shoots Jameson after he refuses to call off the wedding to Susanna Kittridge. She doesn't want her Tommy back; she only asks that he spare Susanna the pain of being scuttled by an ageless mate. His refusal to comply with her wish creates for him the long-awaited consummation he has been avoiding—his death. "Walter Jameson" belongs in an American fictional tradition, swathing Poe, Henry James, and Joyce Carol Oates, that links erotic love to death. Ratifying this honor is the play's enactment of the belief, general in *The Twilight Zone*, that the past is inescapable. Sooner or later, it will exert both its force and its claim with unswerving punctuality. In Ziegler's words, the play's eponym tried to "escape the constraints of logic" (34) by choosing immortality. His identities as Walter Jameson, Major Hugh Skelton, and Tommy Bowen describe the painful lesson learned by overreachers in the zone, that is, that more can be less. In one of *The Twilight Zone*'s most brilliant special effects, Jameson/Skelton/Bowen ages horribly and then disintegrates. When Susanna runs to the man she loves, all she finds are the clothes he was wearing and some dust.

Another character the fulfillment of whose greatest wish recoils on him is Henry Bemis, the Burgess Meredith role, of Serling's "Time Enough at Last" (11/59). This early *Twilight Zone* script fits neatly inside the series' moral landscape. The word "time" appears in the titles of three other *Twilight Zone* episodes, and the motif of the last man on earth actuates at least that many, starting with the series' pilot show, "Where Is Everybody?" (10/59). A gentle bookworm, Bemis is his town's only survivor of a nuclear attack. When the radioactive bomb fell, he was having lunch and reading a book in the basement vault of the bank where he was working. "The worst part . . . is being alone," he mutters to himself after emerging from the rubble. The man who wanted solitude—so that he could read in peace—now has too much of it. He craves human company. Gnawed by loneliness, he wants to shoot himself. But he notices that he's near the smashed remains of the local public library. His need for other people disappears. The bombing has given him all the books he wants and all the time he needs to read them. The burden of loneliness has been lifted.

But just as he starts to settle in for a comfortable read, his eyeglasses break. This bibliophile has been condemned to be surrounded by books he can never read. But why? Is he the victim of chance, the butt of a joke, or an object of punishment? Serling's reference in the show's epilogue to the "best-laid plans of mice and men" implies Bemis's guilt in the destruction of his city, an implication that is false. What is disturbingly true is that Serling, invoking a harsh puritan morality rarely in force in *The Twilight Zone*, makes him imaginatively guilty of the bombing attack, since, for a moment or two, he profited from it. Humble himself, he's reading, at the outset, Dickens's *David Copperfield,* an important character of which is the hypocritically humble Uriah Heep. Though Serling never identifies Heep with Bemis, he does suggest a similarity. Both men, though meek and even simpering, are dangerous to cross; both stand at the center of violence. Yes, Serling condemns in his prologue those "tongue-cluckers" who scorn both Bemis and the life of the imagination he favors; Bemis has to pursue his reading as he would a vice, furtively. And even furtiveness doesn't insure his happiness. His boss threatens to fire him, and his wife destroys his beloved book of poetry. But he's more than a victim. A bank president has the right to demand reliability and efficiency from his employees, services that Bemis defaulted on at the start by inadvertently shortchanging a customer. Helen Bemis also deserves a husband she can count on to be ready with a clean shirt on his back to receive dinner guests when they arrive.

Another first-season play, "The Chaser" (5/60), generates moral ambiguity, as well, but its best effects rely more heavily upon camera angles and repetition than did those of "Time." Again, the play turns on the puritan argument that getting what we want can destroy us. Like Balzac's Old Goriot and Flaubert's Charles Bovary, Chaser's Roger

Shackleforth suffers because of excessive love—his love for Leila and then, after Leila swallows a love potion he puts in her drink, hers for him. Roger is the chaser of the play's title, one who seeks a goal not meant for him to attain. At great personal cost, he learns that, having failed to win Leila by courting her, he should have relinquished the quest. This man who keeps repeating the phrase, "as a matter of fact," has lost touch with factual reality. Even Professor A. Daemon, the provider of the love potion, tells him to forget Leila. But he ignores this advice along with Daemon's addendum that the potion is the cheapest of his wares. As a result, Roger finds himself trapped in a cycle of his own making as corrosive in its way as the ones found later in "Dead Man's Shoes" (1/62) and "Come Wander with Me" (5/64). His entrapment asserts itself through repetition. At the outset, Leila accused him of talking like a baby. The booties she's knitting at the end reveals that she's having a baby. Doors call attention to his enthrallment. To reach Daemon's den of wares, Roger must pass through two doors. While courting her, he had kissed the outside door of Leila's apartment. Yet, after marrying her, he kisses the apartment's inside door on his way out of it. Doors stand between him and what he sees as his best chances. Now he'll never open the right one. The roses and champagne accompanying both his first and last on-camera encounters with Leila describe his life as a closed circle.

But these developments also have pleasant connotations. The play's ending makes us wonder if he can benefit from the fragrance and sparkle of champagne and roses. He changes his mind about giving Leila the professor's "glove cleaner" or "eradicator," a nondetectable poison that costs him $1000. Daemon's first question, after he spots Roger at his door for the second time, "Have you come for the glove cleaner?" reminds us that undoing a mistake can be very toilsome. But Roger must pay the price, which is 1000 times higher than what he paid for the love potion which brought him to Daemon in the first place. He lacks force, a point that director Douglas Heyes emphasizes by placing him below Daemon in each of the men's two encounters. Besides being shorter than the professor, Roger also interacts with the older man when Daemon is on a ladder inspecting his wares. But Daemon isn't Roger's only controller. Just as Leila once controlled him with her indifference, she now rules him with her stifling love. And in that her unborn baby tightens her already firm hold on him, she has blocked his freedom altogether. Should he have given her the glove cleaner as a chaser to the love potion that won her heart? The question will occur to him repeatedly. The end of the play finds him chained to a woman whose love he once prized above everything.

Reversal also governs the *Twilight Zone* episode "The Trouble with Templeton" (12/60). The reversal this time involves kindness and cruelty. Aging actor Booth Templeton learns that his wife and best friend deceived him, despite his having idealized them in the years since their deaths. Living on his happy memories of these deceivers makes no sense; it feeds his spirit with lies, and it saps his initiative. Knowing that his misreading of the past has stalled his acting career, the director of the new play Templeton is rehearsing puts together a scenario to improve his star's hindsight. Though painful to enact, the scenario brightens both Templeton's past and future. More illumination occurs, too. Accompanying the scene shifts during the actor's painful rite of passage are changes in mood and tone that are managed partly by lights. Lighting also accounts for the running together of reality and illusion, a major trope in an anatomy of a deluded stage actor. These brilliant effects, alas, run afoul of carelessness with details on the part of the play's production crew. Though the title character's wife is swimming in an outdoor pool, suggesting that the season is summer, Templeton puts on a three-piece suit, a muffler, and a topcoat before leaving his house to go outdoors.

Another script whose title figure's misreading of the past pushes him backwards in time is "The Incredible World of Horace Ford" (4/63). The play's first two apparitions—a toy mouse moving in circles on a desk and a cap pistol Horace fires at a coworker—get the action off to a fine start. The recoil action of the pistol sends a charge back at Horace, who is an oversized mouse caught in the maze of his childhood fantasies. Another apparent incongruity makes sense at a still deeper level. The scene after the one in which Horace loses his job opens with a shot of the cake his wife bought for his surprise birthday party. What follows makes sense of this juxtaposition. Another searcher for the golden millennium, Horace twice sidesteps his family duties to visit the "dirty old street" where he lived as a boy. His three visits to (Chicago's?) Randolph Street (also the setting of *Twilight Zone*'s "A Game of Pool" [10/61]), rather than maturing him, aggravate his childishness. Besides getting fired, he rejects the friendly help of his boss, wife, mother, and best friend. He also contradicts everybody. After denying his boss's charge that his work has slipped, he tells his wife that he deserved to be fired. This immature, impractical man even forgets to ask if he's entitled to severance pay after being sacked.

His childishness has also apparently killed his erotic urge. The day she takes him home from work, his wife tells him that she's so tired that she wants to fall into bed immediately. Later, she asks him to "stay in bed for a couple of days," presumably so that she can join him there. Her brat of a husband ignores both of these sexual overtures. Does this behavior typify him? Perhaps a flaw in "Horace Ford" accounts for both his having stayed married to Laura and his having kept his job for 15 years, even if the job is that of a toy designer. But any flaws in Reginald Rose's fine script are offset by the skill with which the script uses details to support its main idea. Horace has upset both his intimates and himself for nothing. The golden age of his boyhood was tarnished. His defining moment came on his tenth birthday, when some boys he thought were his friends attacked him and beat him unconscious. Re-enacting this horror, perhaps symbolically, at age 38 shows his childhood to have been "an ugly, sad, unbearable nightmare." Like that of the main figure of Harold Pinter's *Birthday Party* (1958), his new life begins on the anniversary of his birth. Though the process is painful, it exorcizes his childish ways.

Up to now, his ten-year-old self has been ruling him. But he's also a breadwinner and husband. Only when Laura, this second self's partner and stay, enters his fantasy and follows him to Randolph Street does he see his boyhood as the mean, sordid affair it was. "Let's go home," he tells her after she lifts him from the street where his 10-year-old self had been abandoned by the youngsters who pounded him. Having started his life anew, he's ready to celebrate. He deserves the party his friends have planned for him. And Pat Hingle deserves high praise for his interpretation of the title role. With his unruly cowlick and his pampered, pouting face, he looks the part of the spoiled fat boy who must have his way. His impersonation gains added conviction from the sausage roll forming at the back of his shirt collar (he meets a hot-dog vendor three times on Randolph Street) and also from his ability to sulk, giggle, or look dazed as he interacts with others. But whether his voice quakes or shrills, his pudgy, loose-cheeked Horace Ford has a consistency that matches its great emotional range. Deft camera work helps dramatize this consistency. In the play's climax, the camera contrasts his petulance with the patience and common sense of his loving wife. As he recounts the ordeal imposed by his painful reentry into boyhood, this half-lifer appears in profile, whereas Laura faces the camera eye as she takes in his words.

Revealing incidentals can also improve a lesser work, such as the "poorly adapted" "Execution" (4/60), which first saw life as a George Clayton Johnson story (Zicree 110). About to be hanged for shooting a man in the back, Joe Caswell is suddenly canted into the mid-twentieth century by a time machine. He kills the machine's inventor when the inventor tries to teleport him back to his 1880 prairie gibbet. Then, this shedder of blood runs out into the street. His hands red, he passes in front of a Red Cross poster asking for blood donations. The jukebox in a bar he enters is playing "Wrap Your Troubles in Dreams." At a subliminal level, he rejects the advice offered by the song. Reality is always more livable than dreams or miracles in *The Twilight Zone*. Dreams, said Freud in *The Interpretation of Dreams,* move away from the objective world because of their unreason, incoherence, and antisocial bent. Ignoring the restraints of civilized daytime thinking gives the dreamer what reality has denied him; dreams fulfill his secret wishes. The disoriented Caswell wants a reality he can be on a level with. His search is doomed. A sign in front of a cabaret he passes reads "Jim Henry's Paradise." But he has crashed into a world that's hell for him, and he has made it more hellish still. As Ziegler said, gainsaying ordinary logic leads to the imposition of harsher, sterner laws (34). The attainment of the dream in Serling's "Execution" kills both dreams and dreamer. Caswell dies, as he deserves. But so does Dr. George Manion, inventor of the machine that brought Caswell into our century. "Execution" is, in fact, the colorless Manion's story more than it is Caswell's, even though Manion's scant time in front of the camera suggests otherwise. It was Manion who wrenched life's equilibrium by tampering with reality, an act of pride that calls for punishment.

A mediocre play about time travel that suffers from poor production values is "Static" (3/61). The carelessness with which Beaumont's script is treated squanders Dean Stockwell's fine acting together with some inventive camera work. For instance, the Stockwell character, Ed Lindsay, puts a coin into a pay phone before picking up the receiver. The phone eats the coin even though Lindsay made a free call, to Information or Directory Assistance. The play's ending is also mangled. Hearing Tommy Dorsey's "I'm Getting Sentimental Over You" has presumably reunited Lindsay with Vinnie Broun, his fiancée of 20 years before. Though Lindsay agrees that he once loved Vinnie "as much as a man could love a woman" (in one of *Twilight Zone*'s worst lines), he used his mother's illness as an excuse to scrub the wedding. His conduct with Vinnie is anything but loving. The two visits she makes to his room in the boarding house where they both live elicit the same curt greeting from him, "What do you want?"

Finally, their hearing together their favorite big-band tune lacks the bonding force the script claims for it. Even though the tune was special to them 20 years ago, it is now playing on a radio that Vinnie gave to a local junk dealer behind Lindsay's back. Besides, if it didn't link the couple a generation ago, there's little reason to think it can do so now that they're older and more deeply mired in single life. At issue in "Static" isn't ambiguity. Some of the *Twilight Zone* episodes work at a variety of levels and invite a variety of responses. "Static" isn't one of them. Its uncertainties stem from bad direction and confused writing.

4

Ghosts Who Laugh

One of *The Twilight Zone*'s best shows, "Walking Distance" (10/59) depicts both the temptations to, and the drawbacks of, reentering the past. "Serling's most personal and undoubtedly one of the series' most finely crafted" works, it sets forth its major plot lines straightaway (Zicree 45). Martin Sloan, a New York media executive, drives noisily into a rural service station. Looking dusty and tired, he toots his Jaguar's horn insistently, even though the attendant is close by. He wants immediate service. But this brusqueness is a facade. He apologizes for it straightaway. His snappy car and prestigious job haven't satisfied him. His very presence in the "quiet, tree-filled little town of three thousand people" (*Stories* 54) where he grew up signals his frustration. At 36 he is wrung dry, and he has returned to Homewood in order to rediscover the "uninhibited freedom" he associates with the calliope music, cotton candy, and lazy summer evenings of 25 years before (*Stories* 54).

His outlook promises well. His mile-and-a-half walk to Homewood rejuvenates this weary man, despite summer's glare and heat. When he's next seen, downing a three-scoop chocolate soda in a soda fountain he had recalled from his youth, he's sharp and bright. He soon learns, though, that the same past that can be evoked must not be reentered. Serling's shining, moving epilogue to "Walking Distance" calls "trying to go home again" "some wisp of memory not too important really, some laughing ghosts that cross a man's mind" as he ages. These ghosts must be suppressed, a lesson that probably applied more strictly to the nostalgic Serling than to most of the show's viewers. Serling makes this heartfelt lesson vivid. Homewood may be Binghamton, but it is also everybody's home town. An imaginative presence, it beckons every city dweller caught up in the frenzy of competition, whether the New York ad executive Martin Sloan or the Los Angeles-based TV writer Rod Serling. The summer setting adds to Homewood's charm. With school out of session, a youngster can enjoy the parks, playgrounds, and amusement parks during long, carefree evenings. Serling salutes one of his most beloved characters, Lew Bookman of "One for the Angels" (10/59) by calling him in both the play's prologue and epilogue "a fixture of the summer." The slow amplitude of summer engulfs Sloan quickly. But the engulfment has a special mystique. The sight of a new 1934 roadster convinces him that he has gone back 25 years in time to the summer when he was 11.

Serling uses the wisdom-of-children motif to develop his belief that the past must be left alone. Sloan sees his 11-year-old self carving his name on a post. But within moments, the boy runs away, as he will again when he hears Sloan calling him while the two are on a moving merry-go-round. The intergenerational drama intensifies, though changing focus. In one of the canon's most memorable scenes, Sloan addresses a man his own age as "Pop" and is, in turn, addressed as both a son and a contemporary. The double remove works brilliantly. Sloan's remark, "I belong here," is countered by his father's insistence that Sloan's staying in Homewood will cause trouble. "Only one summer to a customer," the father adds; young Martin shouldn't have to share his. But Sloan has already encroached upon it. While jumping off the merry-go-round to flee his pursuing adult self, Martin twisted his leg. Nor will he recover completely. The physical manifestation of Sloan's interference is the limp he drags away from the merry-go-round.

His visit to Homewood 1934 has taught him a lesson served often in *The Twilight Zone*, that the pain we inflict upon ourselves stings more than that inflicted upon us by others. Sloan will judge well to heed his father's advice about fixing his attention on the future instead of the past. As soon as he decides to leave Homewood, the fateful merry-go-round starts turning again, as if in approval. Earlier, the horses on the merry-go-round had looked grotesque; they were photographed at rest from angles and then lit so that the sockets and grooves in their faces clashed with the flat planes. Sloan's giving the garage mechanic who fixed his car a dollar tip before driving away from Homewood shows that he has learned the lesson conveyed by the shift from the grotesque and the stationary to the mobile; he had jumped on the merry-go-round as soon as it began spinning. That the spinning starts right after his father leaves him shows the intransigence of those natural and moral laws Sloan has breached. That both Sloan and the moving steeds are seen from behind reminds us of what a horse's ass he was to attempt the breach. Every scene counts in "Walking Distance." Though the idea undergirding the work is commonplace, even trite, both the moral passion dictating its composition and the artistry with which the passion took dramatic shape make the script a classic of TV drama.

I

Another story about recovering peace and innocence by merging with our pre-urban past, "A Stop at Willoughby," like "Walking Distance," describes some of the psychological fallout of free-market enterprise. A gentle, sensitive person like Gart Williams can't survive the jungle ethics of business. The play's opening image consists of hard, granite skyscrapers towering above the concrete canyons of Manhattan. These symbols of life's severity appear through a window of an office where a meeting has been scheduled. The meeting, though, is canceled because a junior colleague Williams trusted has betrayed him by taking both his services and a $3 million account to a new boss. Williams has cost his firm a great deal of money. Still worse, he has revealed himself to be a poor judge of character, a major setback for an executive in a "push, push, push business" like the ad agency where he works. So pervasive is this aggressiveness that it has also subverted his marriage; rather than comforting him, his abrasive, status-mad wife scolds him. His alternative is 1888 Willoughby, a place of calm and sunshine that exists only in his dreams. He may well prefer it to the hard, fighting world he lives in, one in which he has to hold two phone conversations and receive instructions from his boss in the next office at the same time. The advantages offered by a village "where a man can slow down to a walk and live his life full measure" are clear; we enter the force field that pulls Williams to Willoughby.

But we don't follow him there. When the conductor on the suburban train Williams rides home calls the stop for Willoughby, Williams gets off and dies. There is no such place, as an earlier inspection of old railroad timetables proved. To fend off the pressures of both workplace and home, Williams conjured it up. But conjury isn't reality. His attempt to enter his fantasy kills him. Believing that he had arrived in Willoughby, he jumps off a moving train. But perhaps Willoughby is more than an imaginative projection. The hearse that takes him from his death site belongs to a firm called the Willoughby Funeral Home. Serling has equated the universal quest for the golden millennium with death. Yet, even though Gart Williams touches us as deeply as did Martin Sloan, "Willoughby" falls short of "Walking Distance." Besides lacking the innovative lighting effects of its predecessor, Serling's May 1960 teleplay suffers from weightlessness and flimsiness of texture. Willoughby appears too briefly to take on the imaginative force and thus the gravitational pull of Homewood. Whereas we share Sloan's fondness for our country's small-town heritage, we must take Williams's on trust.

A lesser *Twilight Zone* effort that tallies the prohibitive cost of reliving the past is Richard Matheson's "Young Man's Fancy." A wedding has just taken place. The bridegroom's name, Alex, from the Latin *a-lex*, meaning against the law, gives a clue to his misdeeds in this May 1962 teleplay. Clinging to the past, Alex Walker lets the memory of his dead mother skew his duty to his new bride. He delays phoning the real estate agent in charge of selling the mother's home, where, advisedly, the whole play unfolds. Then he refuses to deed the home to the realtor so that it can be sold. After starting up an old grandfather clock that symbolizes his nostalgia, he goes through his boyhood effects rather than packing for his honeymoon. Finally, his will both materializes his mother and turns him into a little boy of 10 or 12. His bride, Virginia, has been stymied. "The boy was causing it, not the mother," said Matheson of the ensuing confrontation between the two Mrs. Walkers (Zicree 232). The elder woman only walked into the picture because she was summoned (if she had been away at all). Virginia's helplessness before her owes much of its pathos to cleverness in both casting and camera work. Phyllis Thaxter, the actress playing Virginia, is no longer young, a point made by several close-ups of her face. Alex's practice of calling her "Verge" or Virdge" also suggests that she may have been waiting for her wedding night to give up her chastity. Her chastity she will keep, probably. What this woman of high moral standards will lose, though, after 12 years of courtship, is her chance for the warm anchoring security of a home shared with a man she loves.

The hour-long format of "Of Late I Think of Cliffordville," from the series' fourth season, gave Serling the reach to probe different aspects of the dangers of absorption by the past. His April 1963 teleplay belongs to the same decade that introduced a nostalgia wave that gave rise to TV anthologies set in the past like *The Wild Wild West*. Perhaps the best metaphor for this fast-moving decade, which saw the surge of the Beatles and the burning of draft cards, comes from Marshall McLuhan's automobile driver who keeps looking in the rear-view mirror while speeding. "Cliffordville" shows how the fulfillment of a wish can backfire. With $36 million in assets, William Feathersmith is one of the world's most powerful industrialists. But he proves that there's a piece missing from every life, no matter how fulfilled. Perhaps Serling pads the jolt of this important insight by injecting a moralistic bias into his script. As Feathersmith's lifetime business rival Sebastian Diedrich says of him, he's a "predatory, grasping, conniving, acquisitive animal of a man." The accuracy of this assessment makes Feathersmith's woes look more like the justice doled out to a scoundrel than a warning the rest of us might heed. And he's much more than a scoundrel. A man of energy and drive, this financial mogul of 75 longs for the struggle. He enjoys hard work, and he enjoys it most when it bears fruit. But he still feels empty. Though he has achieved and perhaps even surpassed his professional hopes, he wants more.

His crowning act of plunder and cruelty, perpetrated upon his old rival Diedrich, a buyout that both extends and solidifies his industrial empire, has left him drained, like Genghis Khan, to whom he compares himself. The very night he takes over Diedrich Tool and Die, with its 13,000 workers, he gets drunk and make a pact with the devil. He trades his assets, minus a couple of thousand dollars, for the chance to re-enact his triumphs of the past 45 years. The devil needn't force him. As works like "Escape Clause" (11/59) and "Printer's Devil" (2/63) show, the devil never visits anyone uninvited in the zone. What follows Bill Feathersmith's meeting with Miss Devlin proves that the diabolic has already infused itself in the old buccaneer's bloodstream and nervous system. Feathersmith's return to the past defeats him in a way consistent with the ambiguity the people in *The Twilight Zone* often generate vis-à-vis their environment. In fact, the deftness with which Serling explores this ambiguity is the play's outstanding strength.

Yes, Feathersmith's Indiana home town of 1910 has the charm and innocence he remembers its having. But its backwardness—it knows nothing of inoculations or storage batteries—stops him from implementing his scientific knowledge to recoup his fortune. This setback might not have stopped a more patient man from making good on a second chance. No victim of bad luck, Feathersmith is in too much of a hurry; his penchant for grabbing and exploiting, for manipulating and conniving, blots out any ideas he may have had about building and developing. Ironically, his impatience makes a strange kind of sense. He had asked Miss Devlin, the play's Satan figure, to change his appearance, not his innards. Though he looks 30, he's still 75.

The Cliffordville background of the play's three main male characters—Diedrich, Feathersmith, and Hecate, the night janitor—evokes our common humanity. The play goes beyond reminding us that the wicked always suffer. Wicked Feathersmith is. But the revelation that his youthful body depends upon the collapsing viscera and entrails of an elder stirs in us an unexpected wave of pity. If he's a brute, he's a man first. Admittedly, the fusion of delicacy and hardness evoked by his name lacks balance. But it doesn't wipe out his humanity. Like King Lear, he wants to surrender his realm and also hold on to it. And his Lear-like want of self-knowledge constantly trips him up. Pluming himself on his power and his wealth, he tells Hecate that the two of them have the same origins, that they put on their trousers in the same way, and that they both work in the same place. But here, he thrusts in, the resemblance ends. He owns the building in which Hecate slaves for a pittance. What follows this pronouncement refutes it. Bill Feathersmith's trip back in time shows him to be interchangeable with the servile Hecate (whose witchlike name suggests a capacity for the same rank opportunism that drove his alter ego).

The point is clinched in the last scene, in which the two men have switched places. Perhaps Feathersmith is less pathetic than he looks. He's in the big tycoon's office after normal business hours because, as night janitor, it's his job to be there. Hecate, like Feathersmith before him, hangs around because he has nowhere to go and nobody to be with. But if this doubling pattern mitigates Feathersmith's evil, does it also soften that of Miss Devlin? She might have blessed, not cursed, Feathersmith by taking his capital and steering him toward a low-paying menial job. Obviously, the wealth and power he had heaped up as an industrial magnate left his spirit empty. Now his pockets are empty. But his low-paying, mindless job gives him plenty of time to think about his prodigal past and, perhaps, even figure out its meaning. Coping with his sharp comedown could either crush him or ripen him morally. Perhaps he had to lose his fortune to find his true self. The challenge of self-being lies in him. No surprise, though; this same tension distinguishes the best *Twilight Zone* episodes.

Another hour-long work from *The Twilight Zone*'s fourth season that shows the search for the golden age wringing the searcher is "On Thursday We Leave for Home." But "Thursday," which features the strong, nuanced acting of James Whitmore, doesn't merely outstrip "Cliffordville" artistically. It's also one of the most touching, memorable shows in the series. The flow of images and words in Serling's May 1963 script coheres like a good piece of music. Captain William Benteen, the Whitmore role, unifies the flow. He runs a community of exiles who left earth 30 years ago in search of what Serling calls in his prologue "a millennium, a place without war, without jeopardy, without fear." What the exiles found instead on their remote asteroid was a parched, blazing landscape. Fierce meteor storms, the toil of daily survival, and suicide have pounded down the population of the asteroid to 187 (one suicide occurs during the course of the play). The credit for maintaining human life at any level belongs to Benteen. He fixes broken or worn-out equipment, improvising with the materials at hand. He has devised security precautions to shield his people from falling meteors. He rations food and water, assigns jobs, and sometimes touching the people he addresses, tries to maintain the health and morale of his followers. He has also accepted the burden of making hard, unpopular, decisions, punishing shirkers or malingerers. But his greatest feat lies in the oratorical, shaman-like skill with which he convinces his followers that a spaceship will soon fetch them back to an Earth rich in beauty and joy.

The arrival of the long-awaited ship defeats him. His ministry has consumed him to the point where he needs it to live. William Benteen is a benevolent despot, but a despot nonetheless. So long as he remains in charge of them, his people can't achieve full growth, a point he doesn't deny. By asking them to stay with him on their baking, impoverished asteroid, he's rating *his* selfish needs above their welfare. He even lies to them, calling planet Earth a place of horrors where they will all suffer and die. Yet, when a vote is taken, he's the lone colonist who chooses to stay behind. Serling's anatomy of the dangers of political power warrants close attention. As he did in "The Mirror" (10/61), Serling describes power as a cancer; the quest for it ends in apartness and despair. Benteen is mad at the end of "Thursday," addressing a nonexistent audience. He has sacrificed all to a Godgame in which he's the only player. The game metaphor carries forward. Once Benteen's followers decide to play a game of baseball or board the spaceship that has come to collect them, they can't be stopped, even with lies.

And can the leader maintain his power base without lying? Can he make the transition from one sort of society to another as the needs of his followers change, even if those needs exclude him? Shakespeare's Coriolanus and George S. Patton both learned that the leadership skills that made them great generals can clash with the needs of a peacetime society. The same truth crushes Benteen. During the meetings he holds, the camera usually shows him from below and by himself, in order to make him look heroic. His followers, on the other hand, shot from above and in groups, seem foreshortened and huddled together, as if afraid to stand free. But director of photography George T. Clemens changes his strategy in the scene in which Benteen's people disobey his command to repeat the word, "together," betokening their agreement to live as a group on Earth rather than parting company and going their own ways. This act of collective disobedience marks Benteen's overthrow, his plan that his people stay with him on their asteroid having already been rejected.

Heavy with pain and loss, he slouches out of the frame, his shoulders drooping, with the camera placed both behind him and above the level of his head. This inventive photography shows him ending his career as a slowly departing back. But this diminishing image doesn't negate the value of 30 years of service that held his community together. His tragedy and triumph flow from the same source. Had he not played the Godgame, his followers all would have died. Yet this same Godgame proves life-inhibiting. "Thursday" is a great teleplay because, besides extending Serling's thoughts on the dangers of seeking the millennium, it blends inevitability with mystery in a way that questions our own political morality. Such uncertainty is healthy. As D.H. Lawrence showed in *Women in Love*, any artifact powerful enough to make us feel unsafe compels our imaginative commitment.

II

Politics in *The Twilight Zone* can abut on many other issues. Serling writes about history and loyalty, the solace and loneliness of family duties, the grip of everyday reality, and the dangers of both forgetting one's ghosts and giving them the upper hand. He explores these large issues through characters frayed, damaged, and often lacking the habits of mind that can lift them into middle-class respectability, like Al Denton of "Mr. Denton on Doomsday" (10/59), an ex-gunfighter turned town drunk, or Joey Crown, a broke, jobless trumpeter in "A Passage for Trumpet" (5/60). Serling's affection for these small-timers shows in the minor victories they win. On the other hand, the grandees of "A Thing about Machines" (10/60), "The Silence" (4/61), and "A Piano in the House" (2/62) all come to grief. This leveling social morality recalls the Columbo series, whose evildoers, regardless of gender or race, always enjoy fame and wealth and are also always apprehended. Commoners from *The Twilight Zone* whose pride has pumped them up with self-importance, like the protagonists of "Mr. Dingle the Strong" (3/61) and "A Kind of Stopwatch" (10/63), also suffer deservedly.

No scourge, Serling will reward virtue, too. John and Mary Holt of "The Trade-Ins" (4/62) go to the New Life Corporation to renew themselves. But the $5000 they have brought will only pay for one renewal. Hoping to double his cash, John joins a poker game. He's cleaned out quickly. But the calamity helps him. His opponent, unaccountably, returns his money. Even a hardened gambler can help a sucker, in his own stronghold, no less. In the fullness of time, John parlays this compassion into the recognition that love is better than youth. He reverses the operation that restored his vitality, removed his pain, and divided him from Mary. The Holts will share their remaining days secure in their mutual love. Both everything and nothing have happened to them. Though they leave the New Life Corporation physically unchanged, the resolve and self-acceptance they have gained make their visit a blessing.

A careful blend of sugar and sting gives "Trade-Ins" more integrity than the usual heart-warmer about the goodness of good people prevailing over the wicked. Inner truths also outpace tangible results in "The Man in the Bottle" (10/60). The more grandiose Arthur Castle's wish, the harsher its recoil. Castle's ambition to become an absolute dictator lands him in Hitler's bunker wearing a toothbrush mustache the very day the Allied Forces take Berlin. With his usual tenderness for decent, gentle people, Serling, in one of his rare interventions, helps Castle out of this trap. And as usual, both Castle and his wife benefit from Serling's act of grace. Having learned the truth that all fulfilled wishes carry a surcharge, they return gratefully to their prior threadbare existence, cured of any temptation to leave it.

"Cavender is Coming" (5/62) describes another failure to reorder life. Miracles aren't miraculous, Agnes Grep, the Carol Burnett character, learns. The help they provide goes against the grain of the daily routines we have put in place for ourselves. Though not consciously chosen or implemented, these routines probably suit us most of the time. Their persistence also confirms our right to seek happiness in our own way. Our efforts don't insure happiness. But they succeed more often than any scientific or supernatural paradigms imposed on us from without. The contentment that replaces the Castles' search for gold carries the weight of a steadily lived reality that has withstood years of setback and shock. Thus the rooming-house resident, Agnes, feels lost amid the glitter of a high-society party. After returning to her old life of seediness and uncertainty, she hears Cavender, her guardian angel, tell her, "You're the richest woman I know. You have an abundance of life." Cavender might have added that this abundance comprises friends, neighbors, and artifacts made familiar and comforting by the passage of years. His last words about Agnes, "She's six times happier than when I found her," calls up another important truth. Like Arthur Castle in "Man in the Bottle" and Mr. Bevis, Agnes's appreciation of her daily routine sharpens when she's jerked away from it. Her disclaimer, "No Morgan Mansion, No Sutton Place," shows that, rather than living her life according to received social standards, she has the courage and wit to create her own.

Serling commends this creativity. A believer in self-reliance, he told *Gamma* magazine that "every man can and must search for his own personal dignity" (74). The search may segue into conduct that is blameworthy. But blame or disapproval shouldn't deter the searcher. In a misreading, Farber and Green call George Clayton Johnson's "Kick the Can" (2/62) a "sweet-tempered . . . insipid fantasy about old people" (174). What they miss is both the redemptive force of magic and, more importantly, the need to believe in this force. An elder shocks his friends when he says, "Maybe kick the can is the greatest magic of all." The empty can he's holding as he speaks just diverted and delighted some local youngsters. Why can't it also grace the life of aging Charles Whitley? It does become a talisman to him. He makes most of his pronouncements about youth while holding it. In the play's closing scene, Ben Conroy, his cynical boyhood friend, has it. But Ben's cranky, carping ways seem to have cost him the second chance so vital to *The Twilight Zone*. At least for now; his very act of holding the battered can marks his acceptance of the truth that the commonplace, and even the despised, can house magic, wonder, and the power to transform. The flustered old man holding the can may stand closer to the boy who used to kick it than he knows.

Another obsolete man whose obsolescence stems from within is scarred, battered-looking Bolie Jackson, a 33-year-old boxer attempting a comeback in Serling's "Big Tall Wish" (4/60). Serling's reference to "the strange and perverse disinclination to believe in a miracle" in the plays's epilogue explains why Jackson's ring comeback fails. Watching the fight on television, his nine-year-old neighbor Henry concentrated his mind and made a big tall wish that Jackson be the winner. The wish works. Though Jackson is knocked out, the force of Henry's spirit reverses the identities of winner and loser. It's only Jackson's faithlessness that reverses the reversal and turns him back into the whipped pug splayed on the ring canvas while the referee counts him out. "I can't believe," he tells Henry; "I'm too old and too hurt to believe." "Kick the Can" proves him wrong. Loss of faith in himself has cost Jackson his boxing career. It also reflects the all-too-human tendency, enacted in "The Grave" (10/61) and "The Dummy" (5/62), to subvert one's best chances.

Another work that probes the question of alternative realities is "The Sixteen-Millimeter Shrine." Like "A World of Difference" (3/60), "Shrine" pits Hollywood celluloid against the real world. The October 1959 teleplay starring Ida Lupino recalls the 1950 film *Sunset Boulevard* with the love story replaced by a mystical turn of time. Former film idol Barbara Jean Trenton spends most of her time in the screening room of her extravagant Beverly Hills mansion, itself a throwback to the 1930s, the heyday of her movie career. By 11 A.M. on the day that "Shrine" begins, she has already watched two of her old full-length films and downed a drink or two. Her agent, a role enacted with insight and sympathy by Martin Balsam, calls her screening room "dark, damp, and full of cobwebs." Both the ratchety whirr made by the projector and the flashes of light created by the projector's turning reels augment the atmosphere of foreboding.

Serling's complex attitude toward Barbara, avatar of this sinister make-believe world, combines nostalgia for the silver screen of his youth and hardheadedness. "If I wish hard enough, I can wish it all away," says Barbara of the film industry that has forgotten her. She wants to return to the "carefree world" of the 1930s, equating it with the charm, polish, and romance of the decade's movies. Her having forgotten that this breezy elegance clashed with the day's economic woes implies that she has always been a dreamer. The implication acquires force, lending both speed and pressure to the plot. Barbara retreats every deeper into her fantasy, spending more time drinking, watching her old movies, and thus denying the passage of time. The play's powerful closing sequence shows her on the screen in her projection room. She has left our world for that of both the screen and the screenplay she has conjured into reality. That her agent, Danny Weiss, views this alarming spectacle from the chair she always sat in to watch her old replays and that he smiles when he picks up the handkerchief she throws him from the screen both call into question the fantasy-reality dualism. Do movies have a reality of their own? Barbara has forsaken her flesh-and-blood self for the realm of celluloid. But she has preserved both the style and the tone of the Hollywood star she once was, and she also wrote and directed the movie in which she appears; others are acting *her* script. Plausibly, Danny's smile tells us that she's happier now than she has been for years. The questions raised by "Shrine" run deep. Economical, fast moving, and provocative, the work dares both to teach us and to do it in the best, but hardest, way—by withholding answers.

Charles Beaumont's "Miniature" (2/63) provides another lesson at once partial, ambiguous, and momentous. The show's main figure, Charley Parkes, like Barbara Jean Trenton before him, either slips into a fantasy or chooses creatively and wisely. His apartness is made clear from the start. The opening scene differentiates him from his coworkers. Whereas these men leave the office together at noon to have lunch, he keeps working. And when he does eat, he doesn't go to the diner used by his coworkers, but to the cafeteria of a nearby museum. Even here, though, he bucks the common tide. A touring party of visitors to the museum descends the staircase leading to the cafeteria, taking him back down to the ground floor with them.

His alienation soon seems complete. After his second visit in our presence to the County Museum, the camera cuts to his family's breakfast table. His uncouth knuckle-cracking brother-in-law and his domineering mother both try to foist their values on him. Both talk with full mouths, too, whereas fastidious Charley, clad in suit and tie, only sips milk. His boss has just fired him because he "doesn't fit in." But the joy Charley takes in whistling a song he first heard that same day shows that the day was a good one for him. The source of this goodness lies close by. Earlier, at the museum, he had seen an encased nineteenth-century miniature townhouse. In it was a beautiful figurine seated at a harpsichord, which he soon hears her playing. It's natural for him to endow her with life and to fall in love with her. Nobody he has interacted with in our presence has so much in common with him. Besides being neat and ceremonious, he and the figurine both move deliberately and precisely. Most of all, they have similar problems, both being menaced by coarseness and brutality. Charley angers a young woman his sister introduces him to by rejecting her kiss. Then the figurine has to repel a visitor's rough pass. Charley's saying of this incident "he tried to kiss her last night, but she wouldn't let him" shows that he has confused the two events—and probably also the identities of the reluctant parties in the two aborted love scenes.

His involvement, or confusion, builds. Neglecting all his duties, he spends four or five hours a day looking at the girl. He calls her "trusting, innocent, and helpless," which is the way other people see *him*. He tells her he loves her: she's the only one he has met capable of understanding him because they're both outsiders. He wants to forget the socialized people of the world; only *she* is in sympathetic attunement with him. The last scene finds him sitting alongside her in the townhouse, a well-dressed suitor paying court. The warm smile on the face of the museum guard who sees this ceremonious pair recalls that of Danny Weiss bidding his last goodbye to Barbara Jean Trenton in "Shrine." But does it also reflect our approval? Both Beaumont's text and Walter E. Grauman's direction are slightly ambiguous. Prior to the finale, Charley had hidden in a mummy case just before closing time in order to spend some after-hours time with his ladylove. The link between death and his ruling passion is clear. Clouding it, though, are the energy and wit infusing the passion. He tricks his psychiatrist into thinking he has outgrown his fascination with the doll. For the first time in the play, he lets his mother remove his shoes. He defies the museum guard who chides him for spending four or five hours a day gazing at the model townhouse. Both Charley's explanation that he's not breaking any rules and his request that the guard leave him alone reveal his strength of purpose. In the best tradition of courtly love, he has found the woman he wants and pursues her regardless of what others think.

Do his ingenuity and drive serve his delusion? Perhaps; American literature bristles with such unfortunates. But Charley's splendid energies confirm another patently American theme—the individual's right to snub vested authority in his/her quest for authenticity. Remember, one of the authority figures Charley stands up to, the museum guard, smiles when he sees Charley with his ladylove. His approving smile recalls a warning dramatized in *Twilight Zone* episodes like "The Obsolete Man" (6/61) and "Mute" (1/63), that nonconformity is a right that any just gov-

ernment must protect for its own sake as well as for that of the nonconformist. "Miniature" works both as a political statement and a human
drama because of its ability to find the precise point where the seemingly
false turns out to be true.

5

The Abyss

The landmark January 1955 *Kraft Television Theater* production of "Patterns" featured a motif that recurs often in Serling, that of the obsolete man. As has been seen, the young industrial planner and production engineer from Cincinnati, Fred Staples, replaces Andy Sloane, "the last of the original bunch" that helped found Ramsie and Company. The firm's chief, "a freak . . . an organization marvel with no compassion for human weakness," forces Sloane out of the firm even though Sloane's ulcer, bad heart, and 56 years all hurt his chances of finding work elsewhere.

Office politics also develop the motif of obsolescence in "They're Tearing Down Tim Riley's Bar," which played on NBC's *Rod Serling's Night Gallery*. Like Andy Sloane, Randolph Lane is a decent, high-minded executive in a large, thriving company. Also like Sloane, he's being edged out of his job by an ambitious young colleague (a "hot-shot peddler" called Doane). The action of the January 1971 teleplay featuring him takes place on the day Lane is celebrating 25 years with Pritken's Plastic Products. His mood isn't festive. Worried that he's going to lose his job, he gets drunk—in Tim Riley's Bar, site of his first date with his now-dead wife. The bar stirs other memories. Randy Lane equates it with "an age of innocence" that includes rumble seats, saddle shoots, and "pre-Pearl Harbor long summer nights," a time he calls "the best years of my life." These years have passed. Both Lane and Tim Riley's Bar are obsolete. The bar is being razed to make way for a 20-story bank building, and Lane's decline in productivity at Pritken's has already prompted his chiefs to groom Doane to replace him as Director of Sales. In a stroke of unity worthy of Chekhov, both Lane and Tim Riley's must yield to progress; neither pub nor man can survive the changes dictated by advances in technology and business.

But people are more than tradesmen and technocrats; they have inherent worth. Like Chekhov, Serling understands how the passing of a local landmark, let alone of a person, can wrench hearts. Lane's rich, inventive language (articulated stunningly by *Twilight Zone* alumnus William Windom) discloses a keen wit. Though Serling bought into his society's get-ahead secularism, he also clung to the traditional ideals of neighborhood, home, and family. Several *Twilight Zone* episodes treat issues raised by what passes for obsolescence in our confrontational materialist society. And he directs these large issues back to himself, a motif hinted at by his having made Lane the same age as himself, 45, and by his mentioning Lane's dead father (Serling's own father died in 1945 [(Sander 50)]).

The December 1963 script, "Ninety Years without Slumbering," though not by Serling, features in Sam Forstmann an elder who, besides sharing Serling's father's first name, would have been about Sam Serling's age had Sam lived to see the script produced. Unlike most of the zone's obsolete men, Sam Forstmann invites obsolescence. Though the retired clockmaker admits that his 76-year-old grandfather clock is just a machine, he identifies with it to the point of believing that its collapse will cause his own. The script makes good the identification. Sam first appears repairing the clock and singing to it, even though the hour is late. Then he's seen in the reflection of the glass door in front of the pendulum. Man and clock seem joined. When told by a psychiatrist that he's obsessed by the clock, Sam remains unmoved.

Richard de Roy's slack script deserts this promising plot line. The pregnancy of Marnie Kirk, Sam's granddaughter, is gratuitous and irrelevant. The script peaks in Sam's rebirth, an event that occurs when, without motivation, Sam puts aside his obsession with the clock. His renewal violates plausibility elsewhere, too. All too conveniently, the scene following Sam's decision to sell the clock introduces a neighbor who offers to buy it. A regimen snaps quickly into place. The neighbor and her husband admit Sam into their home every other day for two weeks to wind the clock. But then they leave town for a weekend without leaving Sam a key. This last development is absurd. The Chases know that the clock needs winding. They also know of Sam's obsession with it. Thwarted, Sam returns to his room after trying to break into the Chases' home, and he starts to die. But just as his spirit begins squiring him to the afterlife, he snaps out of his doldrums. He wants to go on living. None of his previous actions have changed his mind. He merely starts believing what his family and psychiatrist have been telling him all along because he would rather live than die. How does his decision affect us? We can only hope that his remaining days will be happy. Our hopes end here. Any play whose resolution violates plausibility insults its audience.

I

A work of greater intelligence and polish that treats the issue of obsolescence is "The Obsolete Man" (6/61). That *obsolescence* is the third word spoken in the work discloses an attentiveness that helps lift the work to the top tier of the *Twilight Zone* canon. The dictatorship in which the work unfolds has banned books. And if books no longer exist, neither can libraries or librarians; Romney Wordsworth has become obsolete, says the law of the land. Knowing that any police state breaks on the rock of the individual, the librarian's accusers address him as Wordsworth, Romney. But their inversion of his first and last names, rather than blurring his individuality, sharpens it by identifying him with the language's best poet since Milton. Names continue to bear thematic weight. The Chancellor, Wordsworth's chief accuser, has no name that we know of. That he's always seen wearing a uniform bleeds still more humanity out of him. This loss of self comes from the functionalism that rules the state: rather than standing freely, individuals exist to serve their country, enacting a loveless creed that dwarfs human purpose. The belief that a person's reality stems from his/her political usefulness disclaims the person's value as an independent center of significance; it robs us all of self-justifying existence, as well.

Like most fascist writ, this bleak functionalism trivializes morality. For one thing, it has extruded metaphysics. Necessity has decreed that the state embodied by the Chancellor outlaw religion; to worship God is to acknowledge a force more potent than government. Yet the Chancellor's constant practice of calling the condemned man "Mr." Wordsworth, though meant as a slur, suggests a hidden admiration for the independence and individuality fostered by the librarian's religious faith. Ironically, the Chancellor denies God while standing on a pulpit and intoning his pronouncements in the sonorous cadences of a minister, cadences whose authority he enhances with ministerial gestures. His pulpit performance, though moving to others, has left him feeling dry and empty; it confirms the power of the tradition he ostensibly denies. He needs more self-assurance. Thus he orchestrates Wordsworth's execution as a media event with microphones and TV cameras in place so that his fellow citizens can witness both Wordsworth's death and the cringing pleas for mercy preceding it. Allegedly to make sure that his viewers will get a cowardly performance from Wordsworth, the mighty Chancellor even visits the librarian's humble room 45 minutes before the room is slated to explode with the librarian inside it. Now any nation that scorns the civilized controls of reason, justice, and decency can declare a citizen obsolete and then wipe him/her out at will. What the Chancellor has failed to see is how closely any leader lives to this same pit of obsolescence. He overreached himself by visiting the man he condemned to death in order to make him grovel. But what would such cowardice—if cowardice it be—prove? Lack of conviction brought the Chancellor to Wordsworth. What occurs next is a consummation he may have been wishing for in his innermost heart; the framers and enforcers of unjust laws are those laws' true victims, and they know it.

After admitting the Chancellor to his room, Wordsworth locks the door and pockets the key. The Chancellor flusters when, the clock fast approaching Wordsworth's doom stroke, he finds himself also looking at death. Nor can he forsake rational control in his attempts to persuade Wordsworth to free him; the scene is being watched on television by millions. He has been stymied. The rescue of a high-ranking state official is unlikely, particularly in front of a large TV audience; nobody will break in Wordsworth's door to free the Chancellor. The strong, erect authority figure must die alongside the despised, obsolete librarian. But aren't the two men, so different on the surface, dying for the same reason? The reluctance of the Chancellor's colleagues to save him shows that his duping by the lowly Wordsworth has made him obsolete. The creed he serves demands his death. He has become the obsolete man of the teleplay's title.

Driving home the inevitability of this gripping finale is the last exchange between the two men. Enacting a perfect stroke of justice, Wordsworth gives the desperate Chancellor his key, allowing his foil to flee the room that will explode within seconds. Wordsworth meanwhile stays put. He dies a hero's death, dignifying his last minutes by reading aloud from the 23rd Psalm. The Chancellor's atheism, on the other hand, has made him Wordsworth's inferior. Sweating and panicky, he shrinks in dignity as his death moment approaches, begging Wordsworth to spare his life and then grabbing Wordsworth's door key so that he can flee. But his survival is worthless. Having forfeited the dignity that goes with his high post, he has also forfeited the post itself—a hard truth he overlooked in his zeal to escape death. He's alone overlooking this logic. Greeting his return to the courtroom where he had condemned Wordsworth to die is the verdict of his ex-colleagues, now his judges, that he is obsolete.

What follows this verdict could have been foreseen. All dressed alike, his accusers, who pronounce his doom in unison, close in on him. Die he must. Lacking a job in a state ruled by the law of functionalism, he has already renounced his claim to life. Finally, his last words to his jailer Wordsworth, "for God's sake," betray both his individualism and the piety that the state must crush in order to survive. A hero in his own right, the Chancellor dies within minutes of the time he began to live. His triumph inheres in the ease with which he recovers his humanity; his tragedy, in the inescapability of the death sentence which he, as a political leader, has pronounced on himself. Like a king from antiquity, he consents to his death. He rushes back to the courtroom right after leaving

Wordsworth, and the feebleness with which he resists his attackers depicts the sad victory of his politicized self over his instincts. A political lesson his death is. It shows his fellow citizens that no act of heresy in the state goes unpunished, regardless of its perpetrator. Besides getting the public's attention quickly, such lessons drive home the advantages of obedience.

"Mr. Denton on Doomsday" (10/59) also uses the obsolescence motif to questions received notions about failure and success. The play's basic components look frayed and shopworn. Set in the American West of the nineteenth century, "Denton" uses the clichés of the town drunk, the good-hearted prostitute, the local bully, and the young sharpshooter who wants to supplant a tired, aging one. What's more, the plot's resolution depends upon a deus ex machina, a peddler of magic potions audaciously called Henry J. Fate. Fate gives some of his potion to Al Denton, an ex-gunslinger who has degenerated into an alcoholic wreck. Denton needs it. A virtuous man who would rather destroy himself than others, he has been drinking to crawl beneath the challenges he once routinely faced from would-be top guns who rode into town looking to depose him. He continues to crawl. Mixing method with madness, like Charley Parkes of "Miniature" (2/63) (or Melville's seagoing Ahab and Claggart), he sings a chorus of "How Dry I Am" to cadge a drink from the sadistic Dan Hotaling rather than accepting one free of obligation from local bar girl, Liz Smith. Serling's script turns on a brilliant stroke of misdirection. What looks like moral decay on Denton's part owes its life to both patience and calculation.

His perseverance repays him more than he had thought possible. Drinking Fate's potion restores his old skill as a sharpshooter, lifting him out of the gutter and winning him the respect of his townsfolk. But word of his reclamation has spread. The young desperado Pete Grant challenges him to a duel, news of which reaches H. J. Fate. The peddler then gives both Grant and Denton a potion that will guarantee them perfect accuracy with their handguns for ten seconds. Just before their showdown, each man watches the other drink the potion. Then each fires. But the bullets that strike their marks prolong life rather than ending it. Neither man has shot to kill. By shooting the pistols out of each other's hands, the two adversaries—or collaborators—inflict injuries that preclude future gunfights; after this standoff, neither man will be able to draw or shoot well enough to win any duel. Fate's potion has made winners of them both. But Denton's victory means more. Not only has he acquitted himself honorably from future gunfights; he has also won the satisfaction of knowing that he has spared Pete Grant, a stripling young enough to be his son, the anxiety of looking down the bore of every fast gun who believes he can outdraw him. The blessings mount. For what better gift can any father, literal or symbolic, offer a son than an added sum of years to his life expectancy?

"The Changing of the Guard," like Denton before it, shows an obsolete man transcending his obsolescence by interacting with youth. But this time the discard interacts on camera with many young men rather than just one. Professor Ellis Fowler must step down from the teaching job he has held for 51 years. Played insightfully by Donald Pleasance, who had won fame in Harold Pinter's 1960 play, *The Caretaker*, Fowler considers shooting himself. He believes himself a failure; he has left his mark on nobody. He has thus betrayed his master, the great educator Horace Mann, whose statue he visits (a version of which also stands at Antioch College, Serling's alma mater). Fowler's despair soon lifts. His dead former students, given a short reprieve from the grave in order to visit their beloved ex-teacher, explain to him his importance to them. The seed is sown in many ways, Serling believes. Whereas Al Denton helped one youth, Fowler helped many, and he did it cumulatively, by example, rather than through a single act. Perceiving the value of his legacy brightens Fowler's heart. The closing scene of this June 1962 work shows him eating. His Christmas dinner fuses celebration and communion. Though alone, he's one with the human family. No longer needing his job for self-validation, he welcomes his mandatory retirement. He's also glad that he didn't shoot himself, an act he had postponed to listen to Handel's *Messiah*. As in "Denton," chance, or fate, has intervened to help a right-minded loner manage those first few steps on the path of moral reform. The intervention is crucial: no Hallelujahs are sung for suicides. A violator of both secular and scriptural law, the suicide forfeits the triumph and the joy set forth so thrillingly by Handel's Christmas favorite. Another detail in the play, though, reveals less care. It's the A.E. Housman poem, "When I was One-and-twenty," that Fowler reads to his students at the beginning. Dealing with the pitfalls of youthful sexual love, the poem bypasses altogether the problems that await Fowler. Nor could Serling have known that Housman was born the same year, 1859, that his hero, Horace Mann, died, even though the coincidence tallies with the notion of continuity evoked by the play's title. Now, since the coincidence tightens the play, we should be grateful for it. We should be more grateful, though, if it looked less accidental. Serling has Fowler call the poet by his full name, Alfred Edward Housman, a designation that never appears either in collections of his work or in anthologies.

"Kick the Can" (2/62), though artistically inferior to "Guard," uses details more consistently. The play rises to a visual climax when elderly

Charles Whitley thinks, talks, and even bounces around like a youngster. This climax impresses us all the more because of the gloom and weariness it offsets. The dreariness declares itself straightaway. Whitley tells his co-residents at the depressing senior citizens' home where they live that his son is coming to fetch him away. When David does arrive, he shrinks from taking his father home to live with him. Either Whitley misunderstood David's words or David changed his mind. The sad old obsolete man must trudge back to the same rest home he had pranced so hopefully from just moments before. His escape from fatigue and grousing seems to have failed. But for the game of kick the can, called by him "a summer ritual," he would subside into the quagmire of age, a numbing regimen enforced by the director of the home, a male authority figure advisedly called Cox.

Both the joy Whitley takes in kicking the can and the moral prod he uses to rouse his counterparts, "I can't play kick the can alone," show that obsolescence can be fought. Though Serling uses film noir techniques, he rejects the moral nihilism associated with the genre. Charles Whitley and Ellis Fowler are but two of his *Twilight Zone* creations who withstand the entropic drift. Getting sucked into the drift usually means surrendering to denial. Michael Grady, the jockey in "Last Night of a Jockey" (10/63), closes out his turf career by wishing himself ten feet tall. He hadn't reckoned on the leniency of the local racing commissioner, who reinstates Grady after his alleged participation in a horse-doping incident barred him from the track. But Old Testament retribution can influence *The Twilight Zone*'s outlook on obsolescence as much as New Testament mercy and forgiveness. A good example of a character crushed by the consequences of his misdeeds is Martin Lombard Senescu of Jerry Sohl's "The New Exhibit" (4/63).

Senescu protests the demise of the wax museum where he has been a curator for 30 years. And his efforts do bring about a temporary reprieve. If the museum must give way to a supermarket, its quintet of figures comprising Murderers' Row can be spared. He stores them in his basement, where he devotes increasingly more time, money, and work to their upkeep. This devotion gets out of hand. He needs the figures more than they need him, a sign of which is the way his tendance of them warps him. Warped he is. He blames them for murdering the three people closest to him—his ex-boss, brother-in-law, and wife. Naturally, he did the murders himself. The figures were merely a convenient excuse; wax dolls lack the sentience to commit any human act, be it murder or anything else. But how did Senescu die? The play's final scene shows him alongside the dolls in Murderers' Row in a Brussels wax museum. His kinship with the dolls drove deeper than he knew. By killing three people, he put himself on a par with the notorious Jack the Ripper and his ilk. The merging of life and art in this scene also puts an intriguing new spin on the play's title. Devoting oneself to dead things can make one deathlike. As with "The Obsolete Man," the eponym of "The New Exhibit" reveals his identity only at the very end, an identity he had been creating all along.

II

Arlen Schumer's June 1991 statement, made in Chicago, that loneliness recurs often in *The Twilight Zone* reminds us that loneliness leads to madness in much of American literature. Numerous *Twilight Zone* scripts also show that the unfamiliar and the strange are always more menacing and thus more conducive to madness when faced alone. "The major ingredient for any recipe for fear is the unknown," said Serling in the prologue to his teleplay, "The Fear" (5/64). Works like "Fear," "Nightmare at 20,000 Feet" (10/63), and "Stopover in a Quiet Town" (4/64) all carry the point a step further by showing that people in transit, i.e., those lacking the comforts and securities of home, are particularly vulnerable. The vulnerability can chill into panic. Soon after landing on an asteroid millions of miles from Earth, Colonel Adam Cook of "Probe 7—Over and Out" (11/63) learns that our planet has been destroyed by nuclear war; he must stave off loneliness while trying to reinvent himself in a strange setting. Had a woman not shown up on his asteroid, his ordeal might have crushed him.

"The worst fear of all is the fear of the unknown working on you, which you cannot share with others" said Serling(qtd. in Zicree 62). And who would quarrel with him? Though we claim to welcome the challenge of the strange and the new, we're usually less open-minded and flexible than we believe. The Serling script "And When the Sky Was Opened" (12/59), haunts us because its three main characters vanish mysteriously; and if their disappearance weren't unsettling enough, every trace of the men's existence also disappears. David Gurney's loss of his identity in "Person or Persons Unknown" (3/62) challenges the very notion of a continuous, abiding self. Gurney's waking up in bed one morning after having known for a day the loss of self lends but little comfort. He hasn't awakened from a nightmare. But has he awakened at all? The woman who spent the night with him and who talks to him with the easy familiarity of a wife turns out to be a stranger. We feel his anxiety. How can a person face the future when his past has become opaque? The script plays on in our minds after its final camera shot, making us wonder if Gurney is either a literary symbol or a character in someone's dream rather than a person in his own right.

"Where is Everybody?" (10/59), the first *Twilight Zone* show, defined humans as social creatures; our well-being requires both social interaction and companionship. Mike Ferris finds himself in a ghost town. Despite the presence of stores, homes, and a movie theater, no people can be found. Ferris gets a recorded message when he dials the operator from a phone booth, and a mannequin (whom he addresses as "doll") falls to his feet when he opens the door of the truck in which she had been sitting. These two events constitute his closest approach to other people. And neither comes very close. Rather than wandering around an empty town, Sergeant Mike Ferris had been inside an isolation booth as part of an experiment. His chiefs used him to simulate the conditions of a rocket trip to the moon. The worst of these conditions was the loneliness. After spending 484 hours inside his isolation booth (upped from 284 in the printed text [*Stories* 114]), Ferris can take no more. Looking down on him as he lies on a stretcher, a medical examiner says of the experiment that nearly snapped Ferris's mind, "There's one thing we can't simulate. . . . And that's a very basic need. Man's hunger for companionship. That's a barrier we don't know how to breach yet. The barrier of loneliness."

Loneliness would persist as humanity's worst foe in the zone. In his prologue to the aptly entitled teleplay "The Lonely" (11/59), Serling calls James Corry, a prisoner serving a 50-year sentence in solitary confinement 9 million miles from Earth, "a man dying of loneliness." What follows justified this description. So lonely is Corry that he wonders, "Can I believe in myself any more?" Later, he tells the man who brings provisions to his asteroid three or four times a year that he's about to lose his mind to loneliness. Another script from *The Twilight Zone*'s first season, "People Are Alike All Over" (3/60), revives the threat of isolation. The first words spoken by an astronaut who suspects that his partner is dead, after the two men finish a 35-million-mile trip to Mars, are "Don't leave me alone."

Loneliness always dogs the intergalactic traveler, as Captain William Benteen of "On Thursday We Leave for Home" (5/63) discovered. The astronaut William Fletcher tells his power-hungry copilot in "The Little People" (3/62), after hearing his decision to stay on the rocky planet where their spaceship had touched down for repairs, "You're . . . going to die of loneliness." Fletcher is wrong—but only because a gigantic spaceman, many times Peter Craig's size, accidentally crushes Craig when he picks him up. Perhaps this quick death was a stroke of luck. For the inhabitants of the zone, any quick death, regardless of its violence, outpaces the bleak wastes of loneliness. The main reason why little Billy Bayles of "Long-Distance Call" (3/61) wants to join his dead grandmother is that she's "lonesome"; thus he jumps in the path of a moving car and then tries to drown himself. Although only five years old, Billy wants to protect his grandmother from the madness that prolonged solitude always brings. He has judged her situation well. Paul Radin, the multimillionaire who lives alone in a huge building in "One More Pallbearer" (1/62), goes mad because he thinks the world has become depopulated. A female counterpart, Miss Menlo of Serling's "Eyes," a November 1969 work shown on *Night Gallery,* will die because her wealth—not her blindness—seals her off from others.

The Twilight Zone will force us to reevaluate standards and guidelines. Paul Driscoll of "No Time Like the Past" (3/63) rejects the love of beautiful Abigail Sloan, a schoolteacher he meets after going back in time to the Homewood, Indiana, of 1881. A twentieth-century person, he knows too much about her world to fit comfortably in it; his sole attempt to prevent a disaster he has foreknowledge of not only causes but probably also worsens the disaster. Driscoll's plight is both rare and representative. If his dreadful prescience alienates him, the natural flow of events proves just as isolating to the ungifted (or uncursed) in the zone. To provide a short list, the main figures of "One for the Angels" (10/59), "Nightmare as a Child" (4/60), "Nothing in the Dark" (1/62), "Four O'Clock" (4/62), and "He's Alive" (1/63) all live alone. These solitaries recall Didi and Gogo, who spend most of their time in Samuel Beckett's *Waiting for Godot* (1952) caught in the trap they most want to avoid, that of waiting. Many of the zone's haters of loneliness also find themselves alone.

Why? Does some built-in destructiveness cause us to sabotage our best chances? Individuality in *The Twilight Zone* is both private and mysterious. The point is made often. In "A Kind of Stopwatch" (10/63), Serling draws some of its sting by using both a nerdlike protagonist and a light comic tone. Patrick Thomas McNulty can't discuss his miraculous stopwatch with anyone since it halts all activity, including thought, except for his own. The watch, his very claim to uniqueness, deprives this chatterbox of the audience he has always craved. His revelation recalls that of Archibald Beechcroft of "The Mind and the Matter" (5/61), i.e., too much of oneself is worse than too much of others. That both Beechcroft and McNulty unearth self-truths when alone limns a point central to both *Twilight Zone* ontology and technique: the nonsharable truth is always vital and profound. An early sole witness, aging pitchman Lew Bookman, is the only person who can see Mr. Death most of the way through "One for the Angels." Joe Britt of "What's in the Box" (3/64) sees his infidelity, his murder of his wife, and his death sentence enacted on a TV channel that had previously transmitted only wavy lines. But his viewing experience is private; anyone else who looks at his TV screen will only see the jumble of waves.

Machines will also humbug their owners in "A Thing about Machines" (10/60) and "You Drive" (1/64) when nobody else is on the scene. These two teleplays set forth an important paradigm, as well. The inanimate object that springs to life in order to punish a person is often a machine, and the victim is often the machine's owner. Secret sins also gnaw at the main figures of "King Nine Will Not Return" (9/60), "The Arrival" (9/61), and "You Drive," and as we know, there's nothing like a secret sin to galvanize a person. In all three plays, private guilt injects life into a machine to enact justice. The pattern varies in "The Thirty-Fathom Grave" (1/63). Seaweed strews the deck near the sick bay where the delusional Chief Bosun's Mate Bell thought he saw his dead ex-shipmates beckoning to hem. Though only Bell sees the men he believes he betrayed 20 years before "calling muster" on him, everybody on his destroyer witnesses the clumps of seaweed his pain had presumably invoked. What's the truth about these two apparitions? And how is our grasp of this truth affected by the discovery, on the submarine in which his mates died, of Bell's old dogtags? The diver who finds the tags knows nothing of Bell's trauma. Though his find defies explanation, it does stimulate thought. One of the great values of *The Twilight Zone* stems from its ability to spark dialogue. A Washington, D.C., man who's slipstreamed from the world of 1961 to that of the April 1865 assassination of Abraham Lincoln in "Back There" (1/61) returns to his own time with a monogrammed handkerchief of John Wilkes Booth in his pocket. Neither he nor Chief Bell has changed the past; President Lincoln takes Booth's fatal bullet in Ford's Theater, and Bell's ex-mates continue to rot on the sea floor. All these victims are past saving. But both Peter Corrigan and Chief Bell, their would-be saviors, make us wonder if we participate in different realities simultaneously, a question reintroduced by "Mirror Image" (2/60) and "The Parallel" (3/63), works that posit the notion of parallel universes.

Everyday reality has become tricky and deceptive, an omniform, multilevel shape whose depths glide in and out of view. Those who winnow an important truth from this shifting mass are forever changed. Their epiphanies, or theophanies, make us ask whether we are more real when alone or together, in groups. The key truths of existence come to the zone-dwellers in terror, not in fact, and the truths bring irreversible changes. The climaxes of "The Hitch-Hiker" (1/60), "The Passersby" (10/61), and "Nothing in the Dark" (1/62) come in the main characters' discovery that they're dead. These shocking finds underscore the point, general in *Twilight Zone*, that all truth is self-truth. Dr. William Loren of

"The Lateness of the Hour" (12/60) creates a robot-daughter so human that she defies him. Over the years he has come to love Jana, defiant spirit and all. But in order to keep her at home, he must reprogram her as a maid, a role in which she's less likely to rebel.

Aesthetics and morality collide again in "The Dummy"(5/62), another work that describes an artifact both edging into and claiming a place in reality. Only ventriloquist Jerry Etherson can hear the voice of his "knotty-pine partner," Willy. But this voice is a torment, symbolizing the way any career in art can engulf the artist. This symbolic shorthand for the tyranny exerted by imaginative creation, which will recur in "Caesar and Me"(4/64), a *Twilight Zone* script about another ventriloquist bullyragged by his dummy, argues that an artist's personal welfare exists inversely to his professional success. Whereas Jerry's routines with Willy are funny, the ones he does with the dummy called Goofy Goggles get few laughs. Jerry's commitment to an art that harrows him declares itself in his attempt to destroy Willy. Bursting into his darkened dressing room, he flails away recklessly. But the dummy he smashes is Goofy, not Willy, whom he needs.

Artists are driven by forces beyond their control. Had Jerry wanted to destroy Willy, he'd have snapped on the light of his dressing room before starting to flail away. Yes, Jerry's drinking curbs his artistry; he'll never be booked as a headliner into a prestigious club. But the bite he gets on his hand from Willy after leaving the stage with his hand clapped over Willy's mouth shows him a true artist. Even to his self-detriment, the creator must let his creations defy him if he wants them to spring to life. Spring Willy does, reciting lines on stage that Jerry neither rehearsed nor even scripted. The "old switcheroo" that turns Jerry "from boss to blockhead" in the play's finale enacts Jerry's undoing along with his self-transcendence. We should not be surprised. The reversal of roles enacted by ventriloquist and dummy has been occurring all along. All serious artists are dominated by their muses. As kingpin novels like Thomas Mann's *Doctor Faustus* (1947), Patrick White's *Vivisector* (1970), and John Fowles's *Mantissa* (1982) show, artists submit themselves to chaos and agony as they lift pen, brush, or violin bow. The artist in William Gaddis's *The Recognitions* (1955) forfeits friendship, marriage, and health for the sake of his canvases; as his art thrives, he wilts. The annihilated one in "The Dummy" is Jerry Etherson; as *his* art thrives, he wilts. But he has believed strongly enough in his vision to sacrifice himself to it, an act repeated by Jonathan West of "Caesar and Me," another artist-mystic who either misjudges his art or is betrayed by it.

Matheson's "Nightmare at 20,000 Feet" (10/63) shows again in *The Twilight Zone* the same interest in private experience. Robert Wilson is flying home with his wife after having spent six months as a mental patient. Another of *Twilight Zone*'s lone witnesses to a dread event, he sees a monster, or gremlin, on the wing of his homeward-bound plane. Only he knows of the calamity the gremlin is trying to cause—the destruction of the plane and the death of everyone inside it. Wilson's attempts to convince the others on the plane of the disaster awaiting them come to naught. Whenever anyone else looks out of Wilson's window, the gremlin disappears. Wilson's panic level rises; he wonders if the mental hospital released him too early. In his tumult, he enacts an argument found in Dostoevsky, among other writers, that truth comes mostly to the outsider or outcast, and that it comes in hallucination or nightmare, a point also argued in *Twilight Zone*'s "Shadow Play" (5/61) and "Night Call" (2/64). Wilson's vision, though outlandish, is more vital and penetrating than the mundane reality perceived by the plane's other passengers and crew. At an altitude of 20,000 feet, the overwrought Wilson lacks stability, ballast, and the other controls usually associated with the land. He is also ready to erupt. We viewers share his fears. Crashing through a plane window, he seems to be causing the very catastrophe he wants most to avert. Yet it soon comes out that he *has* saved lives and property. The next scene shows his plane safely on the ground. In view of the camera is the steel plate standing away from the plane's wing, where the gremlin had pulled it loose. Yet none of the passengers, flight crew, or ground staff have a camera's eye view of the wing's upper surface. Isolated in his dreadful knowledge, only Wilson knows the truth about the gremlin. The others have dismissed him as a lunatic. How long it will take his sanity to be acknowledged and acclaimed is an open question.

This drama will occur off camera because it is secondary. No middle grounder, Wilson will keep to the edge. But he will stay there with conviction and courage, having acquired self-trust. A wife of 27 years in "What's in the Box" (3/64) says to the husband who watches terrible images pass before him on a nonexistent TV channel, "What you see is in your mind, and what you hear is in your conscience." Wilson can ignore such taunts. Thwarting his nemesis has made him a freestanding, clear-sighted man capable of withstanding crises. It seems churlish to find his heroism less impressive than the show's producers would have liked. But the teleplay featuring William Shatner as Wilson does violate plausibility. No rain falls at an altitude of 20,000 feet. And, even if the wing of Wilson's plane were dry, the wind currents would have swept the gremlin into space. Even suction pads on his feet would not have helped. Another cavil: sitting as close to a propeller as he does, he would have been sucked into it and sliced to bits.

III

Though necessary for self-knowledge, introspection can veer into the self-absorption that paralyzes action of the kind undertaken by Wilson. Shallow, vain Paula Harper of Serling's "The Masks" (3/64) looks in the mirror incessantly, justifying the claim of an observer that, to her, "the world is a reflection of herself." Forget her narcissism. Any closed space, however comfortable, will smother those living inside it. *Twilight Zone* teleplays like "Nervous Man" (10/60), "A Most Unusual Camera" (12/60), and "Last Night of a Jockey" (10/63) eliminate outdoor scenes, leaving their people trapped in the claustral oppressiveness of a single room. Other forms of malaise assert their force through mirrors. Right after his grandmother's death in "Long-Distance Call" (3/61), Billy Bayles appears as a reflection in the fish pond in which he'll later try to drown himself. The symbolism is as clear as his image. Just as windows abet interchange, the mirror in *The Twilight Zone* often suggests trouble. Frustrated loners address their alter egos in the glass in "Nervous Man," "The Mind and the Matter" (5/61), and "Jockey." The grubby, hectic jockey and nervous man don't even have matches to light their cigarettes. They lead furtive, isolated, self-hating lives, their mirrors depicting to them their failures to transcend grunge.

It is material that these mirror meetings occur when the characters are alone; revelations experienced alone touch us most deeply. Also, mirrors always tell the truth, even if the people looking into them deny it. The denier can smash the mirror, as in "A Thing About Machines" (10/60), "The Mirror" (10/61), and "Last Night of a Jockey." People who can't forgive themselves try in vain to destroy the secret sin that blocks them from the second chance that could redeem them. Some mirrors reveal surprises that rivet the onlookers rather than twitching their destructive impulses. "Mr. Bevis" (6/60) first sees his guardian angel in the glass. Joey Crown's experience of looking into a mirror and seeing no reflection in "A Passage for Trumpet" (5/60) warns him that he may be dead. The hitchhiker who reveals to Nan Adams of "The Hitch-Hiker" (1/60) that she's already dead appears to her several times as an image in a car mirror. Mirrors also vex Sgt. Mike Ferris of "Where Is Everybody?"(10/59). After addressing his reflection in one glass, he runs into another one with such force that he shatters it. But shattering a mirror can't erase the pain that he's trying to deny.

Lt. William Fitzgerald of "Purple Testament" (2/60) has a terrible gift; just before his platoon goes into battle, he knows which of its members will die. Then comes his biggest shock. He sees in a shaving mirror a reflection of his own face surrounded by the same deathly halo he had witnessed in his doomed men. No slave to *cinéma vérité* or any other mode of screen realism, Serling will wrench probability to gain dramatic force. When the mirror falls and breaks, each shard of it bears a complete image of the lieutenant's face. The cheap grifter Max Phillips's breaking of a mirror in "In Praise of Pip" (9/63) proves just as wrenching. The play's climax takes place in the house of mirrors of an amusement park where Max had spent an hour with his small son. Seen from many different angles and perspectives, Max will face the ultimate reflection of himself in his only child.

Slanted mirrors recur often in *The Twilight Zone* for another reason—to show how characters look from the side and even the rear as well as from the front. This camera technique tallies well with an art form that is not only basically visual but also corseted by a 24-minute format. The angling of mirrors on a shooting set can create both depth and surprise. Occasionally, we will be witnessing a conversation between two people, as in "The Jeopardy Room" (4/64), only to find out, when one camera lens yields to another, that one of the people has been addressing the reflection of another. Mirrors can add important information as well as enriching awareness of the possibilities inherent in the human transaction. Maj. Bob Gaines of "The Parallel" (3/63) sees in his reflection that he's wearing the eagles of a full colonel. Why should his discovery of his elevation in rank reach him in this bizarre way? Has he, in fact, been elevated?

The question gnaws at him. Though they always tell the truth, mirrors can provide information that's unwelcome, mostly because it can't be ignored. Michael Kerbel refers to the Edmond O'Brien role in Serling's Emmy-winning "The Comedian" (2/57) as "the conscience figure" (59). A version of the term appears in J. E. Parker's discussion of "Nervous Man," "the story of a man who battles his alter ego for control of his soul" (172). John, the title character in "Nervous Man," Parker claims, is "the moral conscience" of the "despicable little crook" Jackie Rhoades (172). Called by this moral conscience "cheap, weak, scared, half-vulture, all mouse," Jackie needs to build self-trust. His outlook is bleak. Rather than obeying his instincts, he has always tried to show off to others. He took dares, joined gangs, and committed crimes—all to win the approval of others. Though he hides behind tough talk, saying things like, "Dames I can leave alone," he also calls himself "the half-way boy." The term is accurate. It also discloses a redeeming self-honesty. This stuttering ex-reform-schooler and jailbird is tired of being everyone else's pawn. Looking into the mirror of his grubby room shows him that his worst enemy has been himself. The ensuing dialogue with his upstanding self-image empowers him to defy the gangster who has been threatening him with death unless he agrees to murder someone who angered the gangster's boss. The inversion of selves that takes place before Jackie/John's second on-camera meeting with George, by the way, occurs brilliantly. The mirror through which Jackie and John interact spins cap-à-pie to some otherworldly music just before what is probably the ex-crook's last meeting with his would-be controller.

"Nervous Man" contains one of the few happy endings in the *Twilight Zone* series. The title figure calls himself John, not Jackie, Rhoades at the end, as he leaves his dingy digs to look for a job and perhaps also some female company. Yet his triumph is muted by Serling's belief that we're all self-divided. Jackie/John now brims with hope and purpose; he has left his mousy, fumbling self in the mirror of the room he has just vacated. But this self can't be denied completely. The gutter remains a possible direction for John Rhoades. As his last name implies, he'll have to go a great distance to gain the stature his newfound self-respect has taught him to prize. Between him and his goal stand many obstacles, any of which could halt his progress. On the other hand, his mirror meeting with himself has taught him that our instincts can befriend us. The time he spent cowering in his four-dollar room showed him the squalor that awaits him if his resolve flags and he starts to backslide.

The mirror offers less consolation or hope in "Mirror Image" (2/60), another study of the loss-of-identity theme that permeates *The Twilight Zone* (Zicree 107). Twenty-five-year-old Millicent Barnes is the sole possessor of an outlandish truth. Others find her delusional or mad; at times, like Robert Wilson of "Nightmare at 20,000 Feet," she questions her own sanity. She also resembles Wilson by being in transit. But rather than riding in an airplane, she is sitting in a bus terminal in upstate New York. The drabness of her surroundings clashes well with the wildness of the events breaking around her. First, her suitcase moves. Acts she remembers performing only once, other people claim to have happened at least twice. She even wonders if she's in two places simultaneously. Looking in the mirror through a bathroom door, she sees herself sitting in the waiting room. Later, she will faint when she sees this same self already seated in the bus she's preparing to board. As the young stranger who befriends her says, "This one's tough to figure out."

Serling's "Mirror Image" takes its life from the dark, threatening, Jungian precept of the double. Millicent Barnes and her mirror image are competing for life; because the world hasn't room for both, one has to destroy the other. Both the visitor's headstart and her foreknowledge of Millicent's private history have given her an advantage. She uses this advantage well. Having come to Earth from a parallel universe, she drifts in and out of view, visible only to Millicent. Perhaps she'll supplant Millicent by driving her mad. This plan is already working well. Catching sight of the visitor on the bus dressed exactly like her gives Millicent a nervous breakdown that could reduce *her* to a pale mirror image. Perhaps this development even encourages her new friend Paul Grinstead's alter ego to slip into our world and put Paul through her ordeal at a different level.

Twilight Zone episodes succeed best when they either defy or force us to re-evaluate ordinary causality. "Where is Everybody?" lets us down because it misleads us; it commits us to one set of realities only to change them for a more prosaic set. Unlike the switch that occurs at the end of "Mirror Image," one so cogent that it changes the meaning of the work's title, that used in "Everybody" cheapens the action preceding it. The disclosure that Sgt. Mike Ferris has just spent 484 hours alone in a box makes his ordeal look both padded and thin—thin in meaning and padded in the arbitrariness with which it inched ahead.

A script featuring mirroring relationships that surpasses "Everybody" artistically is "The Mirror" (10/61), a political drama set in a Latin American country meant to evoke Castro's Cuba just after the 1959 junta. Like Millicent Barnes, Gen. Ramos Clemente, the Castro figure, learns to his dismay that mirrors tell the truth. The truth in his case, so common yet so fearsome in *The Twilight Zone*, is the encroaching specter of loneliness. Clemente hears, after killing the last of his lieutenants, "Now you will be alone. Now I'm afraid you will be very lonely." These words strike home. But if loneliness is life's worst blow, its pain sharpens when it is self-inflicted. The head of state Clemente has deposed tells him, first, that he'll die in office and, next, that the identity of his assassin will come to him in a mirror hanging in the presidential suite. General De Cruz is right on both counts.

A high-ranking pol himself, De Cruz knows that rulers care mostly for themselves. Time turns revolutionaries into copies of the leaders they deposed. As the burdens of state force the new chief to compromise his ideals, they also persuade him that he no longer has any friends, only followers and rivals. His puritanism sours into fear and self-indulgence while the democratic beliefs that helped lift him to power harden into tyranny. One of Clemente's first presidential acts consists of ordering the execution of 1000 political prisoners awaiting trial. Then he kills his top aides, convinced that they've combined against him. His surviving aide tells him he's demented. Then the aide is shot.

All that remains is for Clemente to kill himself. Political power is supposed to enhance the self. In *The Twilight Zone*, it doesn't. Power infects whatever it touches, leaving the leader alone with his corrupt self-image. This ugly spectacle repels him so much that he destroys it.

Yet De Cruz's statement to his deposer, "You are me," falls off target. First, Clemente had called De Cruz "an old man in a dirty uniform." De Cruz's age is irrelevant, and his uniform has fewer symbolic bloodstains than that of Clemente. Clemente will also predecease him. Yet, in another regard, Clemente's description carries force. De Cruz's years show that he served as president longer than Clemente, whose incumbency ended after a couple of weeks. De Cruz may well have disregarded benevolence and justice while running his country; perhaps his ouster was deserved. But his succeeding his successor in office also reflects his ability to stave off the fear, arrogance, and cruelty that goaded Clemente.

Goaded Clemente was during his weeks as head of state. Conjuring up conspiracies against him everywhere, he suspended due process and ordered mass executions. The bloodshed soon reached the point where the only person left for him to kill was himself, the real wrecker of his peace. His madness, though, didn't devour all. He never practiced clemency, as his name implies. But he gave no order, in our presence, anyway, to execute De Cruz. Perhaps, knowing how much power corrupts, he believed that he could sting De Cruz more deeply by letting him live and thus force him to serve again as head of state. This indirect hit would have made Clemente's revenge upon his hated predecessor perfect. It would have also chimed with the artistry infusing the play's production techniques. At the outset, director Don Medford contrasts the elegance of the chambers occupied by the newly empowered revolutionaries with the drabness of the revolutionaries' field jackets and jeans. Medford then calls our attention to the red herring he'll later strew across the action by both placing Clemente alongside De Cruz and facing the two men in the same direction right after De Cruz voices his belief in the sameness between Clemente and himself.

What helps make De Cruz's statement a red herring is the violence sparked by Clemente's short incumbency. This carnage also reveals Serling's skill as a writer. The same script that demands the annihilation of anyone who threatens Clemente also varies the ways his victims die. This blend of freedom and fixity works well on the small screen. After one of Clemente's victims dies of poisoning, another is stabbed; others will die from bullet wounds inflicted by a handgun and then a machine gun. Meanwhile, still another falls to his death from a window (a device also used in *The Twilight Zone*'s "A Most Unusual Camera" [12/60] and "What's in the Box" [3/64]), while two more, whose deaths Clemente orders by telephone, die off camera. The many way in which these murders are performed enrich "Mirror." While creating visual variety, they also convey Clemente's madness.

Another *Twilight Zone* show whose main action consists of a stricken soul alone in a room confronting his mirror image is "The Last Night of a Jockey" (10/63). Like Ramos Clemente before him, ex-jockey Michael Grady, "a short man with a short memory," has to swallow the consequences of some bad choices. Or does he? A force tries to persuade him he can undo these consequences. The force lives in his mind, and it calls itself Grady's memory, conscience, or alter ego. It's the self that can't be lied to or shrugged off. What it teaches Grady is that no outsider can either boost or sink a person's spirit. Like the opinions of outsiders, secular success and failure are both evasions or impostors. Real change comes only from within. And it may take strange forms. Grady keeps smashing the objects on which the face of his better self appears, like a coffee pot and a plaque, as well as a mirror. But he can't escape his reflection. Sooner or later, the conscience will rein us in.

Paul Radin of Serling's "One More Pallbearer" (1/62) also suffers from self-division. And, like Grady, he throws temper tantrums, during which he smashes things—a loudspeaker and a TV screen. But these acts of destruction cannot wipe out the unwelcome messages he sees and hears any more than Grady can suppress the outcroppings of his conscience. Both men are wretched. Both destroy material objects because they are afraid of yielding to an inclination to destroy themselves. But yield they do. Driven by both self-contempt and respect for justice, they want to end their sad, empty lives. Radin has been drifting toward death for some time. The bunker this multimillionaire builds 300 feet below sea level, allegedly as a bomb shelter, has aggravated his antisocial life style. Like the many burrows in Kafka, his bunker offers only a false security, encouraging him to brood about his warped sense of fairness, dignity, and injured merit. His ex-teacher's words to him, "Your whole life has been a fantasy," refers to this obsessiveness.

His business acumen, though, makes "Pallbearer" a Marxist's nightmare. Despite emotional problems reaching far into the past, he has earned a fortune. It's doubtful that he earned all of it honestly. "A devious, dishonest troublemaker," according to a former teacher, he cheated on a test as a schoolboy and then tried to blame someone else for his misdeed. He also disgraced himself in the army. Because he disobeyed an order from his commander, he caused the death of half a company of soldiers. Then he drove a girl who loved him to commit suicide. Now, years later, he has brought together the three figures whose verdicts have been vexing him—a minister, an army colonel, and a schoolteacher. His purpose? He uses his high-tech audio and visual gear to convince his visitors that the city 300 feet above them is being razed by bombs. They can remain safely in his lead bunker on one condition: that they beg his pardon for causing him so much grief. None of the three complies. Each claims that he/she acted correctly by denouncing him. Honor counts more to them than life. They ask to leave the bunker, preferring to die alongside those they love to owing their survival to a scoundrel.

But Radin is less of a scoundrel than an object of pity. As he admits, "lifetime habits aren't easily put aside." The apologies of his three guests wouldn't have helped him. As is implied in the punning title of the script featuring him, he has been swathing himself in a thick, heavy pall since high school, a pall he will never shed. The final scene shows him on a busy city street. He thinks the street is empty; all the city's inhabitants have died in the bomb attack he conjured into existence. Serling judges well to call him, in the play's epilogue, "the last man on earth." His mind gone, Radin needs to be helped to his feet by a policeman. The man who wanted to transcend the law can't escape authority figures. No sooner does he see the last of his old teacher, minister, and colonel than he finds himself helped by a policeman. But his madness hides this irony from him. The man who "wants to settle three old scores," as the script notes, is more a victim than ever.

"Pallbearer" exposes the dangers of retribution, its main figure dramatizing the recoil action of both harboring resentment and refusing to forgive. The play's deft orchestration of visual motifs sharpens the danger. The three authority figures summoned to Radin's bunker are first seen from behind. Then they walk from darkness into light—Radin's light—where they follow his instructions about preparing for what will follow. They sit while he stands, an erect, dapper figure with a cultured, confident voice. But the advantage that has been building in his favor will soon dissolve. His three passive visitors soon take life. They turn down his offer of drinks before refusing to beg his pardon. At the end, they're walking, whereas he's last seen whining and groveling. As in "The Mirror" and "The Little People" (3/62), power has once again recoiled on the power hungry, all the more violently because Radin's bid for control has left him unable to manage the rudiments of daily existence.

IV

Characters do prowl through ghost towns in "Where is Everybody?" "Two" (9/61), and "Stopover in a Quiet Town" (4/64). In "Stopover," a married couple, Bob and Millie Frazier, "average young New Yorkers" according to Serling's prologue, wake up one Sunday morning in a strange bed. Their anxiety builds with each new attempt to get their bearings. A refrigerator contains fake food; a car they try to start has no engine; a stuffed squirrel is perched on an artificial tree that's sitting on a papier-mâché carpet instead of grass. Even the town and all its buildings are deserted . Hope does surface in the form of a train sitting in a local station. But the relief felt by the Fraziers when the train leaves the station sours quickly. Within moments, they're back in Centerville; their train has gone in a circle. The giggles they hear enforce their impression that though they're in a ghost town, they're also being watched. And their watcher? Looming above them is the gigantic child whose pets they have become. Although probably normal, seen from below in close-up the child looks menacing. Without intending to, she could easily crush the Fraziers. By how thin a strand do their lives hang? And does their plight resemble any that we might face? By naming the model village which has become their prison Centerville, author Earl Hamner, Jr., invites the possibility.

A different kind of couple actuates "Two," a teledrama that unfolds in a town devastated by war. The couple are strangers. They even lack names, and they don't speak each other's language. All they share is a mutual suspicion. Each wears the uniform of warring armies. But even though the armies have disbanded and the war is long over, the military programming each ex-combatant once underwent still sticks. The woman's first reaction to the man is to attack him. Soon, though, the need for companionship overrides the dictates of military or political partisanship. Though the man sends the woman away, he also has with him two bottles, one of which he intends as a gift to her. The sight of her, even in the uniform of his country's former enemy, has already moved him. He had gone into a derelict barber shop to shave. She, too, has washed her face. Montgomery Pittman's fine script keeps faith with the ambiguity that has characterized the couple's relationship from the start. So pervasive has been the woman's political programming that the sight of some war propaganda posters sparks her warlike impulses, and she attacks the man—but with a divided heart. Though she fires her rocket blaster at him, she deliberately misses.

The ambiguity persists. Our couple walks off the set side by side, a development she had heretofore resisted by always walking a few cautious steps behind him. They've also given up their uniforms for civilian garb. But along with their mufti, they're still wearing their rifles. Mutual trust, if it ever comes, will have to wait. Do they have the patience and good will to put it in place? No answer comes to mind. A sign of hope does emerge, though, in the lone word the woman says during the play. It's the Russian word for beautiful, which he repeats, as if in approval. The pair would do well to take their cue from the word. They're closer than they know to total loneliness.

Life's worst blow recurs often in *The Twilight Zone*, starting with the weekly anthology's pilot show, "Where is Everybody?" It can uncoil from politics, as in "The Little People" (3/62) and "On Thursday We Leave for Home" (5/63). In "Two," the motif sprouts from a military context, as it does in "Still Valley" (11/61), which features a battalion of soldiers all silent and immobile. Usually, it's equated with a lust for power. As in Henry James, the zone dwellers who make large demands get nothing. Garralous Patrick McNulty of "A Kind of Stopwatch" (10/63) craves an audience, just as the prospect of ruling a society of mitelike people in "The Little People" keeps astronaut Peter Craig on the remote planet where his spaceship had touched down for repairs. Henry Bemis of "Time Enough at Last" (11/59) fits the pattern; because this bookworm broke his eyeglasses, he can no more read than McNulty can address an audience of listeners.

The solitary often do their utmost to be with other people. Often, they're too late, having committed themselves to mental habits that block social bonding. Paul Radin leaves his bunker for the city streets he imagines were destroyed by nuclear bombs because he can no longer face being alone. Like him, Captain William Benteen of "Thursday" discovers too late his need for other people. Luckier than these two are the couples in "Two" and "Probe 7—Over and Out" (11/63), who both overcome barriers of language and cultural difference to be together—perhaps to start new civilizations. The misanthropic Archibald Beechcroft of "The Mind and the Matter" (5/61) also enjoys good luck in social bonding even though he lacks the incentive provided by sexual magnetism. Beechcroft has a unique gift; by concentrating his will, he can make bizarre things happen. To remind us of the dangerous political offshoots of his gift, Serling has him paraphrase Hitler: "Today myself, tomorrow the world," he intones, anticipating a program of self-enhancement that backfires on both him and, later, on the title figure of Jerry McNeely's "The Self-Improvement of Salvadore Ross" (1/64).

Godgames are always dangerous, regardless of the rules they're played by. Instead of freezing the world, like McNulty, Beechcroft depopulates it. A stroke of his will empties a subway station, a train, and his normally busy office, Serling having put him in settings conducive to stress. But Beechcroft discovers worse problems than stress-driven ones. Addled by loneliness, he repopulates the world—but with clones of himself. This arrangement depresses him; he tries the patience of his gloomy, short-tempered counterparts more than they do his. "A lot of me is as bad as a lot of them," he realizes. For all its faults, he decides, the world we know is the best imaginable one. Fortunately, he's able to reinstate it, a place that thrums with active perceivers, all of whom differ from each other. He counts himself lucky. He should. In the epilogue to "One More Pallbearer," Serling says Radin is "doomed to a perdition of unutterable loneliness because a practical joke has turned into a night-mare."

Freud saw jokes edging into the reality they spoof. The presence of robots and mannequins, the persistence of the loss-of-identity theme, and the thoroughness with which the Godgame grinds its perpetrators all describe the fragility of the human self. Works as different as "Time Enough at Last" and "The Mirror" show that one misstep can whip us out of existence before we're able to get our guard up.

6

Almost Human

Identity remains a major question posed by *The Twilight Zone*. Fantasy and reality may collide at any time, along with past and present. Nothing seems stable. Characters walk from one time frame to another; they can even infiltrate our world from a parallel universe. This instability can jar us. The person we're maneuvered into identifying with in "The After Hours" (6/60) turns out to be a mannequin; in both "The Lateness of the Hour" (12/60) and "In His Image" (1/63), it's a robot. Surfaces command serious attention in *The Twilight Zone*. Nearly all the inmates of the futuristic nightmare of "Number Twelve Looks Just Like You" (1/64) have had an operation that makes them look the same as millions of others. The operation, or transformation, goes beyond cosmetics. It aims to enforce conformity and obedience through beauty. Physically beautiful people surrounded by mirror images of themselves will have few grounds for complaint. In the process, politics disappear from the state; look-alikes who enjoy the same decent standard of living have no needs. If they did, they couldn't meet them, anyway, since they lack bargaining chips. So thin is their reality that they're interchangeable. A different threat to selfhood occurs in "The Four of Us Are Dying" (1/60). The main character of this play can change his face, a gift so bizarre that he exploits it at will to shirk accountability for his misdeeds. But like all of his counterparts in the zone who exchange ordinary reality for one that looks more promising, he suffers deeply.

The impulse to take drastic steps to improve oneself is understandable. The opening scenes of "One for the Angels"(10/59) identify a pitchman with the toy robots he sells. One of these robots malfunctions. The juxtaposition of the malfunctioning robot and Mr. Death, the immortal who drives the plot, invokes both the fragility and frailty of human life; our unconscious operates by image and symbol, not by logic. Like the robot, the mannequins in "Where Is Everybody?" (10/59) convey a vulnerability and a helplessness that Sgt. Mike Ferris applies to himself:

He went toward the service entrance of the department store . . . and stuck his head into a dark hall loaded with mannequins piled nude on top of one

95

another. The thought hit him that it was like World War II pictures of the gas ovens at the concentration camps, the way they were piled on top of one another. He was disturbed by the similarity and hurriedly backed out into the delivery yard. (*Stories* 100)

In another jarring effect, Millicent Barnes of "Mirror Image" (2/60) is seen from the rear lying on a hard bench. Meanwhile, just beyond her, it's dark and raining outside. This low-placement composite image creates a hostile world, one which might welcome a double of ourselves, despite knowing that the double intends to thrive at our expense.

So often do Serling's people reel around in confusion that they make insecurity the norm of life in the zone. Groping for his bearings in "A Hundred Yards Over the Rim" (4/61), Christopher Horn exclaims, "Who are you and where am I? Where is this place?" The Major in "Five Characters in Search of an Exit" (12/61) asks his four counterparts, "What's going on here? Where are we? What are we? Who are we?" The answer he gets from the Ballerina keeps his nerves frayed: "None of us knows, Major. We don't know who we are. We don't know where we are." Nor do the answers posed by the others trapped on the bottom of a huge, smooth cylinder bring comfort—that the five figures including the Major are on another planet, a space ship, or in a dungeon for the unloved. The telescript's ending surprises us. The five figures aren't people at all, but dolls lying on the bottom of a Christmas barrel. At the Major's instigation, they had formed a human ladder that the Major climbed till he reached the rim of the cylinder. Then he lost his balance and fell—into snow. Our first reaction to his fall is to feel cheated. But the resentment wanes. No, we haven't been watching the actions of people, as we had thought. On the other hand, the five dolls displayed so much passion and such a gift for cooperative effort that they enriched our sense of the possible. If, as dolls, they're less than we had believed, they regain stature quickly, having outstripped our expectations of them.

The Twilight Zone will often provide this enrichment; life is fuller or stranger in the zone than it is in the plod of daily existence. It also holds more dangers. The ventriloquists' dummies in "The Dummy" (5/62) and "Caesar and Me" (4/64) exude a greater menace than we had expected. Two newlyweds stranded for a couple of hours when their car breaks down in "Nick of Time" (11/60) must deal with weird portents in a prosaic Ohio diner called the Busy Bee Cafe, where they have lunch. Busy the Carters must quickly get if they want to leave town with their sanity intact. Terror also erupts from homeness in "Stopover in a Quiet Town" (4/64), a work that also sinks its barbs more deeply into us by unfolding in the daytime. "Stopover" begins with a couple waking up one Sunday morning fully dressed.

"Person or Persons Unknown" (3/62) varies the format. It, too, opens with a couple waking up in the morning to a great shock. But the day is a workday, and the room the couple wake up in seems familiar to both of them. Yet David Gurney's wife claims that Gurney is a stranger, and she threatens to call the police unless he leaves straightaway. Surprised that his clothes are missing from the bedroom closet and dresser drawers, he goes to work, anyway. But here he's thwarted again. None of his co-workers recognize him. A stranger is sitting at his desk, and when Gurney tries to oust him, he's marched away at gunpoint. Later attempts to prove who he is fail. All of his identification is missing from his wallet; then his best friend and his mother both deny knowing him. Tension keeps rising. People whom Gurney calls by name all treat him like a stranger or a madman. Whom to believe? His waking up at the end of the play wearing the same clothes he had on in the opening scene brings no answer. What it does unearth is a glimpse of the unpredictability of the world. Like absurdist drama, *The Twilight Zone* suspends natural law to seek new ways both to describe reality and to disclose its heartbeat.

I

Not only did Serling have an instinct for quality. He also knew when the quality chimed with *The Twilight Zone*'s format and outlook. Though budgeting helped dictate his choice, he used whole cloth the 1962 Cannes Film Festival winner for best short subject as the 28 February 1964 *Twilight Zone* episode. The French film adaptation of Ambrose Bierce's "An Occurrence on Owl Creek Bridge" uses imagery rather than dialogue to portray a reverence for ordinary life displayed elsewhere in the series. Like "Execution" (4/60), "Dust" (1/61), and "I Am the Night—Color Me Black" (3/64), its central scene discloses a condemned felon on a hanging platform. The occurrence of which Bierce (1842-c.1914) wrote is the execution of a Confederate spy by some Union troops. A mood of grimness and desolation is established immediately by the images of a charred post, some gnarled, leafless trees, and the barren winter landscape. The lone note of joy that breaks the gloom seems nearly irrelevant: the only well-barbered, neatly dressed character on the set is the doomed spy.

Surprisingly, the cheer holds. No sooner does the rope supporting the weight of the hanged man stiffen than it breaks. The drab embankment through which the man runs has grown verdant and vibrant. After swimming away from his pursuers, he rejoices in the experience of clutching the sand on the shoreline when he clambers out of the river. He looks at some leaves and insects, which the camera frames in close-up; he's photographed touching and smelling flowers. The English-language song accompanying the sound track at this point begins, "He walks around; he turns around." Having barely escaped death, he now invests reality with a wonder he had never imagined it held before. But the wonder bursts. Just as he's about to kiss his wife, he jerks backward, and he's next seen in a long-range shot dangling from his noose above the river which supposedly took him to safety. Like the lushness surrounding his family estate, his escape was an illusion. But not a mockery; it taught him to cherish a reality forever out of reach. Ironically, only by forfeiting this reality can he perceive its shimmering worth.

"And When the Sky Was Opened" (12/59) also probes the ideas that gain is intertwined with loss and that being may exist inversely with perception. Three astronauts crash-landed in the desert two days before they come before us; they have returned to earth from a 31-hour journey into space. But, unless they're being punished by the gods, who resented being disturbed by them, the calamities that squeeze them are terrestrial. These calamities wipe out everything. Not only do all three astronauts vanish or die; all evidence of their existence also disappears. Each disappearance creates immediate changes; the hospital ward in which the men were recovering will contain one less bed, and succeeding newspaper accounts of the space flight the men were on will refer to one less astronaut. The imponderables mount. One of the men notes that his name is missing from a phone directory where he had seen it many times before. In the same sequence, another astronaut, after asking about the whereabouts of his buddy's glass of beer, hears the bartender tell him that he entered the bar alone.

That buddy had already been shocked when he saw no reflection of himself in the mirror above the bar. Neither did his anxiety-level drop when he phoned his parents in Des Moines and learned that they'd never heard of him. Are they telling the truth? When he vanishes, he leaves no trace of having existed. The space probe's lone survivor, who reads a news story about a spaceman who just returned to earth after a solo flight, feels that he has lost track of reality. His memory clashes with both the written record and the spoken testimony of those near him. Then he, too, disappears. And the contradictions that haunted him? Does their disappearance free us to forget them? "And When the Sky Was Opened" questions the subject-object dualism. It also challenges accepted ways of locating reality. What claim on solid existence has a man who lives 30 years and then vanishes without leaving a sign of himself behind? That "Sky" invites such questions without answering them reveals both an open-mindedness and a flexibility that could promote an

ontology from which reliable answers might evolve. The burden of finding them is ours, as the play's title implies.

While pondering connections between events, *The Twilight Zone*
also looks for a connecting principle. The eponym of "Long Live Walter
Jameson" (3/60), for instance, has lived many lives dating from Plato's
Greece. His essence is indeterminate except for an ongoing need for
love. This need betrays him into committing one of the heart's worst
betrayals—marrying women he knows he will discard when the march
of years ages them while leaving him untouched. "Long-Distance Call"
(3/61) proposes a betrayal just as vile. Five-year-old Billy Bayles is
picked up and carried by his grandmother, but not his mother, whose
marginality in the Bayles homes comes across in director James Sheldon's practice of positioning her in shadows, often to the side of a frame.
Billy's mother, Sylvia, understates her case when she calls the tie joining
Billy to his grandmother "too close." Grandma Bayles calls Billy her son
and make a deathbed wish that he follow her to the hereafter.

Her heart attack and ensuing death plague her survivors. Billy says
that he wants to join her in death. He also claims to speak to her regu-
larly on the toy telephone she gave him as a birthday present the day she
died. Are Billy's phone conversations with her imaginary? The viewer is
perplexed. Sylvia thinks she hears the grandmother breathing through
the receiver of the telephone. If Grandma *is* on the other end of the
phone, she has been saving her words for Billy. These words form the
play's chief mystery. Like the children's classic, Frank Stockton's "The
Lady and the Tiger," "Call" probes the nature of love by pitting sacrifice
against selfishness: in this case, does a dead woman want her beloved
grandson so badly that she'll connive at his death to have him join her?
The answer set forth by the William Idelson–Charles Beaumont script
makes for a happy ending; Grandma Bayles sends her healing spirit out
to Billy and restores him to life. The greatest of our hopes always consists of avoiding death. Like the rest of us, the people in *The Twilight
Zone* want to stay alive as long as they can; Walter Bedeker of "Escape
Clause" (11/59) even trades his soul to the devil for immortality. Such
bargains are empty. *The Twilight Zone* strips away death's malignancy
and horror. A work like Serling's "The Masks" (3/64) presents death as a
deliverer, a permanent release from the pain of dying. Romney
Wordsworth, the condemned man in "The Obsolete Man" (6/61) finds it
more welcoming than threatening. His calling it "the equalizer" also
makes it a force for justice more potent than all the injustices of a dictatorship combined. To Romney Wordsworth, death transcends distinc-
tions of social status and political power: it joins us "in the eyes of God."
This lost unity, a favorite subject of English Romantic poets like William

Wordsworth, also informs Shakespeare's statement in Serling's "The Bard" (5/63), "Death is relative and need not be the end." To some it can bring the rewards of rest, peace, and the healing company of those we have loved; James Edward Parker calls it "friendly, soothing, compassionate" (151). These blessings are glimpsed but never savored in "Death Ship" (2/63); Captain Paul Ross, the Jack Klugman role, forces his two fellow crew members to keep repeating their last living act, their landing on the asteroid where they accidentally crashed and then died. Naval Captain Carl Lanser of Hitler's Third Reich forfeits the consolations of death in "Judgment Night" (12/59) for a different reason; he must relive throughout eternity the horror of riding on the unarmed civilian ship that was torpedoed at sea in 1942 at his command.

Nearly any fate improves upon that of knowing again and again that, although one's ship will sink, one can't help keep it afloat. Even those who clutch most greedily at life would prefer death to this soul-grinding cycle. The people in *The Twilight Zone* have still more reason to welcome death. No fire-breathing dragon with scorched wings, Mr. Death in "One for the Angels" acts like a bureaucrat, a man aware of the pressures exerted by the celestial order he serves. He's also a neatly groomed, well-spoken 40-year-old with a kind heart; at play's end, he assures the main character that he's going to heaven. Death's incarnation in "Nothing in the Dark" (1/62) exerts no menace, either. A handsome young man played by Robert Redford, he wins the heart of the elder he has come to fetch. The horror she has been avoiding but that she invites into her home proves anything but horrible. In fact, Wanda Dunn neglects getting him the medical attention he needs for his bullet wounds because she wants to prolong his time with her. The joy she takes from his company sheds intriguing light on the play's title. Ultimately no ordeal can undo us unless it includes the threat of death. But death gives no cause for fear or anxiety. The drawing of death's sting both quiets our nerves and confirms our place in an all-swathing process that's both benign and just; we awaken in the good place where we belong.

The arrangement of the furniture in Wanda's room makes the place look like a barricade or a prison cell. Fittingly, Wanda first appears to us through the bars of her bedstead. She's a prisoner of both her age and the grubby, furtive life she has adopted. She's the sole occupant of a condemned building; an utter loner, she even lacks a phone. By never leaving her nasty basement flat, she has made herself a living death. And she wants to die. Death beckons her as a reprieve from the cringing loneliness that has overtaken her. But as grim and lowdown as it is, her subsistence is all she has, and she's loath to throw it away. Incentive arrives in the form of a visitor. A representative of the world of living values, a subcontractor has come to say that he has been hired to tear down the wreck in which Wanda has been clinging to the last shreds of her waning life. The visitor stands for progress. He explains that until the place comes down, a new, more livable one can't replace it. What's more, the razing of the condemned pile is long overdue, just like the death of its sole occupant. That occupant's talk with her visitor shows her the futility of her attempt to stave off death. When she directs the man's attention to the third party in the room, she sees puzzlement in his face. Only *she* can see the third party. She has already admitted death into her home; Wanda Dunn is done wandering. Her timely passing will also coincide with that of the eyesore of a building that has brought her more torment than peace.

Mr. Death turned up at her door as the fulfillment of her greatest— and most suppressed—wish, a handsome lover-son who can end her stifling fugitive routine. When she walks into the bright street with him— which is set significantly at a higher level than her drab flat—she looks happy and relaxed, an older woman who fancies herself a debutante promenading with her beau. The death she was dreading has already occurred, proof of which is the haggard corpse she looked down upon before leaving her burrow. She died painlessly, too. Her greatest fear was groundless. Scarcely a second passes before she realizes that she's happier than she has been for years.

When Wanda first sees Mr. Death masquerading as the wounded policeman, Harold Beldon, slumped near her door, she accuses him of unfairness. She knows that, overturning years of caution and suspicion, she's going to admit him into her home. Death is the lover-son she has been secretly craving most of her adult life. Nor does she regret her hospitality. Even the most reclusive old crone will cave in to a handsome youth. Yet he's no more blameless than she. Like the handsome youths in Edward Albee's "Sandbox" (1959) and "American Dream" (1960), he has a deathly agenda which includes deceit. He comes to Wanda from the snow, a symbol of death and thus his natural element. But his deceit becomes gratuitous. By the time the subcontractor knocks on her door, Death has lowered her guard. And by calling her Mother, he destroys whatever scraps of resistance she has retained; within seconds, he's strolling with her in the sunshine adjoining her squalid flat.

Director Lamont Johnson's running of the credits of the teleplay against a background consisting of the clasped hands of Wanda and Mr. Death imparts a crowning unity. Reinforcing the notion that life and death are inextricably bound has been the play's casting. Whereas life's exemplar is an old hag, death stands forth as a radiant young man. The third speaking part, meanwhile, acting the Vishnu-like role of preserver, is middle-aged. George Clayton Johnson's "Nothing in the Dark" is a powerful meditation on death and dying. Though nearly motionless, it blends excellent camera work with thematic unity in a way that makes it one of the strongest entries in *The Twilight Zone*'s third season.

An earlier work that also describes death as a male intruder is "The Hitch-Hiker" (1/60). But the woman death intrudes upon is only 27 years old, and death, no handsome lad like Harold Beldon or well-groomed bureaucrat like Mr. Death in "One for the Angels," has a vague, paltry look. Yet the doggedness with which he keeps thumbing Nan Adams during her cross-country drive exudes menace. Each manifestation of the hitchhiker chips away at Nan's composure. Though carefully pointed, the play's ending shocks us, largely because of Serling's well-articulated script and Inger Stevens's smart, winning portrayal of Nan. Surely and steadily, Nan's self-control gives way to fear and finally to hysteria as she comes to realize that the hitchhiker, who's visible only to her, incarnates a unique dread. The dread uncoils smoothly. Like "Walking Distance" (10/59) before it and "Nick of Time" (11/60) after it, "Hitch-Hiker" opens in a service station which the play's main figure has pulled into for a fill-up or repair. Unfortunately, the car trouble being righted in the work's opening scene occurred in an accident in Pennsylvania that killed Nan, a symbol of which is the detour Nan soon takes into an eerie byway. The celebrated plot twist we've been expecting comes in her revelation that she's dead. But the revelation implicates us, too, since she has been dead the whole time she has been in our presence. What distracted us from this important truth was the sound track. As in the narration at the outset of the film *Sunset Boulevard* (1950) by hack journalist Joe Gillis, who's shown lying face down in a pool, the voiceover in "Hitch-Hiker" comes from a corpse. This effect also turns the mind to Belgian painter René Magritte. Just as Magritte fuses ordinary forms in extraordinary ways, so does the Serling of "Hitch-Hiker" interweave the living and the dead to call forth life's underlying mystery and strangeness.

II

"A World of Difference" (3/60) uses point of view in the same way. The character who has lost his identity is the one we sympathize with. He's the first character we see and the one who feels the most insecure and anxious. He also builds a good case for himself as the person he claims to be. He knows everyone at the firm where he says he has worked for seven years; his keys fit the ignition of the car he drives; he knows by heart the phone numbers of the people he calls his best friend and mother. Yet he's blocked wherever he turns. And though he sticks to his original story, his slowly diminishing faith in it shows in his voice, gestures, and face. The play's opening scene withholds all indications of the events causing this distress. After business executive Arthur Curtis reports to work, he chats with his secretary, Sally, and he approaches a desk on which sit photos of his wife and daughter. Everything looks as normal and commonplace as could be wished. Then, after Sally leaves Curtis's office, the ordinariness is broken by the word "Cut!" The integrity of Curtis's life has been challenged. He's on the shooting set of a film studio, and he's looking into the backlit faces of the production crew. His bewilderment deepens. When he opens his secretary's door, he's addressed as "Mr. Raigan." But Sally's feet are perched on her desk, and, rather than attending to business, she's reading a magazine.

Is he really Arthur Curtis, as he claims? One of the play's most arresting visual images shows various members of the production crew shuffling past him as he tries in vain to get his home telephone number from Information. Have Jerry Raigan's boozing, his divorce, and his professional problems deluded him into thinking himself Arthur Curtis, the rising young entrepreneur he's portraying in a movie? He does seem threatened, an impression that builds from the scene in which he dials Information; for as soon as he leaves the film studio, he's nearly run down by a car. What's more, the concern that the other characters show for him sounds genuine, even out of his presence. The director of the film-in-the-making he's starring in claims that he's having a nervous breakdown. Along with several colleagues, he also refers to the man who would be Curtis as Jerry Raigan. Who's to be believed? Is Arthur Curtis only a movie role? These questions matter because the filming of the script in which Raigan appears has been halted. Most of Arthur Curtis lies on the cutting room floor. The urgency mounts. A telephone operator tells Raigan/Curtis that the firm where he has worked for seven years doesn't exist. Then, when he drives home, his daughter denies knowing him.

Reacting quickly, he rushes back to the shooting set as it's being dismantled. He uses some of the remnants from the set of the canceled film either to conjure up or to preserve his Arthur Curtis identity. Then he and his wife leave the set before it's completely broken down. Artistic invention has replicated itself. Like the characters in Pirandello's *Six Characters in Search of an Author* (1921), he has used some materials from an acting set to create a character. But the character is himself. What remains a mystery is whether his act of creation has helped him re-enter or depart from life. In either case, he wins. Having his wife at his side frees him from the burden of loneliness. Regardless of the hurdles he faces in either inventing or re-inventing himself, he'll be helped.

The main figure of "Queen of the Nile" (3/64) is also a film star, the beautiful actress Pamela Morris. Unfolding at her Hollywood home, the work treats the question of identity differently from "World." Rather than chafing about the loss of self, Pamela enjoys a selfhood as solid and sustained as that of Walter Jameson. Furthermore, she has no death wish. It's unlikely, too, that any prior intimate will re-enter her life intending to end it, as did Laurette Bowen that of her truant ex-husband, Jameson. This literary descendent of the destructive siren or Lorelei has blocked all trails leading back to her. She's even called with accuracy a *femme fatale*. Immortality in "Queen" is a function of vampirism, as journalist Jason Herrick learns when he goes to her house in search of a story. Herrick visits Pamela to unravel the mysteries she has generated over the years. But the more he finds out, the thicker the swathings around her become. His Chicago editor has press clippings citing roles she played in the 1920s. But this surprise pales before others Herrick stumbles upon. The 70-year-old who lives with Pamela isn't her mother, as the actress claims, but her daughter. And, most spectacularly, it's surmised that Pamela, who once played the role of Cleopatra in a Hollywood film, is the Serpent of the Nile herself.

Most of the evidence supporting this identification stems from Pamela. Her ability to combine elegance, warmth, and seductiveness touches us immediately, thanks largely to the acting skill of Ann Blyth. First seen in her swimming pool, she then shows her lovely body to Herrick. What follows looks just as calculated. Though some of his questions seem to shock her, she marshals the poise and control to recover quickly. Her brief show of bafflement and the charm she displays during this first interview lower Herrick's guard. He never learns that, rather than taking charge of his exchange with Pamela, he's being toyed with. What we learn is that this scenario with a hidden agenda has played many times in the past with the same fatal outcome. Any beautiful, socially dazzling charmer can always attract and win admirers, particularly when she has 2000 years of courting experience. The ringing doorbell at the end signals the start of a new cycle, as another eager young reporter has come to Pamela's mansion in quest of her story.

But the story will include him, as it did Herrick. Aided by a scarab, or beetle, Pamela sucks the blood from her victims. These men, it needs saying, come to her voluntarily, just as the devil in "Escape Clause" (11/59), "Printer's Devil" (2/63), and "Cliffordville" (4/63) is either actively sought or invoked. Blinded by erotic attraction, Herrick and his kind invite their destruction. But even had they participated less willingly, they would have surrendered to Pamela. The script Jerry Sohl built around her injects this note of fatalism by changing an important element of the Cleopatra prototype. Whereas Cleopatra used an asp to poison herself, Pamela will drug her suitors and then suck blood indirectly from their unconscious bodies. After the scarab drinks his fill, she fastens it to her own flesh in order to transfer the victim's life fluid to herself.

Meanwhile, her withered daughter, Viola, stands by helplessly. Like the maids in Ionesco's *Bald Soprano* (1950) and *The Lesson* (1951), she has foreknowledge of the imminent devastation, which she deplores but can't stop. One might even argue that she abets it, since she always seems to usher Pamela's victims into the mansion. "Queen" may say little about the tie joining victims to their predators. How often, for instance, does Pamela need a transfusion? It can also be argued that "Queen" lacks structure; Pamela could have drugged Herrick's coffee at any time. On the other hand, the play portrays the persistence with which humanity has always cooperated in its undoing. That it effects the portrayal through the medium of beautiful actress Ann Blyth also performs the useful service of showing us our own vulnerability and plain good luck. Jason Herrick's galvanized response to Pamela is both normal and, in most cases, appropriate. Blyth's ability to enchant us along with Herrick reminds us how close we are much of the time to the edge of the chasm of dissolution.

III

Like E. T. A. Hoffmann's *The Sand-Man* (1816), in which a man falls in love with a automaton, *The Twilight Zone* addresses both the complexity and difficulty of artificial intelligence. It asks, for instance, if a robot looks, talks, and acts human, *is* it human, especially if it stirs deep feelings in people? And doesn't the other side of the coin deserve a look? The feelings awakened in a robot in "Uncle Simon" (11/63) and in a computer in "From Agnes—With Love" (2/64) disjoint human lives. These disjunctures serve notice that *The Twilight Zone* cares less about technology than about people and the stresses that the new technology begets in them. Though morally neutral, knowledge of any kind has byproducts that can inflict psychological pain, most often when they refer to one's private past. But knowledge can also heal the wounds of the past and point a hopeful future. Our folklore is full of this ambiguity. Ursula K. Le Guin has discussed both the positive and the negative aspects of the myth of scientism that prevails today: "Science is all powerful: it can create anything (destroy everything). Science will save us (destroy us). It can solve any problem (it is the problem). It is the essence of the human (it creates monsters). The scientist is superhuman (subhuman). Science is purely rational process (the scientist is mad)"

(23). Le Guin grazes two large issues also worried in *The Twilight Zone* —what is the highest type of robot that can be developed and can it help humanity evolve into a higher life form. Shows like "Simon," "Agnes," and "You Drive" (1/64) show machines becoming human. *The Twilight Zone* forecasts the way computer programs today not only replicate themselves but also evolve into more complex forms. Though threatening, these forms serve natural justice, either clarifying or speeding descents already underway. The main figures in all three plays foil themselves; like the tightly wound Franklin Gibbs of "The Fever" (1/60), they all cause their undoing. Yet elsewhere in the series, highly intelligent machines can be benign. In the epilogue of "In Praise of Pip" (9/63), Serling notes that "the ties of flesh are deep and strong." The foregoing action had shown a "drab and undistinguished" bookie bargaining with God. Max Phillips offers to trade his most cherished possession, in this case his life, to secure the welfare of a loved one. This possession may be as nasty as "a bundle of dirty clothes." But it's still the best that Max can muster, after a long, sordid career spent mostly with lowlifers. Forget that Max is already dying. God accepts his offer, a sign of which is the recovery of Max's son from life-threatening injuries incurred in Vietnam.

Serling's closing words, "You can find nobility and sacrifice and love wherever you seek it out," reminds us that love can flourish in the twilight zone. Judged on the basis of his long record of misdeeds, Max has failed. Yet the greatness of his last living act redeems him. Pip's recovery spells out his father's success in the private sphere; God has responded to Max's prayer.

The love that redeems Max can also declare itself in the world of robots, even though the declaration is qualified. James A. Corry of Serling's "The Lonely" (11/59) proves that, if loneliness is life's worst blow, then relief from loneliness in the form of companionship qualifies as life's greatest blessing. "Dying of loneliness," Corry is serving a 50-year term of solitary confinement on a parched, gritty wasteland nine million miles away from earth. His only human contact during the first four years of his sentence is the crew of a spaceship that flies in provisions every three months. The crew relieves the agony of Corry's loneliness with some longed-for conversation and perhaps even a game of checkers. This agony upsets the crewmen. Captain Allenby, the chief, both sympathizes with and recoils from Corry. His benevolence, though, carries the day; he risks a court martial by bringing Corry, in the hold of his spaceship, a female companion—a robot called Alicia.

Though made of springs, wires, and flashing lights, Alicia knows hunger and thirst, warmth, cold, and pain. She can also think and speak.

Most important, she outdoes most people in her capacity for loyalty, patience, and kindness. These gifts soothe the embittered Corry. When told that his government has revoked its policy of shipping convicts to asteroids, he answers, "Good." But he had to overcome a great deal of prejudice before he saw any goodness in Alicia. Whereas she accepts him straightaway, he feels repulsed by her. Accepting her means overcoming his category crisis—allowing the warmth she stirs in him to prevail over his resistance to being intimate with a robot. How well he succeeds is an open question. Though he can't define his growing love for Alicia, he does accept it cheerfully enough to spend 11 happy months by her side. His falling in love with a machine confirms the power of the heart to raze barriers—imposed by age, race, language, and social class. But how strong is the confirmation? The play ends with an unscheduled visit by Captain Allenby; Corry is told that he has been pardoned and that he must immediately board the spaceship that will take him back to Earth. When Allenby adds that Corry may only bring 15 pounds of personal gear onto the ship, he's told that the woman-sized Alicia's weight exceeds that limit.

Now Corry prefers staying on his baking asteroid if leaving it means bidding Alicia a permanent goodbye. Allenby responds to this news by shooting Alicia in the face, his bullet exposing "a mass of smoldering wires" (Zicree 38). This violence makes sense. Corry could never have remained with Alicia. The pardoning of convicts sentenced to remote asteroids has put a stop to the flights that kept the convicts supplied with food and other essentials. Without his quarterly dole, Corry would die. And he knows it. Yes, he called Alicia a woman. But he didn't try to deflect Allenby's aim when he saw Allenby's handgun pointed at her head. He's now adrift without love. While seeing Alicia sprawled on the ground, clockwork face upward, he hears Allenby tell him, "All you're leaving behind is loneliness." Perhaps his memory of the throes of isolation stops him from replying to these words with anything stronger than the ironical, "I must remember that. I must remember to keep that in mind." The truth that irony usually entails distance implies that Corry has already started to overcome both his shock and grief. And perhaps Serling commends his resilience. Though warm and gentle, Alicia was only a toy or an instrument. And instruments are supposed to have instrumental, not terminal, value; an instrument is something to be used.

Alicia's ability to sustain Corry raises doubts addressed in "I Sing the Body Electric." The robot in Ray Bradbury's May 1962 telescript known as Grandma speaks of her ilk attaining real life within 300 years. Her own goodness ratifies her claim that science will only need three centuries to bridge the gap between people and machines. Nor should this advance worry us. Judging by Grandma's example, robots can be sweet, giving, and wise, perhaps even surpassing people as purveyors of human warmth. Grandma throws herself in front of a speeding car to save the life of an 11-year-old. But her sacrifice doesn't move us as much as it could. Though it fuels the belief, dramatized in "The Lonely," that machines can love, it also invites moral qualifications. The same speeding car that might have killed Anne Rogers would have only sent Grandma to the repair shop.

The juxtaposition of the cozy and the unsettling in the play's opening scenes foreshadows this ambiguity. The camera doing its customary downpan from a clear, starry sky discloses a solid-looking, well-landscaped home in what looks like a rich suburb. The lush, melodic violin music accompanying this pleasant imagery stops when the camera moves indoors. Three well-dressed children inside the genteel home are eavesdropping on their father and aunt. The father, Mr. Rogers, has been looking at an ad for a robot "in the shape of an elderly woman with the incredible ability of giving loving supervision to your family." The meddling Aunt Nedra loathes the idea of introducing a mechanical surrogate mother into the home. She's not alone. Anne also protests, claiming that, unlike her two sibs, she doesn't need a Grandma.

The camera conveys her objections. Anne, the worrisome child in the family, usually stands apart from the others and wears darker clothes. The psychological realism carries forward. As Grandma's saving of Anne's life shows, the girl needs a surrogate mother more than her sibs do. She objects to Grandma because she sees Grandma as an extension of her mother, whom Anne still resents for dying. With the mother gone, Grandma takes the brunt of Anne's resentment. Grandma's saving of the girl's life, though, brings needed assurance; Anne won't be abandoned by an older woman she has come to depend on. It's safe for her to love Grandma. Directors James Sheldon and William Claxton had already clarified Anne's resistance to Grandma before the car incident. As the camera photographed the shop or studio where the robotic grandmothers are made, it played into our misgivings, too. Cameo lighting was used to show body parts like the ones that would later comprise Grandma; the bright-looking arms, ears, and eyes, disturbing enough on their own standing free of a body, took on an added threat projected against a contrasting black background. Yet the threat dissolves. The brightly lit set in the play's finale, which shows Grandma telling the family goodbye, puts forth the same uplift and cheer conveyed by the three-point lighting used routinely in TV quiz shows and domestic comedies.

We're meant to approve of Grandma's leave-taking. Bradbury treads safer ground in "Body Electric" than Serling did in "The Lonely." First of all, the later work avoid sex; at no time is it even whispered that a romantic bond has developed between Grandma and the children's father. Grandma's loving example persists to the end without causing strain or discomfort. She doesn't deceive Anne any more than she lusts for Mr. Rogers. Her leaving the Rogerses after having spent eight loving years in their home shows the college-age children that nothing lasts forever. They accept the sweet sorrow of this lesson, too. Grandma is nobody's property. Rather than belonging to their family, she will use the nurture that was programmed into her to help other children.

Another benign, productive robot who overcomes a setback is the eponym of "The Mighty Casey" (6/60). This outstanding southpaw can throw a fast ball that's faster and a curve ball that's curvier than any known in the past. The struggling Hoboken Zephyrs enjoy unprecedented success as soon as his creator talks Zephyr manager, Mouth McGarry, into letting Casey try out for the team. This success ends when Casey is hit on the head by a line drive back to the mound. The doctor who examines him discovers that he has no pulse or heartbeat. Then the doctor reports his discovery to the Commissioner of Baseball, who bans Casey from playing with the Zephyrs; the major leagues are off limits to robots. Can Casey be deroboticized? McGarry wonders. Casey's creator builds the pitcher a clockwork heart, which will qualify him as a person. Meanwhile, in a deft stroke of irony, McGarry tells his players before a game that Casey is in a hospital "struggling for his life." The struggle leads to a surprising plot twist. After veering briefly into darkness, "Casey" ends happily. Dr. Stillman implants the "heart" he had built for Casey. But the same heart that allows Casey to meet the Commissioner's requirement for human status and thus restores him to the pitching mound also wrecks his effectiveness.

Casey has shocked his creator. In his first start for the Zephyrs after being released from the hospital, he gives up 14 runs without retiring a batter. His new heart has given him compassion; foiling the opposing batters would endanger and perhaps ruin their careers. But the ex-fireballer finds a life after baseball that puts his heart to good use. Following the example of Mountain McClintock, the old boxer in Serling's "Requiem for a Heavyweight" (10/56), Casey becomes a social worker so he can help people.

What needs help that he can't give is the script in which he appears. The tightly built, well-timed script, unfortunately, betrays Serling's ignorance of baseball. The Zephyrs' general manager mistakenly calls his team "a last-division club." The teams in each of the major leagues belong in divisions, all (or both) of which are equal. The term, "last-division club," makes no sense. The general manager meant to say "last-place club." Nor would McGarry have assigned Casey the uniform number that he wears. A pitcher wouldn't wear number 7 any more than Casey's awkward pitching delivery would get him through one inning; any robot with his supposed speed and accuracy would have been programmed to have a smoother pitching motion. And he'd probably have a different name, too; the Casey of baseball folklore was a slugger, not a pitcher.

Richard Matheson's "Steel" (10/63) also centers on sports. But the sport is boxing (which Serling indulged in as a paratrooper). Details are managed more carefully, and the play's bittersweet ending grows out of a more provocative script and better camera work. The action unfolds in Kansas in 1974. Boxing as we know it has been banned. The only prizefights allowed by law pit human-looking robots against each other. A stunning visual irony opens the action. The robot-pugilist Battling Maxo, en route to a six-round bout that calls for a $500 purse, is sitting impassively in a bus, his head hooded, while the two men flanking him, his manager and his trainer, argue hotly about him. As his impassiveness implies, Maxo dwindles in importance as the script moves ahead; in fact, he never makes it into the ring. His place will be taken by his manager, Steel Kelly, an ex-heavyweight who was never knocked down in his ring career. This switch makes Steel unique in *The Twilight Zone*. Whereas works like "The Lateness of the Hour," "Casey," and "In His Image" all show robots acting like people, in "Steel" a person both looks and acts robotic. The impersonation fools everybody, Lee Marvin, the Steel Kelly role, wearing the blank look and copying the mechanical movements of a robot. But Marvin criticizes the Kelly imposture as he plays it. Not only does Kelly use robotic, as opposed to human, boxing techniques in the ring to avoid detection; he also shows outstanding greed, stupidity, and, as it turns out, courage to box a robot in the first place. Like his charge, Battling Maxo, Kelly is unfit to fight. The two are metaphors for each other.

Even if he were properly maintained, Maxo would be outmoded and obsolete. He's a B-2 matched against a B-7; what's more, B-9s will soon be ring ready. Many of Maxo's essential parts are no longer made, like an important spring. Some are subpar. He also needs an overhaul, a job that can't be done without a substance called oil paste. But no oil paste is to be had in Kansas. Called by his handler a "steamshovel" and a "piece of dead iron," Maxo will fall quickly to any B-7. His unfitness strikes us straightaway. As soon as he's taken off the bus, a ball bearing fall off one of his boots. Yet as sorry a specimen as he is, he alone stands between his manager Steel Kelly and the gutter.

Kelly knows this. As the scurvy Maish Loomis did with McClintock in "Requiem," Kelly only sees Maxo as an investment. Yet perhaps he learns something by standing in for his mirror image, even if it's only a respect for property, a lesson driven home by his first-round knockout at the hands of the B-7 he's overmatched by. His impersonation might have taught him something else—the parity of existence. While he's putting it together, simulating robotlike movements and mannerisms, his charge, Maxo, begins to look more human. Perhaps he's sad because he can't keep Kelly out of the ring with a B-7. The mechanism of deceit has been set into motion. By impersonating Maxo, Kelly has taken on some of the fish-eyed inertia the robot seems to have shed. Nor will we mourn the switch. People who act like robots take on robotic traits that stick to them.

These traits can infiltrate the bloodstream. At the heart of *Twilight Zone* ethics lies the imperative that we're better off improving the lives we have than escaping into new ones. Those who ignore the imperative often use some mechanical device to improve their lots. Works like "The Nick of Time," "Uncle Simon," and "The Brain Center at Whipple's" (5/64) thus make machines look hostile to humanity. And evil does often operate in the zone through the medium of an artifact. Yet the artifact, except for the robot in Uncle Simon (11/63) and the computer Agnes in "From Agnes—With Love" (2/64), lacks consciousness. It's the misuse of technology that corrupts life. After endowing a slot machine with human traits in "The Fever" (1/60), Franklin Gibbs soon empowers it to destroy him. Mischief always starts with the individual in the zone. When asked if he invited the devil to his printing office, a publisher in "Printer's Devil" (2/63) confesses, "Well, in a way I did. . . . And I'm going to spend the rest of my life making up for it, too." That one of the devil's names is Nick yokes the confession to "Nick of Time" (11/60). By feeding coins into a diabolic-looking fortune-telling machine, Don Carter relinquishes his ability to choose.

Franklin Gibbs of "The Fever" gives up a lot more. He and his wife, Flora, have won two free nights in a Las Vegas hotel. Differences between the Gibbses surface immediately. A wearer of flowers, Flora smiles during the opening sequences, whereas Gibbs scowls into the camera photographing him and Flora. He lacks balance, cheer, and a gift for fun. Like some other brittle, defensive people, he proclaims himself "normal, mature, thoughtful." Yet his reserves are shallow. His lack of self-confidence has driven him to adopt a facade. He flusters when the good-natured Flora puts a nickel into the one-armed bandit. This overreaction prefigures his ensuing collapse; in good art, small touches are telling touches. Now that he's away from home, his facade crumbles quickly. Nobody forces him to put a silver dollar given to him by a drunken passerby into a slot machine; nobody forces him to pull the lever of the machine, either.

These actions define his obsessiveness; the moment he performs them, he's lost. The sound of the coins spewing from his slot machine reminds him of his wife's voice. But it charms him more than Flora does. Having outlived his passion for her, he sleeps alone. Yet his heart still pumps blood. He views the one-armed bandit that gives him a trough-full of coins as a seductive siren. Though she repels him morally, she heats his blood. He tells Flora that his new money is tainted and that he wants to feed it back into the machine whence it came. What he omitted to tell her about was his fantasy depicting his stack of coins rising higher and higher.

His fantasy drives the action at two levels. Before he knows it, Gibbs loses his reason. He never takes the shave he says he needs in the early going. Gambling through the night, he loses everything. His exchequer turns out to be his most trivial loss. Ignoring the people watching him, he grows more badgered and hectic as his losses mount. The mechanical whore he condemns has claimed him. Telling Flora to shut her mouth, he pushes her away from him. His only concern is the slot machine, which he has endowed with cunning and guile, weapons he knows will defeat him. Like a child, he accuses the machine of theft and knocks it over. Conveying the force of his shocking decline are the skewed camera angles both of the row of machines where he's transfixed and of actor Everett Sloane's face; along with his quaking voice, Sloane's feverish expression brings to life the frenzy of Gibbs as he careens toward the punishment he craves.

Gibbs's endowing the machine that gulps all his money with both a mind and a will of its own stems from his collapse. After an employee of the casino puts an out-of-order sign on the machine, the camera cuts to an exhausted Gibbs lying on his bed upstairs. He has just emptied his seed into the whore he loathes, and he must live with his degradation. Can he recover self-respect? His all-night rut has erased all moral differences between him and the whore. Both need a rest. The whore has done her job well, taking all of Gibbs's money and, for good measure, ripping away the facade Gibbs had put in place to hide from himself. This unmasking is crucial. Ranting and grunting about the whore's fiendishness, Gibbs is no longer human. When he hears her call his name, he follows the sound, ignoring his wife's request to go back to bed. Again, he chooses recklessly. Seeing the machine close in on him, he leaps through the window. The cry accompanying his leap merges into Flora's. Part of his wife has died with him. She's not seen after his fatal jump.

Reinforcing the conservative morality set forth by this symbolism is Gibbs's total depletion. There's a brief silence before Flora's scream merges with his; a brief lapse into adultery can smash a marriage. By contrast, Flora's voice and the sound coming from the machine melt smoothly—in Gibbs's ears. The self-styled moral paragon can no longer distinguish between a woman and a machine—or between a loving, caring wife and the whore who stripped him of both his money and his self-respect.

Though predictable, his downfall has a drive that holds our attention. Enhancing the drive is Gibbs's growing alienation from his wife, the natural flora, some artful lighting, and the jazz rhythms that slice through the action. Irradiating it all is Serling's critique of gambling. The jut-jawed players lined up at the slot machines disclose a seriousness of intent completely at odds with the mood of lighthearted recreation that gambling casinos promote. In this regard, Gibbs is the casinos' ideal client, or mark. His first name suggests the balance, moderation, and thrift that are more difficult to sustain in today's pluralistic culture than in Ben Franklin's day. From his last name is invoked the founder of the concept of entropy, Yale mathematician and physicist Josiah Willard Gibbs. Entropy, or inertia, the second law of thermodynamics, decrees that all energy runs out, bringing everything to a state of rest. But the entropic drift continues. The equalizing of pressure and temperature both within and around a static object will reduce the object to a homogeneous blob—which is what Franklin Gibbs has become. Could he have avoided this collapse? Carping and puritanical, he always wears dark outer clothes, whereas all the other speaking parts except for one wear pale tones that match the trappings of the Las Vegas casino where much of the play takes place. Although these bright, airy trappings are a ruse, installed to corrode the mark's moral scruples, they do signal Gibbs's need to lighten up and relax. Perhaps, like a Flora, he could have gambled away a few dollars, walked away from the casino, and enjoyed his all-paid vacation.

But he never had the gift of enjoyment any more than did Barbara Polk of Serling's "Uncle Simon" (11/63). Barbara has been living with her sarcastic, abusive uncle for 25 years because she wants to inherit his money. One day, she grabs the chance to come into her inheritance early by pushing her hated uncle down a flight of steps. But her peal of glee, voiced moments after Uncle Simon dies as she flings open the windows of her dark house, "Hey world, I'm back; I'm really back," sends out a false hope. Having cowered too long in shadows, she can't return to the light. She has seen too much of her self-esteem chipped away by her uncle's barbs. In view of her past, she might have expected the clause in her uncle's will mandating her to take care of the robot he had finished building just before his death. The mandate looks harmless enough. But then changes occur in the robot that make Barbara wince. Serling had already introduced these changes in his 1954 radio play, "A Machine to Answer the Question." In the following passage, the machine's inventor is explaining how his invention will eventually gain the wit to answer questions beyond the scope of man: "This machine can do much—ultimately. But it's like a newborn child. It must be given a chance to grow. To develop. It can't be given too much as yet. At present, it can only answer the simplest questions" (95). Uncle Simon's robot also acquires powers instilled in him by his inventor—the power to prod, taunt, and belittle Barbara. Yes, the robot was custom-made to vex her. But she's no victim of a cruel joke. She has conspired in her downfall, a truth stemming from her freedom to leave the house lodging the robot at any time. At the end, she looks as drab and speaks as lifelessly as she did before her uncle's death. She droops with reason. Whereas her enemy, Uncle Simon, lives on in the robot he invented, she has never lived at all. As Serling says in his epilogue, "Once a bed is made, it's quite necessary that you sleep in it." Barbara set the mechanism of her bondage going by moving into her uncle's house when she could have found work and supported herself while living elsewhere. Now she can only watch the mechanism grind on till it crushes her.

Another notable *Twilight Zone* female victim is Jana Loren of "The Lateness of the Hour" (12/60). But she's more sympathetic than Barbara Polk, and, rather than being ground down by a machine, she *is* a machine. Significantly, her discovery of her identity comes only at the end of the play, long after Serling has committed us to her, both morally and emotionally. Director Jack Smight's mastery with details helps develop the disturbing likeness between the human and the mechanical. Gothic conventions ratify the ensuing disturbance. An eccentric, perhaps even mad, scientist lives in an isolated mansion made of masonry blocks and first seen at night under pelting rain. Jana, the scientist's daughter, is peering out of the window into the storm with all the helpless longing of a trapped heroine. The contrast between her immobility and the wildness of the slashing, whipping rain leads to others. Also counterpointing the frenzied storm is the elegant sterility of Dr. Loren's home. Later, Jana will mime the words passing between her father and the butler as the two men enact their nightly ritual of lighting the father's after-dinner pipe. Earlier, when the camera had first moved indoors, it tracked from the detached, neatly clad doctor at his book to his sybaritic wife, who was moaning with pleasure across the room while her neck and shoulders were being massaged by a housemaid.

But if the Lorens' daughter, Jana, by wanting to leave her parents and start her own family, is too human, then the robot Alan Talbot of "In His Image" (1/63) lacks humanity. His programming was skewed. A woman he remembers lunching with a week ago has been dead for three years; he can't find a trace of the university he remembers attending; a stranger is living in his home. His design flaws can bring on violence. An electronic whirr in his head upsets him so much that he pushes a woman off of a subway platform into the path of an oncoming train. Then he forgets the incident. In creating him, Dr. Walter Ryder encroached upon the Frankenstein myth more deeply than Dr. Loren did with Jana. Ryder has created a monster. Besides killing an innocent woman, Talbot attacks Ryder, and barely stops himself from murdering Jessica Connelly, his fiancée of three days' acquaintance. But Ryder doesn't become a monster himself. He grows more human. This self-critical man wanted to build an automaton that looked like him but was sweeter and milder. In his lab, he displays earlier, more flawed versions of Talbot that fell short of his hopes. Then he shows Talbot *his* flaws. Talbot learns here that he's just a machine, which makes him subject to malfunction and breakdown at any time. But even if he remains disorder-free, he can't marry Jessy. He will stay youthful; she will age.

Talbot reads in his creator's logic a dire outcome—his own deactivation. And he's human enough to fight it. To preserve his being, he tries to kill Ryder. But he's defeated and dismantled in a barehanded fight that occurs off camera. Ryder goes in his place to Jessy, whom he plans to marry. Violence usually causes devastation in *The Twilight Zone*. It solves nothing. The meaning of any violent act consists of living through the act's effects. Ryder has already done some of this. Having put aside his monomania, he can now turn his energies to other people. His failure to build a perfect robot in his own image inspires him to remake himself. He had chided himself for forgetting to grow up. He even wanted to die.

But his life signs are stronger than he had credited, allowing him to invert the Frankenstein archetype. By copying the flawed copy of himself that he had made, Talbot redeems himself. This moody recluse can enjoy the love of a beautiful woman because another incarnation of himself has already won that love. It's up to him to sustain it. If "Image" doesn't end with a crescendo of joy, it does put joy within its main character's reach. The surprises unleashed by the Godgame can bring hope and cheer. A record of pain, "In His Image" ends on an upbeat note. Unfortunately, much of it flags dramatically. Its moral issues are rehearsed in a 12-minute dialogue that relies more on words than on images and thus loses much of its power to move us. Much but not all; "Image" retains enough merit to convince us that, had it appeared at any other time than *The Twi-*

light Zone's fourth season, it could have played as a half-hour show and thus lent more speed and shape to its defining motifs.

IV

Like the robots in "Image" and "Lateness" (and also like the extraterrestrials in "The Gift" and "To Serve Man"), some of the mannequins in *The Twilight Zone* cause grief, whereas others are helpful. In either case, they make their presence felt. Schumer sees them comprising "one of the key motifs in the Twilight Zone," as he noted in his Chicago talk of June 1991. Vindicating his insights, Serling put one into *Twilight Zone*'s pilot show, "Where Is Everybody?" And a mannequin is the first object seen in John Furia, Jr.'s *Twilight Zone* episode, "I Dream of Genie" (3/63). The mannequins in *The Twilight Zone* fit Freud's definition of the uncanny as the uncertainty roused in us by something whose reality is doubtful. Like a Duane Hanson sculpture, the mannequins in *The Twilight Zone* have a similarity to us that rankles. They make us feel unsafe, sometimes even impugning the integrity of our lives. If our externals can be copied so accurately, then how private are our psyches? And how disposable and replaceable are *we*? Some simulations that shoulder into reality pose such threats. The well-made mannequin shatters our reserves. But so does the ill-made one; its inaccuracies and distortions make us wonder whether it has caught aspects of us that we've denied or suppressed. Is that awkward gesture or that ugly grimace of a smile an artistic flaw or an emblem of a trait we possess? The differences between us and the ill-made mannequin can menace us more than the similarities found in the true copy.

All these issues are called forth by "The New Exhibit" and "The After Hours," works from different hands divided from each other by nearly three years. In "The After Hours" (6/60), a young woman is waited on by an insolent saleslady she later identifies as a mannequin. But Marsha White's own identity is also suspect. Both the shock she gets from seeing herself in a mirror and her ordeal of being locked inside a department store after closing time summon up the last-man-on-earth motif that haunts the whole *Twilight Zone* series. The mannequins Marsha sees as she wanders through the deserted store resemble some of the employees she dealt with earlier that day. These and other mannequins, many of whom are seen close up, speak to her. Then they frighten her as they leave their platforms and encircle her (including in their number an elevator man, played by John Conwell, who looks just like Bing Crosby).

But they don't hurt her. Marsha's resemblance to them had already told her that she's a mannequin, which is scarcely news, since she has been one all along. She has just finished a month's leave, which she spent mingling with "outsiders," or real people. "When you're on the outside, everything seems so normal," she says of her time away from the store. Obviously, she felt so comfortable around people that she forgot she was a mannequin. "The After Hours" turns on a double-whammy ending that shifts the work's fulcrum from the aesthetic to the moral sphere, where we have more at stake. We've been identifying with a heroine who's not human; if the identification appeals to our sense of openness, it also impugns our judgment, a quality we usually pride ourselves on. In some cases, it might send the mind back to "The Lonely" and make us wonder what we'd do if we were in Corry's place confronted by an Alicia.

But "Hours" sets challenges of its own. Should we have known earlier than we did that Marsha was a mannequin? And now that we do know, what does our knowledge tell us about ourselves? Have we been manipulated to open our hearts to a mannequin who's also a wrongdoer? If anyone is guilty in the play, it's Marsha. The supposed victim turns out to be the troublemaker. She enjoyed her vacation so much that she overstayed it, forgetting that her errantry bit into the vacation time of one of her counterparts. All of the bizarre developments that blitz her during the after hours began with her miscalculation. But she's not punished. The mannequins who surround her comprise a benign, evolved society governed by a gentle justice. Marsha is assured that her tardiness has caused "no serious harm." Her reintegration smooth and thoroughgoing, she then joins the others in wishing her successor a happy vacation.

Plausibility both underlies and strengthens the mysteries that keep us riveted during the play, like the presence of a ninth floor in the eight-floor department store where Marsha buys a thimble. But Serling also leaves us plenty to ponder. In a sense, his mannequins are more real than people, whom they can identify without being identified in turn. Other questions suggest themselves. For instance, could we duplicate Marsha's feat in reverse by spending a month a year with only store mannequins for company? In a way, the question is fatuous because none of us would consider it; we have lives to lead. But we also lack the physical and mental stamina for the feat; spending eight hours a day for a whole month staring into the middle distance while immobilized in a store would violate our basic nature. Need it, though? Perhaps what happens to Marsha White suggests new ways to self-enhancement; both the camaraderie and the justice that restore her to the sales floor include her. She's a belonger, not an alien. As the play's title implies, the store where she models clothing enjoys a life as vital and intriguing after hours as it does during its time of normal business. Yet none of us will know this life firsthand, perhaps to our detriment.

"The New Exhibit" (4/63) offers a different slant. As has been noted, changes in public taste have made the museum where Martin Senescu works obsolete. But Martin believes that the five life-size wax dolls (which he never calls dummies) are meant to live forever. He has rejected the forward flow of time, and he pays heavily for doing so. One form of payment exacted from him comes in the confusion that besets him. After stowing the five dolls from the defunct museum in his basement, he numbers himself among the many husbands who bring their work home. Then, after committing a murder, he scolds the dolls, using the language of an angry father. His recognition that he'll have to stand trial for murder further disorients this childless man. He rebukes the wax figures in the same way a wife would rebuke an errant husband. Calling them "heartless monsters," he tells them that he gave them his "best years"; he explains how he cleaned their clothes and protected them; he insists that he was the "best friend they ever had."

As Franklin Gibbs of Elgin, Kansas, did with his slot machine in "Fever," Martin Senescu gives the five wax figures his top priority. His brother-in-law speaks more truly than he knows when he accuses Martin of keeping the basement as carefully guarded as Ft. Knox. Violating the spirit behind all museums, Martin forbids access to the basement, even pulling down the basement blinds to stop outsiders from looking in. He stops his wife, Emma, from doing laundry in the basement because the moisture put out by the washing machine will hurt the figures. The figures always come first. He depletes the family savings to buy them, first, new clothes and, next, an air conditioner to keep them fresh and perky. Symbolizing his obsession are the ribbons from the air conditioner, which always seems to be going. So long as the ribbons stay aflutter, neither he nor anyone close to him can live normally. It's fitting that he murders his three closest intimates—his brother-in-law, his ex-boss, and his wife.

Of this hapless trio, his wife suffers the most. He says to her fresh corpse, while digging a grave for it, "If I went to prison, as I probably would, who'd take care of the figures. . .? It's better this way." He'll hide Emma's death from the police, burying her, instead, in the same basement where he keeps the figures. This insult reminds us that the way people treat their dead can say as much about them as the way they treat each other. Martin has disregarded the difference between the living and the dead. When asked by a gas man if he's sure that the figures aren't alive, he answers, "not altogether." At the museum, where they first appeared to us, these "rare and valuable" denizens of Murderers' Row were bathed in light. They also stood on a platform raised above floor level, which made them look bigger and stronger than the spectators viewing them from a shadowed area. Doubtless, this arrangement was the work of their curator, Martin Senescu.

Again recalling the compulsiveness of Franklin Gibbs, Martin begins sleeping in the basement after Emma's death. And why not? He belongs there. He has treated his wax figures better than he treated Emma, having disrupted her routine, ignored her, and raided the family's savings behind her back. She was never a serious rival to them. As soon as they entered the basement, she couldn't compete with them for Martin's attention, let alone his love. A sign of this love is the way he rhapsodizes over them. He notes the "tenderness" and the "shy, frightened little choir boy" lurking inside one of his serial murderers: "To take a life again and again with your hands and not be able to stop yourself. Can you begin to imagine the horror of that?"

He knows the torment of an Albert W. Hicks because he's a soul in chains himself. His wife never inspires the imaginative flights elicited by the figures. And because of it, he gives rein to his cruelty, an impulse that resembles in kind, though rarely in degree, the cruelty we all harbor. The likeness is made subtly. Martin restores the knife with which he killed Emma to the waxen hand of Jack the Ripper. This harmless-looking act conveys his madness. By yoking his violence to that of Jack, he labels himself Emma's executioner, not her killer. But Jack murdered only prostitutes, sometimes aging ones. He probably also believed that his victims deserved to die. What this mad self-justification says about Martin's opinion of Emma is too horrid to dwell upon—as are the implications boiling up from the likeness between Martin's first name and that of Martin Balsam, the actor portraying him. (Another of *The Twilight Zone*'s more provocative accidents occurs in "Little Girl Lost" (3/62), the rescuer figure of which is played by actor Charles Aidman).

No such implications rise from Serling's "The Dummy"(5/62). Like the Anthony Hopkins character in *Magic* (1978), a ventriloquist endows his dummy with so much life that the dummy controls him. We see some of the effects of this role reversal before we're made aware of the cause. On stage, Willy jokes at ventriloquist Jerry Etherson's expense, gives Jerry bad cues, and tells stories that Jerry claims he doesn't know. The first sign of the dummy's malignancy comes when Jerry claps his hand on Willy's mouth while leaving the stage and has his finger bitten. As soon as he goes to his dressing room, he displays the tooth marks. The question he asked Willy at the outset, "What would you do without me?" has taken on a sinister meaning. Whatever power Willy has comes from Jerry. And Jerry knows it. He also knows that his obsession with Willy rules him, and he hates himself for it. As in *The Twilight Zone*'s "Time Enough at Last" (10/59), "Purple Testament" (2/60), and "Penny for Your Thoughts" (2/61), the motif of broken eyeglasses conveys a character's warped vision. The point is made in other ways, too. When Jerry talks to a woman, both his voice and hers sound warped. The camera underscores the madness suggested by this distortion. Much of the action near the end is seen from an angle. Both the tilted street Jerry walks and the high-contrast slanted lines that break the plane between the camera lens and the horizon portray his distress.

In the play's next-to-last scene, Jerry bows his head, as in deference to Willy, who appears on screen with him. He's conceding victory to the dummy he was supposed to manipulate and control. Willy's statement that Jerry made him real is true. And it has alarming consequences. Jerry is the worst kind of slave, the kind that creates tyrants and perpetuates tyranny. As in "The New Exhibit," we feel the desperation that costs Jerry everything. The changes that take place in Willy's physical position, in the tilt of his head, and even in his facial expression describe the anguish Jerry is putting himself through—chiefly by dedicating himself to his art. But surely something here is wrong. Aren't artists supposed to be driven by Jerry's kind of dedication?

The question recurs in "Caesar and Me" (4/64). Ventriloquist Jonathan West has a sweet, gentle nature probably traceable to his Irish background, another legacy of which is his lyrical speech. But, like Jerry Etherson before him, he drinks too much. And his lack of a green card, a steady job, or a marketable skill suggests his failure to adapt. He connects himself to the world mostly through his dummy, Caesar, artists often confronting reality through the imagination. Resembling Willy of "The Dummy," Caesar is the voice of truth, rough justice, and retribution. Through him, Jonathan voices realities he can't speak directly, since most of them are ugly and hurtful. Caesar tells Jonathan that his jokes are bad, that his stage career is over, and that the only way a loser like him can get money is to steal it. Jonathan believes him. Following Caesar's advice, he commits some robberies. He's finally caught and arrested. Caesar remains silent during his interrogation by the police, making Jerry feel cheated and abandoned. He has reached the point where he must act for himself but can't. To jail he must go.

Beautiful but damned, he must face his guilt alone. And the guilt is his. Not only is Caesar sometimes called Little Caesar; his speech also harks to that of Edward G. Robinson's in the 1930 gangster film, *Little Caesar*. Of course, the speech comes from Jonathan. And its vileness reflects Jonathan's dark side. Caesar calls everything by its nastiest name, and both his cruelty and his indifference to suffering reveal the toughness of the born ruler. Jonathan's soft, wondering side might have helped him suppress this malevolence. Instead, it remains frozen and allows his criminal tendencies to surface. It might do still worse. The bond Caesar forms with an obnoxious little girl after Jonathan's arrest implies that Jonathan's moral paralysis has launched a monster of metaphysical evil.

This evil exerts great force in "Living Doll" (11/63). As in "Caesar," an innocent-looking artifact voices threats that can only be heard by one person (until the end, when it addresses another listener). The play's subject matter has a maturity seldom found in network TV. Erich Streator blames himself for whatever is missing or wrong in his home. His inability to have children with his wife, Annabelle, probably stems from his sterility, since Annabelle already had a daughter prior to marrying Streator. The guilt that dogs Streator finally defeats him. Besides withholding love from his stepdaughter, Christie, he also resents her, a sign of which is his denying he's her father after she calls him Daddy. He should have been more self-accepting. His bitterness ignites a charge that kills him and sends shock waves through his family.

Though beyond forgiveness, his pain is real. Its first manifestation infuses a homey, commonplace situation with terror. A mother and her small daughter are getting out of a station wagon in front of a suburban home, their arms full of bundles. One of these contains the doll Talky Tina. A symbol of the domestic harmony and sweetness that Streator has denied himself, the doll sparks a fierce quarrel. Streator doesn't want it in the house. Despite being overruled, he removes it from a sleeping Christie's bed. Then he tries to destroy it with a vice, a blowtorch, and an electric saw. These scenes of stunning visual incongruity describe him as past reclamation. And, as in "Exhibit," his self-alienation shows him violating proper family relationships, a sign of which is Annabelle's resolve (which he later overturns) to leave him. He lies to Christie about Tina's whereabouts after stuffing the doll in a garbage can, and he sends Annabelle away when he's trying to decapitate it. Tina's head stays attached, and after being dumped in the garbage, the doll reappears in Christie's bed.

Streator has been perpetrating one of life's worst betrayals. Because Christie represents the anchoring family warmth he hates, he resents her. He directs his resentment to the doll she loves. Tina is thus more than a doll. His guilt and his inferiority complex will soon empower her to kill him. Each of his plans to dispose of her grows progressively more self-defeating. Dramatic tension builds quickly in "Living Doll," the hatred generated between the desperate grown man and the angel-faced, honey-voiced doll taking on a tragic drive. Streator can't escape Tina. He picks up the phone and hears her say that she's going to kill him. For a while, he thinks that Annabelle and Christie have equipped the doll with a walky-talky to punish him for his wildness. When he sees his mistake, he realizes that his doom is near. Author Jerry Sohl makes the point by restoring the motif of the sole witness to a dread event from earlier *Twilight Zone* shows like "Death's-Head Revisited" (11/61) and "Nightmare at 20,000 Feet" (10/63). Only Streator sees Tina wink; only he hears her say things like "I think I could even hate you" and "I'm going to kill you."

Tina is both his nemesis and his deepest wish. He knows the home to be a place for love and sharing. Having violated this precept, he must suffer. The speed with which the poison engulfs and then kills him makes us gasp. His sins call for such punishment. Despite removing Tina from the garbage can where he had put her a second time and then restoring her to Christie, he's lost. Tina won't forgive him, which is to say that he can't forgive himself. Hearing some noises in the middle of the night, he starts looking around. But unless he had put her there himself, Tina stationed herself at the top of the staircase—just where he'd be most likely to trip on her. Trip he does and spills down the stairs to his death. He dies with his face alongside Tina's. Which is as it should be; after taking away her power to delight Christie, he used her to punish him, as he deserved. Now he can look at his punishment and ponder the justice of it.

His entrapment takes life from Sohl's audacious script, from Telly Savalis's strong, assured acting, and from visual incongruity: witnessing Savalis/Streator's progressive loathing and panic as he plots against sweet-looking Tina makes us wonder if our inner demons will ever let us relax. And so do the play's closing moments. Finding her husband dead at the foot of the stairs, Annabelle picks up the doll and hears it say, "My name is Talky Tina, and you'd better be nice to me." Either Tina has tapped into our secret fears, or in allowing himself to hate her, Streator has unleashed a virus of evil. Subject to the tensions of a daily living, Annabelle might anger Tina accidentally; or, worse, anger her by design to ease the strain of living under a reign of terror.

These fraught possibilities support Marc Zicree's belief that "Living Doll" is "an episode that can stand with the best of any season" (391). Any TV play that rivets us with its challenging insights and its probing, evocative images deserves this praise. Inspiration in "Living Doll" doesn't give way to doggedness or willpower. The work's details and shifts of focus are both so well grounded in our subconscious that their implausibilities keep the wheels of the plot turning. In our deepest selves, we know that Erich Streator always acts plausibly. Here is no dreamlike suspension of logic and common sense. Streator's behavior reveals the quiet desperation underlying our every move. The way he acts with Tina, recalling Jerry Etherson's conduct with his wooden dummy and Barbara Polk's with her robot in "Uncle Simon," discloses the strange, disturbing, yet important link between psychopathic behavior and behavior considered normal. What perhaps rankles us most about this disclosure is its inference that we often can't bridle our demons any better than did Barbara Polk or Jerry Etherson. The highly complicated toys in *The Twilight Zone* suggest that we're all guilty of being human. What's the moral distance between Streator's compulsiveness with Tina and the overattention we lavish upon an O.J. Simpson, or a Jeffrey Dahmer? We're the ones who create the demand for what we read, listen to, and watch.

7

Slippages and Constancies

John E. Mack's *Abduction: Human Encounters with Aliens* (1994) deals with the capture of ordinary people by technologically sophisticated, nearly omniscient space aliens. Though this interplanetary drama occurs but once in *The Twilight Zone*, in "To Serve Man" (3/62), it does challenge some of the same norms *The Twilight Zone* questioned in each of its five seasons. For instance, *The Twilight Zone* dismantles received ideas about objectivity and subjectivity. It discloses striking similarities amid differences. It joins the quest for truth to the loss of certainty. But underlying this junction is a familiar caveat. While suggesting that accepted guidelines block us from participating in a larger, more generous reality, the series also warns us that, inhibiting though they may be, these same guidelines prepare us to cope with the reality that suits us best.

Such fixtures have been debated before. A phrase like "man's battles against himself," from Serling's prologue to "Two" (9/61), suggests that the events enacted in *The Twilight Zone* have all happened before, they happen every hour, and they will happen tomorrow. The problems the show's characters face resemble our own. Thus they make us look closer at ourselves and our surroundings. What appears outlandish may be normal. Only our preconceptions about the order of things make it look as if natural laws have been breached. For instance, the desert in works like "King Nine Will Not Return" (9/60), "Dust" (1/61), and "The Rip van Winkle Caper" (4/61) symbolizes the loss of civilization; it's where we confront our basic impulses and needs. By leaching out patience and good will, it brings out our essence. Analogously, the stripping away of our civilized veneer occurs much faster on those dry, bleak asteroids where several *Twilight Zone* episodes unfold than on earth. People on asteroids have to work much harder to get along with each other. Often they fail. Works like "Elegy" (2/60), "The Invaders" (1/61), and "Death Ship" (2/63) show earthlings coming to grief on asteroids; our planet is the best place to put down roots. William Fletcher of "The Little People" (3/62) has the right idea. As soon as he repairs his damaged spaceship, he leaves the asteroid where he had landed. But even *he* muses about having a statue built in his honor, like the one put up for his power-hungry crewmate, Peter Craig. Like Fletcher, the second relay of astronauts who land in the bleak, sterile canyon where the play unfolds plan to leave as soon as they fix their ship; they have no ambitions to explore or to colonize. Yet one of them accidentally kills Craig.

To leave the earth's orbit is to invite danger. "People Are Alike All Over" (3/60) shows two astronauts traveling 35 million miles to Mars. The idea referred to in the title isn't lived through at an intriguing level, though, Serling having commented more trenchantly on the perils of space travel in other *Twilight Zone* episodes. On the credit side, the photography deserves praise. The two astronauts picked to make the long space flight first appear to us through the interstices of a chain link fence. This arresting image foreshadows their entrapment at the end— one of them by death and the other by his Martian hosts. Sam Conrad is last seen looking through the bars of the cage the Martians lured him to right after welcoming him to their planet. "You're people, just like I am," Conrad had first said to his new hosts, echoing the words voiced by his partner at the outset. He's right. The Martians who gaze at him through the vertical bars of his cage, his only access to the outside from the facsimile suburban home to his rear, do resemble earthlings. The resemblance builds. Though they would probably claim to be virtuous, they're deceitful and treacherous. They've displayed some of humanity's worst traits. Unfortunately, these traits are indwelling, a truth recorded on the stricken face of Conrad as he looks out to his viewers, his hands clutching his unyielding prison bars. This concluding image of helplessness gains scope and resonance from several earlier images, i.e., the spaceship's lift-off, the sight of Mars from a distance, and the approach to Mars. But this deft editing doesn't save the play, which is little more than an anecdote. The idea of "People" can be summed up quickly; character doesn't develop; the dialogue is commonplace; the Martians act from predictable motives, even though the motives are hidden from us.

"Third from the Sun" (1/60), another play dealing with intergalactic travel, also shows life's basic realities mocking our drive to self-improvement. The play's shock ending reveals that the characters whose activities we've been watching are not people. The action has unfolded on an alien planet exactly like ours but which turns out to be 11 million miles away. Like us, the aliens drink lemonade and play cards, sometimes in comfortable suburban homes. But the all-too-human bent for envy, rivalry, and self-destruction has brought on a global catastrophe. In less than 48 hours, their planet will be destroyed. The play's last scene shows two families riding on a spaceship to their designated new home, planet Earth, ironically, a science-dominated, faction-ridden nightmare almost as close to undoing itself as the place they just left.

Another early *Twilight Zone* play, "I Shot an Arrow Into the Air" (1/60), again uses space flight to argue that any radical attempt to better oneself usually ends in loss, defeat, and frustration. Arrow I, "the first manned aircraft into space," suddenly crashes, killing five of its eight crew members. As with Peter Craig of "The Little People," being stranded on a dry, rocky canyon slope brings out the scurviness of one of the survivors, Flight Officer Corey. The craft's skipper, Colonel R.G. Donlin, remains hopeful about both the air quality and the radiation count on the asteroid where the craft presumably crash-landed. Corey, on the other hand, moans about wasting the craft's limited water supply on a mate near death. Then he fatally attacks another mate, warning Donlin, "Don't give him my water," after Donlin leads him by chance to his dying victim. Corey is soon seen gulping from a canteen; despite his fine words about water conservation, he drinks so greedily than the precious water runs to waste down his neck.

If "Third from the Sun" shows a spacecraft bound for Earth, in "Arrow" the craft that's launched to explore the heavens stays inside the earth's orbit, landing in Death Valley less than 100 miles from Reno. This harsh setting helps drive home an important aspect of Serling's morality—the belief that people need other people. Feeling himself adrift in a place so bleak that he can supplant the dictates of justice, reason, and fairness with those of brute survival, Corey murders his two mates. His ensuing discovery that he's still on Earth shows him (and the viewer) the inevitability of the punishment that awaits him. Regardless of where we are, we must obey those laws and codes that divide us from the void. Colonel Donlin's respect for these norms comes across straightaway. Donlin is first seen recounting Arrow I's mishap in a logbook. He's using discipline, protocol, and the civilized process of communication to make sense of the mishap. Corey, who represents anarchy and the creed of self, yanks the logbook from his senior officer's hands, growling, "This is no time to write your memoirs." The specter of thirst has blinded him to decency and decorum. Later, when Donlin tries to solve the cryptic message left by Corey's first murder victim, Corey, the foe of dialogue, remains silent. And within seconds he kills his Colonel.

A bomb threat posed by some UFOs in "The Shelter" (9/61) also shows the need to rule our lives by decency and love wherever we are. Resembling Corey's delusion that he's on a planet millions of miles from Earth, the bomb threat doesn't corrupt Dr. Bill Stockton's well-to-do neighbors so much as bring out their essence. Stockton has built a bomb shelter with only enough air, space, and food for himself and his family.

This arrangement clashes with his professional ethics. Though pledged both to protect and save life, this doctor must turn his neighbors away from the shelter and perhaps expose them all to fatal nuclear fallout. The neighbors, frightened of dying, bicker among themselves. The threat of death has brought out the hostility they've felt for each other during their 20-year acquaintance. Then, intuiting the destruction that could result from further bickering, they turn their collective wrath on the Stocktons. The neighbors who once laughed at Bill Stockton's advice that they all build bomb shelters now resent him: Why, they protest, do he and his family deserve to survive the nuclear attack that could kill everyone else in the neighborhood?

They answer this question by trashing the Stockton home and then caving in the door of the bomb shelter. At this point, the radio announces that everyone can relax; there's no enemy attack. The neighbors are embarrassed and ashamed. They have transgressed. Lacking the foresight to build shelters of their own, they wrecked their neighbor's when they felt threatened. As the smashed, overturned furniture in the Stocktons' dining room shows, the threat of a crisis can cause as much havoc as a crisis itself. "The Shelter" ranks high in the *Twilight Zone* canon because it describes the speed with which both everything and nothing can happen at the same time and change forever the lives touched by the process.

I

Episodes like "The Shelter," "Probe 7—Over and Out" (11/63), and "Monsters Are Due on Maple Street" (3/60) reveal the mainspring of the human psyche in *The Twilight Zone* to be fear. Perhaps of these three Serling plays, "Monsters" portrays most unforgettably the suddenness with which fear can lurch into hysteria and violence. Called by Lawrence Venuti a reflection of "Serling's concern about prejudice and mob violence" (363), "Monsters" uses setting to underscore the warning it serves. The work unfolds in either suburban or small-town America during the late afternoon and evening of a summer day. That the street-corner signs in the neighborhood have the shape of New York State indicates that this well-to-do enclave symbolizes everything that Serling prizes as good and wholesome. His using the enclave as a seedbed of malevolence voices his belief that nobody is safe from the depredations of fear; the monsters are already well entrenched in the Maple Streets of comfortable middle-class America.

Just below the surface of this genteel, orderly life lie a prejudice, a competitiveness, and a suspicion so deeply ingrained that it can be fatal. An innocent act like that of an insomniac standing in his back yard at 2

A.M. invites charges of subversiveness. As in an Agatha Christie novel, all the people in "Monsters" have something to hide. And they're all so desperate to deflect suspicion from themselves that they'll accuse any of their neighbors of misconduct to avoid being accused themselves. They're fighting the war of all against all. The plot of "Monsters," like that of "The Invaders" (1/61), takes much of its bite from a reality slippage; the action isn't only seen but also judged by extraterrestrials. We discover late in the going that we're not the only observers of the fury that has exploded on Maple Street. Some space aliens who want to colonize our planet show us how easy their job will be: "Just stop a few of their machines," says one of them; "Throw them into darkness for a few hours and watch the pattern unfold. . . . All we need to do is to sit back—and watch."

The pattern stems from the aliens' strategy of divide and conquer. Serling contrasts the escalating panic of his Maple Streeters with the cool detachment of the aliens who set the panic going. Hysteria overtakes everyone with great speed, as an alien camped on a nearby hill predicts: "They pick the most dangerous enemy they can find, and it's themselves." Their moral balance is so shaky because they govern their lives by the machine principle and not by human warmth. Though Serling never called himself a behaviorist, he does show his aliens altering human response by manipulating the physical environment of Maple Street. Their success shames us all. Intelligence and decency stand no chance when pitted against the mob hysteria that can addle us so quickly; being caught up in a collective frenzy blinds us to the evil we enact to stave off fear and insecurity.

As in "The Shelter," the Maple Street rioters wage senseless, random acts of violence that can't be reversed or undone. If these acts didn't forecast the ugly truth that, in the early 1990s, the United States led the world in murders, armed robberies, and rapes, they do display the pathology behind this dishonor. American rugged individualism has run afoul of the doctrine of original sin; preferring safety over danger, the individual hides inside the group. This sad truth is conveyed in "Monsters" by the sight and the crunch of feet belonging to Maple Streeters determined to confront a neighbor about a mystery that puzzles the neighbor as much as it does them—why his car engine keeps turning itself on and off. The questions put to the neighbor, Les Goodman, grow more sharp and nasty. But in the following scene, which takes place some hours later, the same people who crowded Goodman with their barbed questions and crunching boots, back away from him, perhaps out of unconfessed shame, when he approaches them. They've been huddling on the sidewalk fronting his house. The ghoulish effect created by the flashlight he holds under his chin has validated both their fear and suspicion. Is Les Goodman less of a good man than they had believed?

"Young Goodman Brown" isn't the only Nathaniel Hawthorne tale evoked by "Monsters." Like Serling's teleplay, Hawthorne's "Rappacinni's Daughter" describes the pitfalls of defining anything as muddled as a human being in clear-cut absolute terms. The most impetuous character in "Monsters" and the one most hungry for answers that will exculpate him is Charley. Played with both accuracy and insight by Jack Weston, Charley remembers the teasing and the taunting he got as the fat kid on the block. His stoutness, his loud, tasteless sport shirt worn as an emblem of defiance, and a voice that wavers between a simper and a screech convey his zeal for quick, easy answers; his melodrama and his loss of control are both functions of his insecurity. Besides blaming a youngster for the troubles on Maple Street when he comes under fire himself, Charley performs the only killing in the script. His victim is a concerned neighbor who had gone to the next street to see if the same electrical problems had occurred there that had darkened Maple Street. Not only does Charley's lethal bullet rob his neighbors of useful information. By ascribing its deathliness to a wish to protect his family, Charley has also put himself beyond blame within the context of the madness that has suffused Maple Street.

An explanation for the disaster Charley causes comes in two later Serling scripts, "To Serve Man" and "The Gift." These works contend that an inner demon has scrambled our moral sense; even if we had the apparatus for judging fairly and accurately, this demon would foil it. "The Gift" (4/62) shows that foreigners as well as Americans cave in to fear. We dread the unfamiliar. And what we dread we want to smash or kill. This wildness recoils destructively on some Mexican villagers. By attacking a stranger, the people of Madeiro deprive the world of a cancer cure—the gift of the title. Serling helps tally the cost of this blunder by building his script around the trope of blindness. "The Gift" takes place at night, a time when visibility is low, particularly in a poor mountain village; most of it unfolds in a bar, the fumes and wares of which inhibit clarity; included in the script is a blind man. Besides the village doctor who treats the stranger, only a child sees through the suspicion and hostility blinding his elders. But his vision comes to naught. The play lacks dramatic action. Much of the acting is bad, and the artificiality of the stage effects strikes a sour note. The Latino accents wobble. Finally, everything looks too sanitized. The sets on which the play is acted are unrealistically clean and tidy, and the villagers comprising the cast look too well fed and groomed. Yet this lame script raises a recurrent issue in world theology—that any savior or redeemer who comes to earth will face persecution and perhaps death.

Looking at our darkness from the opposite side of the spectrum from "The Gift" is "To Serve Man" (3/62). The space alien in "The Gift" who comes in peace and friendship is killed, and his peerless gift to humanity goes to waste. Conversely, the nine-foot, 350-pound Kanamit who persuades his gullible hosts on Earth of his benevolence has been plotting all along to kill them and then eat them. Serling has segued from humanity's moral darkness to its stupidity. The move is managed smoothly. The surprise ending of "To Serve Man" works as well as any in the series, yoking the play's idea to its structure in a plangent dominant chord. The Kanamits have been claiming to befriend man: they want to teach us how to abolish war, and they can help us turn the deserts of the world into gardens. Their motive? By improving the quality of both soil nutrition and animal husbandry, they'll have tastier fare for their palates—and more of it, since the absence of war will raise the population count. Though adumbrated, this data reaches us in a uncharacteristic way. The first scene of "To Serve Man" follows the last scene in time. In it, cryptographer Michael Chambers speaks to us from the space launch carrying him against his will to the home of the Kanamits.

Some of Serling's best energies went into "To Serve Man." Though the play's title, taken from the cover of a Kanamit book, isn't the "reasonably altruistic phrase" Chambers claims, it has a deadly accuracy of its own. The play also has a documentary flair unique in *The Twilight Zone*. Besides mentioning contemporary trouble spots like Berlin, Algeria, and Indochina, it includes footage of New York's UN Building, Times Square, and Museum of Natural History. More ambitiously, diplomats from France, Japan, and Spain respond to the arrival of the Kanamits in their native tongues. And, finally, in another maneuver unique to the series, the play ends with two narrations; Chambers addresses the viewer while looking straight into the camera at play's end just before Serling's usual off-camera epilogue.

A technically modest work that shows Serling's disdain for humanity's capacity for self-betterment is "The Fear" (5/64). Like "Monsters," "Mirror Image" (2/60), and "Will the Real Martian Please Stand Up" (5/61), this late play shows extraterrestrials doing mischief in Serling's upstate New York. "The major ingredient of any recipe for fear is the unknown," says Serling in the prologue, and he shows fear corroding the poise and self-composure of Charlotte Scott, a self-exiled fashion editor from New York City. When Charlotte sees strange lights in the sky near her mountain cabin, she phones the state troopers. This frightened misfit hides behind her cosmopolitan veneer when she admits Trooper Robert

Franklin into her home. Both she and Franklin have reason to cringe. His car turned over after he left it, and her telephone no longer works.

Then the 500-foot-tall invader who presumably tipped the car on its side appears in a field nearby. Our two earthlings have to resist panic. Yet no real harm has been done. After capsizing the car, the invader rights it, signs of which are the huge fingerprints on the door panels. The invader also avoids the nearby village, where it could do widespread harm. Perhaps it's friendly. But Franklin shoots it, anyway, implying a belief on Serling's part that the best way to banish fear is to shoot our way through it. Reversing the plea for patience and tolerance made in "The Gift," he now claims that destroying what is strange and different works better than trying to understand it. Though flawed, the status quo has survived many tests and thus deserves to be protected. And its protector, Trooper Franklin, the play's authority figure, has won our favor, Serling sharing none of Alfred Hitchcock's fear of the police. Ignoring the overwrought Charlotte's taunts, Franklin quiets her anxieties with his quiet control and cultural awareness.

His emptying his pistol into the invader suggests an authoritarian bias that clashes with Serling's attacks upon conformity in plays like "Eye of the Beholder" (11/60) and "Obsolete Man" (6/61). Yet some new elements that have entered the equation suggest that Serling's involvement in "The Fear" is prepolitical. First, the alacrity with which Franklin acts, with Charlotte standing supportively alongside him, makes him the archetypal dominating male, whereas she's flattened into the passive woman stripped of choice, autonomy, and dignity. Next, the invader that takes the phallic bullets is only a big balloon and not a living monster. The tiny creatures who inflated it plan to flee our planet; they're afraid of being captured or crushed. Their fears are probably justified. Character and idea tug against each other in "The Fear," still another *Twilight Zone* episode the significance of whose title only emerges in the episode's last moments. Though sympathetic, Trooper Franklin stands for a destructive paternalism that subjugates its women and crushes its opponents with money, size, and physical force.

Humanity's attraction to violence helps explain the frequency with which power and its abuses recur in *The Twilight Zone*. As has been seen, Peter Craig's zeal "to give the orders" leads to his death in "The Little People" (3/62). His thirst for power redeems his partner Fletcher's belief that Craig is "the victim of a delusion." He slights duties like checking his grounded rocket's radio charts and hydraulic system; he finds water that he doesn't share with Fletcher. Written from a characteristically conservative premise, "Little People" redresses the imbalance caused by his cheating and his pride. Unfortunately for Craig, redress can only occur in one way— through punishment. As soon as Craig, who called for "discipline above all," opted to become "the number one straw boss," he negated himself. Normal-size people in one world may be giants or mites when they travel to another. Amid such deviation, violence is folly. Only a creature as self-defeating as a person would choose it.

A fuller treatment of the dangers of power comes in the hour-long classic "On Thursday We Leave for Home." Serling's May 1963 telescript unfolds in a galactic outpost so wretched that nine suicides have occurred there in the past six months. What has kept this shocking number from climbing still higher are the efforts of Captain William Benteen. Benteen is a true leader. Fighting great odds, he has organized and maintained life for his 186 hangdog followers on the planet a billion miles from Earth where they went to find peace and plenty 30 years before. Improvising with primitive materials, he has built a radar station, a salt-water converter, and a refrigeration unit. He rations food and water because, without rationing, the strong would take from the weak and eventually implement a rule of jungle ethics that would wipe out the colony.

The same need to protect and maintain life has prompted him to punish infractions like tardiness; every misdeed must be atoned for in this straitened paramilitary society. But this punisher of misdeeds also knows the importance of morale. When his charges line up to receive their dole of "hot, flat, and unforgettable water," they're told that the water is, after all, wet and that in six months' time they'll be drinking chocolate ice cream sodas—on planet Earth, no less. His lectures, or sermons, on the beauties of our world, which contain some of Serling's most poetic prose, keep hope alive among the colonists that a spaceship will soon come to fetch them back to Earth. Benteen's description of himself as a consultant and a guide is too modest. He's a political and military leader who also doctors his charges by dressing their wounds and quieting their spiritual malaise. A shaman or religious prophet with some advanced training in psychology, medicine, and electronics couldn't serve them any better than Benteen.

But he corrupts his great gifts by overextending them. External events challenge and then revoke the power he had deemed absolute. He feels betrayed. When the long-awaited miracle he had touted to brighten morale in the colony does come, he rejects it. He has been treating the colonists like children, telling them when to work, eat, and rest. Defying the rescue team that has come for them, he tells them to stay behind. His earlier words about the earthly paradise now take a dark turn. Once full of joy, the planet of his public speeches now seethes with anger, hatred, and violence; it offers only loneliness and death. The primitive radar device he had built and kept staffed for nearly 30 years despite lack of positive results has done its work—which he now disclaims. But it doesn't matter. His power has ended. His followers vote unanimously to leave the colony. Then they cross him again by choosing to scatter to different parts of the United States rather than living as a group under his aegis.

The speed with which these two setbacks occur demonstrates that once the collective will of any people gathers force, it's unstoppable. "Monsters" displayed the negative pole of the folk spirit; "Thursday" puts the positive pole on show. Against Benteen's wishes, the colonists keep asking the members of the rescue team about contemporary America—baseball, education, the places where they lived. Benteen reacts to this rebelliousness by trying to destroy the spaceship. His failure leaves him but one option—to remain behind by himself. He won't join those who rewarded his many sacrifices with betrayal. Having stayed a bachelor, he denied himself leisure and companionship to serve these traitors—if traitors they be. Being in control for too long has warped him. The man who treated his followers like children is now childish himself. The arrival of the rescue team has filled him with spite. Alone by choice, he realizes that the baking salt flat where he has spent the last 30 years is arid and impoverished. His pathetic last words, shouted to the departed spaceship, "I want to go home," spell out the dreadfulness of his isolation. His spite has recoiled on him. "Thursday" comes closer to tragedy than any other *Twilight Zone* episode. Whatever life waits Benteen can only be scraped out at the most rudimentary level. Having reached too high, he must settle for unremitting harshness. As the title of the play featuring him implies, man is a social being. Yet Benteen has always stood alone, and it's too late for him to change. He thus forfeits his place among the "we" who leave for home on Thursday.

Like other tragic heroes, he lives in our collective imagination after his farewell speech. Much of this indelibility springs from James Whitmore's solid, sensitive acting. Much springs from other sources. Yes, the painted backdrops of the crags looming behind the makeshift colony look artificial. But this artificiality, which was standard for the era, doesn't smudge Serling's brilliant script. The two suns seen at the outset serve notice immediately that we're on alien ground. A glimpse of the lower torso and legs of a suicide victim further rivets our attention: ugly things are happening in this ugly, brutal place. Thanks to deft pacing, the drama moves confidently toward its throat-catching finale. Enriching the flow is a feast of language. Already noted has been the lyrical elegance with which Benteen, ironically the play's enemy of change, lauds the changing hues of the earth, the transits between seasons, and the rhythmical swing between day and night. Counterpointing this eloquence is the nervous tension whipped up by the verbal jousts of Benteen and Colonel Sloane, the leader of the team of rescuers. The dazzle generated by these men of conflicting aims, a treat on its own, leaves the two men close to hating each other. "Thursday" is one of the very few telescripts from *The Twilight Zone*'s fourth season that gains from the hour-long format implemented to rescue the series. Whatever the odd viewer may find wrong in it will prove minor flaws in an otherwise polished, deeply provocative show.

II

The Twilight Zone will puncture the self-importance of the human in different ways, questioning our moral goodness, the formulas we use to interpret reality, and our alleged domination of the planet. Sometimes, the series raises doubts about the autonomy of the self. As has been seen, "Mirror Image" (2/60) shows visitors from a parallel universe infiltrating our world and plaguing their earthly doubles. Rather than enjoying free-standing existence, the people in "Shadow Play" (5/61) belong to a recurring dream of one of their number, a man awaiting execution on death row. This convicted felon has attained an ironical god-like status. Because the reality of his fellow characters is enclosed in his, it follows that his death will also cause theirs. Their interchangeability in the play's last scene— an ex-convict has become the judge who pronounces the felon's doom—further discredits human autonomy. The integrity of the self faces other attacks in *The Twilight Zone*. The arrogant captain of a space rocket in "Death Ship" (2/63) who claims, "Everything has a logical explanation," forces himself and his crewmates to keep dying the same wasteful death because his imagination fails him.

Richard Matheson's one-woman play without dialogue, "The Invaders" (1/61), deflates our self-importance visually. A mean shack contrasts sharply with the gleaming high-tech saucer that lands on it. Any fight that may ensue will leave the frightened, paltry-looking inhabitant of the shack, armed only with her primitive kitchen tools, little chance against the invaders and their electronic weapons. These tiny spacemen, who stand about eight inches high, have terrified a normal-size woman. But the battle lines smudge. It comes out that the terrified can also exert terror. All of the beleaguered woman's attempts to destroy her little attackers fail. They enter her shack firing their weapons with great speed and accuracy. Yet their intended victim is later referred to on the intercom inside their saucer as a member of "an incredible race of giants" mighty and savage enough to deter any future explorers from

Earth. No more space missions from our planet, anyway, will break this woman's peace for some time. She has won a lot of safety. But she feels far from safe, let alone triumphant. She's still exhausted, confused, and upset. What's more, she didn't understand the English-language radio message insuring her reprieve. It's too bad; having felt the sting of human malignancy, she would sleep better knowing that she might not have to face it again.

"Will the Real Martian Please Stand Up" reverses the direction of migration, or invasion. "Martian" opens with an investigation of a possible UFO landing in the snows of upper New York State. One of *The Twilight Zone's* most entertaining episodes, Serling's May 1961 work combines fun with suspense. It also invites a serious issue without slackening its dramatic pace. Some people gather in a roadway diner, six of whom were passengers on a bus making a rest stop. The remaining party may have landed on the UFO being investigated and then joined the other six under cover of night on their way into the diner. Who's the space alien? By misdirecting our attention, Serling proposes different answers only to smile at us for falling into his traps. But he has more legerdemain to offer en route to the solution. He has brought together strangers of vastly different backgrounds forced by circumstances to spend time together. Because heavy snows have immobilized the bus parked by the diner, the seven, including the alien, sometimes astonish us.

Then the all-clear sounds. But the hope it sends out proves to be false. A bridge declared safe for motor traffic collapses, pitching the bus into the river below. The play's final scene brings together two of the parties that appeared in the diner before the bridge mishap—the counterman and a Boston-bound executive. The latter escaped danger from the mishap, a story he recounts while revealing himself to have three arms. And, as his extra arm suggests, he escaped because he's the Martian the state troopers have been looking for. But he doesn't gloat for long. Removing his cap, the counterman discloses a third eye, the mark of a Venusian. He, too, entered our planet from outer space, and, having won a big edge in time over his Martian rival, he can keep all the earthly spoils he has in mind for himself and his fellow Venusians. What remains unsaid but nonetheless matters is that if he has bested his Martian rival, both he and the Martian have outperformed their human counterparts.

Yet the motives of conquest driving these two aliens are rare in *The Twilight Zone*. The two sets of aliens in "Mr. Dingle the Strong" (3/61) have come to Earth to perform scientific experiments. The eponym of Charles Beaumont's "The Fugitive" (3/62) is a benign senior who enjoys playing with children. Finally, three aliens plan to take Frisby back to their planet in "Hocus-Pocus and Frisby" (4/62) because they believe every falsehood this egregious liar tells them. Humankind is shamed once more, lying being unknown on the planet where Frisby's would-be captors live. This disadvantage will recur. Even after making allowances for the evil intruders in "Monsters," "Mirror Image," and "To Serve Man," *The Twilight Zone*'s earthlings usually outdo their intergalactic visitors in malice and stupidity. Will our wrongdoing destroy us? At times, Serling gives the impression that his moral imagination darkened with the years. Yet the artistic comedown reflected in the works of *The Twilight Zone*'s last two seasons also gives signs of fatigue and concentration loss. "The Fear" might be an example of a late script in which Serling found pessimism a convenient shortcut.

"Probe 7—Over and Out" (11/63) qualifies as another. Colonel Adam Cook has hurt himself badly while crash-landing his rocket, Probe 7, on an asteroid several million miles from Earth. A development more dire vexes him anew. Despite his woes, he may stand a better chance for survival than the people he left behind on Earth, where war has been declared and where global destruction is imminent (it took only 12 minutes of nuclear bombing to destroy the eastern seaboard of the United States). As the world unravels, the general in charge of Cook's mission wishes Cook the best of luck in founding a new life order free from hatred, fear, and, anger. How good are his chances? Most of the play consists of Adam Cook's interaction with Eve Norda, a female astronaut from a different galaxy whom chance has also brought to Cook's planet. Forget for the nonce the artistic defects of this lame, predictable script. Both the obvious first names of the main figures and the speed with which they sink their mutual suspicion promise well for their future as co-founders of a new race. But their first names also raise doubts about that race's moral health and outlook for happiness.

Religion also moves to the fore in the more artistically achieved hour-long show, "The Parallel" (3/63). Major Robert Gaines successfully completes the journey that defeated the crews of both "Odyssey of Flight 33" (2/61) and "Death Ship" (2/63). But the journey isn't the one he had embarked upon. Shortly after lift-off, he lost radio contact with Earth. He landed six hours later in a field 46 miles from his launching pad. But he remembers nothing of his flight, claiming to have passed out within seconds of lift-off. What he missed was the experience of slipstreaming to another universe where he would spend a week that translates to six hours of earthly time. This universe resembles ours without copying it. Though small, the differences that break the parallel between Bob Gaines's new surroundings and the ones he left behind throw him off stride. For instance, he's now a colonel. He has the same wife and daughter as before, but the house his family occupies is now enclosed by a picket fence. Other differences, some more subtle than others, convince him and his family that the six unaccounted-for hours in his life hold an unresolved mystery, one deepened by the disclosure that the rocket that brought him to his present milieu differs from the one he first took into orbit.

A puzzled Gaines returns to space and ends his flight in our world. Certain repeated scenes photographed from identical angles and including the same people raise questions about the change in venue. Though nearly the same, these scenes differ slightly from their earlier counterparts. For instance, the general in charge of the space mission confers with a junior colleague outside of Gaines's hospital room after each of Gaines's space probes. He offers the colleague a cigarette during each conference. But the second time the men talk, the General's Pall Malls stay out of view. This small touch has thematic import; an exact parallel between Gaines's two universes would disallow the gap through which he slipped out of one into the other. But another explanation underlies the byplay with the cigarettes: Pall Mall was one of *The Twilight Zone*'s sponsors. These cigarettes were already being sold on our globe. By bringing a pack of them into view in a parallel universe, producer William Froug was implying, tongue in cheek, that the goodness of Pall Malls transcends global differences; smokers from all over our galaxy who crave a good cigarette will muster the ingenuity to find a Pall Mall.

The deeper issue called forth by "The Parallel" harks to the paranoid fiction of Philip K. Dick. Watching "The Parallel" revives some of the spiritual unrest fostered by Copernicus nearly five centuries ago. Wondering anew whether our planet is but one of many hosting complex living organisms questions the worth of our sacrifices. Perhaps as occupants of a negligible star, we wait in vain for divine justice. The injustices we have endured may not matter to God, after all. The blessedness that we have been told awaits us as our reward for enduring hardship patiently may never come. Or, what is perhaps worse, it will grace the inhabitants of another planet, if it hasn't already done so.

No, Serling may not have been thinking about redemption when he was writing "The Parallel." But he did see the issue out of the corner of his eye. His decision to retain the dark echoes in the play, rather than revising them out, adds metaphysical bite to his 1958 statement in *Time*, "Our society is a man-eat-man thing at every level" ("Tale of a Script" 36). Serling showed great courage and integrity by imbuing *The Twilight Zone* with such disturbing tints when it was on probation by both station and sponsor. But his self-confidence was rewarded. Viewers shaken by the reverberations sounded by "The Parallel" had learned that network TV programming could engage issues of weight and seriousness.

III

A character like Bob Gaines may tear a hole in the fabric of the space-time continuum and then turn up in a different era or galaxy. The effects of such a huge leap dictate the mainstream morality voiced by both the Angel Gabriel in Serling's "Passage for Trumpet" (5/60), "Take what you get, and you live with it," and the epilogue to "Once Upon a Time" (12/61), "Stay in your own back yard." The dazzling, the intense, and the spectacular usually sink to earth in the zone. Time travel, for instance, can change some things, but rarely the ones the time traveler wants changed. In different veins, works like "The Man in the Bottle" (10/60) and "The Trade-Ins" (4/62) show characters who have undergone wild transforming adventures fighting to reclaim their frayed old identities. Three soldiers from the year 1964 in "The 7th Is Made Up of Phantoms" (12/63) who stumble onto the site of the 1876 Battle of Little Bighorn get swallowed by history. They survive only as names on a monument honoring the cavalrymen who died with General Custer. Cruel, sadistic William Feathersmith's trip 50 years backward in time to his boyhood home in "Of Late I Think of Cliffordville" (4/63) creates many reversals: a poor man switches places with a rich one; a swindler gets fleeced; the innocent past turns out to be a nightmare. Industrialist Feathersmith is foiled by his poor grasp of history. After returning to the Cliffordville, Indiana, of 1910, he spends all his cash on land he knows to be rich in oil. But he either forgot or never knew that the oil couldn't be extracted until 1937 because of the backwardness of petroleum technology early in the century.

The hero of "Back There" (1/61) also believes foolishly that he can change the past. But, since he re-entered the past by chance rather than by choice, he suffers less than Bill Feathersmith. Engineer Peter Corrigan leaves his club after talking to some of his co-members about time travel. The date is 14 April 1961. He suddenly finds himself transported to the same date in 1865, the very evening when President Lincoln would be murdered at the nearby Ford's Theater by John Wilkes Booth. Hoping to stop the murder, Corrigan warns the local police. But his warnings are dismissed—with one exception. Presumably having heard about Corrigan's urging, Booth himself goes to the police station under an alias and secures Corrigan's release. He then takes Corrigan to his rooms, hears his story, and convinces him that he takes the story seriously. This part of Booth's performance is the truth. He finds the story so impressive that he drugs its teller; Corrigan mustn't stop Booth from killing the President.

And naturally he doesn't. Lincoln dies within hours of taking Booth's bullet. Corrigan learns that, though fixed, the past can change us. The Corrigan who returns to the Washington, D.C., of 1961 has in his pocket a monogrammed handkerchief belonging to his abductor, Booth. We're left reeling with him. Even though the historical record decrees Lincoln's assassination, "Back There" builds plenty of dramatic interest. That an acquaintance of Corrigan's who never knew about Corrigan's journey to 1865 benefits from it revives the interdependence motif central to *The Twilight Zone*; we all participate in each other. Other assets to the play's production include casting and direction, the flamboyant, actorish good looks and theatrical bearing of Booth contrasting admirably with the wholesomeness of his engineer dupe.

Paul Driscoll's failure in "No Time Like the Past" (3/63) to change history with the help of a time machine shows once again the inviolability of the past. Driscoll's knowledge of history both burdens and plagues him. He can't prevent the chaos caused by Hitler. And even though he has foreknowledge of both the sinking of the *Lusitania* in 1915 and the 1945 nuclear attack on Hiroshima, he can't get anyone to take his warnings seriously. These disasters must happen. As Driscoll sees, this immutability is beyond challenge. It has also seeped into and helped create the character of the threatening present. But perhaps not *his* present; he still believes he can flee the specter of nuclear holocaust. He'll do it by going back to our country's pre-urban, pre-industrialized youth.

But his retreat to the Homeville, Indiana, of July 1881 mocks his hopes, a sign of which is his recalling that President Garfield will soon die of bullet wounds yet to be inflicted. "No Time" reminds Serling again that the nostalgia he always felt for the band concerts, merry-go-rounds, and lemonades of summer must be checked. Nor did the brutality of our twentieth century smash this peace and innocence. James Garfield's imminent death proves that all times are one. Though our technology is more advanced and thus more lethal, the violence it serves in today's urban state also drove our forebears a century ago. Driscoll's acceptance of this sad truth doesn't sway him from wanting to stay in Homeville, to be on a level with it, and to avoid trying to change anything. He does nothing, after all, to stop the Garfield assassination. But, like a love-struck spy in Graham Greene or John le Carré, he lets his heart thwart his reason. His foreknowledge of a local fire, gleaned from an old history book, prods him to act when he should have remained passive. The fire took place at a school run by a young woman he had fallen in love with. Director Justus Addiss even suggests that Driscoll is punished for intervening; the tongues of flame blazing from the fast-burning school make it look as if Driscoll caused and perhaps even worsened the very disaster he had set out to prevent.

This hint of retribution lends welcome force to "No Time," one of *The Twilight Zone*'s most serious, ambitious programs. It also helps to mitigate some flaws. Driscoll had failed to seize his chance to shoot Hitler from his hotel room; after fixing the Nazi leader in the cross hairs of his rifle, he unaccountably decides to hold his fire. The very opportunity to kill Hitler defies belief to begin with. German security would never have let a foreigner rent a room in a hotel across the street from the balcony or platform from which Hitler had scheduled a speech without first inspecting the foreigner's luggage. And had Driscoll's bags been inspected, any rifle stowed inside would have come to light, even if it were broken down. Also the way in which Driscoll later tries to prevent the Homeville fire suggests that he's punishing himself for ignoring his own edict about remaining passive while awaiting disaster.

Though it would have been both easier and safer for him to remove the kerosene lamp from the carriage that later careens out of control and destroys the county school, he chooses instead to unhitch the horses pulling the carriage, causing them to panic and bolt. Yet the blemishes in "No Time" don't seriously mar the work's quality. The references to President Garfield and the footage showing Hitler with Mussolini remind us that we always live in both the public and the private sphere. Finally, the futility seizing Driscoll when he realizes, after the school blaze, that he won't be able to ignore calamities he knows will happen in Homeville sparks an action as heart-wrenching as it is inevitable—his renouncing the love of Abby Sloane in order to return to the era of the Cold War. "No Time" is a play with its tale in its mouth. Its circularity helps it end as strongly as any other episode in the *Twilight Zone* series.

Unlike "No Time," "Back There" and "Cliffordville," works like "The Last Flight" and "A Hundred Years Over the Rim" (4/61) see benefits in time travel. But the direction of time travel in these two Serling plays is the future, not the past. Walking mysteriously into 1961 from 1847 shows Christopher Horn of "Rim," arguably *The Twilight Zone*'s best show, the whereabouts of fresh water and game that he and his fellow pioneers would have missed on their westward trek from Ohio to California. Horn's visit to the modern world of paved roads and telephone lines also redeems the many hardships of the long, hard trek. Perhaps his personal reason for segueing to our century also comes forth— to cure his dying eight-year-old son. Malnutrition and fatigue have sapped Horn's strength. But as soon as a modern encyclopedia tells him about young Chris's feats as a California pediatrician, he bolts the New Mexico diner into which he had stumbled to give the boy the penicillin he got from the diner's owners; the child must be helped before he can help other children. A touch of suspense at the end confirms his father's heroism and vision. The local sheriff has arrived at the diner to take this odd-looking eccentric away. But Horn uses all of his waning strength to escape. Exhausted, he drops both the rifle he always carries and the bottle of penicillin pills just as he approaches the rim of the dune he had previously climbed before slipping into the twentieth century. When he rights himself for his final sprint to safety, he takes only the pills. He can forget the rifle. God has shown him that he'll be divinely protected during the last leg of his wagon train's overland pull.

Protection he needs. His wagon train started its journey 11 months before, and the migrants are all tired, discouraged, and scared. The adrenalin rush that Horn won from seeing his ordeal unfold as a physical, cross-cultural, and religious drama helps him inspire his followers to soldier on. Much of this mettle carries forward from the name of the expedition's leader. His first name comes from another stalwart whose faith insures the success of his allegorical journey, the hero of John Bunyan's *Pilgrim's Progress*. His last name both counterpoints and lends depth to this allegory. First, it suggests the animal strength and tenacity that help Chris Horn withstand hardship in pursuit of his goals. It also calls to mind the horn containing the gunpowder for his omnipresent rifle. If he doesn't stand for the church militant, he nonetheless has in him plenty of the tough protesting spirit of mainstream Yankee Protestantism.

"If Horn drove others unsparingly, he spared himself still less," we read of him in Serling's narrative version of his ordeal (*Stories* 104). The doughtiness, resolve, and sense of mission pervading pioneers like him as they crossed our country's dry heart both helped people the continent and make it productive. And *Twilight Zone* producer Buck Houghton found in Cliff Robertson the ideal actor to convey this pioneer grit and sinew. Horn's odd attire, featuring a dusty stovepipe hat, his strangely inflected, out-of-date speech, and the jealousy with which he guards his rifle chime with the confusion he's thrown into by the modern appliances in the diner and also the wariness with which he sniffs and drinks the tap water offered him. He's an anachronism in the world of 1961. Yet we see ourselves in all his deeds, which is to say that everything he does matters. He shows us what we are and where we've come from. "Rim" compels our imaginative participation largely because Robertson's masterly offhandedness gives the images he creates the look of prized snapshots in family albums.

A minor *Twilight Zone* episode devoted to the theme of changing the future is Matheson's "The Last Flight" (2/60), the first non-Serling script in the series (Zicree 59). The strong visual contrast in the opening scene gets the action off to a good start. A World War I biplane lands alongside a bomber or transport craft many times its size. Lieutenant William Terrance Decker has touched down in a French air base operated by the United States Air Force. But the year is 1959, and Decker belongs to the world of 1917. He took off on a joint mission with another RAF fighter pilot, but, when he saw a flock of enemy planes nearby, he deserted his friend. His last memory, before flying above the landing strip where he put down, consists of eluding German fire by heading into a cloud.

Decker returns to the 1917 dogfight in order to save not only his friend's life but also the many lives that his friend, now an RAF flight marshal, would save in World War II. An added measure of suspense had come in the announcement of Decker's arresting officer that Air Marshal Alexander Mackaye is coming within hours to the very air base where Decker is being held prisoner. But Matheson's canny script has more surprises to spring. Decker claims that Mackaye can't be visiting the base because he's dead. What he omits recounting is his belief that Mackaye died because Decker deserted him under enemy fire. Besides showing the rewards of journeying into the future," The Last Flight" has also set forth two of *The Twilight Zone*'s trademark motifs—that of the second chance (Zicree 46, 58) and that of cowardice, or what passes for cowardice. These two motifs coalesce in Decker's escape from prison and his ensuing flight in his biplane back to the 1917 dogfight where he saved Mackaye's life—at the cost of his own.

Time travel would remain a staple of *The Twilight Zone*, often in a military or a paramilitary context. Most of the action of "The Odyssey of Flight 33" (2/61), for instance, develops in the cockpit of a passenger plane flying from London to New York. Heavy tail winds push *Global-33* through the sound barrier and into an earlier time frame, an event that breaks the plane's radar and radio contact with Earth. This part of the teleplay contains some excellent footage. It shows *Global-33* looking down on a Manhattan Island bereft of streets, buildings, or any other signs of urban life. What the crew members see below them is an unpeopled marsh. Instead of being a home to millions of people, Manhattan lodges dinosaurs. Obviously, the plane can't land here. The captain decides to gamble. Despite a diminishing fuel supply, he makes the plane go at top speed; he wants to re-enter the jet stream and then crash through the sound barrier. His plan works, but only to a point. Though the jet does come back to the twentieth century, it only makes it as far as

1939. Nor can it land at LaGuardia Airport, which only accommodates propeller craft. Like the mythical *Flying Dutchman* (the title of an opera by Richard Wagner, who's mentioned in the play), *Global-33* must keep moving till Judgment Day. But here the implied Wagnerian parallel breaks. Their doom isn't linked to any moral or spiritual failing on the part of the crew members or passengers. Nothing that any of the people said or did justifies their being permanently deprived of their jobs, friends, and homes.

The deaths of some armored troops on maneuvers in 1964 who find themselves near the Little Bighorn in 1876 in "The 7th Is Made Up of Phantoms" (12/63) invite the same complaint. Though director Alan Crossland, Jr., maintains dramatic tension with some intriguing props, neither he nor the Serling script he worked with justifies the massacres of the tank soldiers during Custer's Last Stand. The men never volunteered to enter the past; nor could they have resisted whatever magnetic or electronic field canted them to Montana's Little Bighorn River. Granted, they do charge into the fray. But soldiers are trained to fight. To expect them to shrink from combat would be as unlikely as asking them to trade their weapons for an olive branch.

"The Long Morrow" (1/64) combines interplanetary travel and time travel. Commander Doug Stansfield has agreed to do a space probe, but one so ambitious that it will fill up 40 years of his life. While preparing for it, he meets and falls in love with Space Agency colleague Sandra Horn. Defying dizzy odds, the two agree to marry as soon as he returns to Earth. Their extraordinary test of patience and loyalty, trying enough on its own, faces still another fantastic hurdle. Although a hibernation unit in Doug's rocket will keep him young, Sandra will decline into an old woman. Or so it's thought. In a double reversal worthy of Maupassant or O. Henry, Doug disconnects his hibernation system six months into his space flight, and Sandra enters one.

Their long-awaited meeting shocks them both. Contrary to expectations, she's still young, and he's gray and withered. Love impelled both of them to overturn their original agreement. Still ruled by love, Sandra agrees to marry Doug, but Doug, reaching into the depths of his lacerated heart, finds the courage or decency to send her away. "Long Morrow" like "Shelter" (9/61) and "Trade-Ins" (4/62) before it, describes the process by which everything and nothing happen at the same time; the play's real action and meaning both lie on the inner planes of perception, in the heart and along the nerves. Serling's poignant love story gains depth from imaginative camera work. Sandra and Doug's farewell scene is shot with the faces of the two ex-lovers filling the screen and thus capturing the way the two have both been permeating each other's psyche. Intensifying this rich effect is its setting—the same Space Agency corridor where Doug and Sandra met 40 years before.

Unfortunately, this intuitive stroke might have come long after the viewer has lost interest in Serling's plodding script. "Long Morrow" never recovers from its dreary start. Serling's prologue yields to a narrative by Doug. Then Doug and his controller, Dr. Bixler, in an exchange swollen with scientific details, discuss interplanetary travel. A second narration from Serling leads to a long one by Doug, which capsizes the show. Too much of "Morrow" is clogged by Doug's mental activity as he lies in suspended animation in his rocket. Carelessness in production adds further harm. Doug is told that he's going into space in six months. Yet, later the same day, Sandra dates his lift-off a month hence. Also, George MacReady, the Dr. Bixler character who gives Doug his lift-off orders, has what looks like a painful blister or cold sore on his lip during his two on-screen appearances. Physical details like this one are botched elsewhere in *The Twilight Zone*. Anne Francis, the title figure in "Jess-Belle" (2/63), has a mole near her mouth that sometimes casts a distracting shadow.

Is it fair to hold a weekly TV series aimed at a mass audience to such strict accounts? The answer is yes, because *The Twilight Zone* usually met very high standards despite backward lighting and makeup techniques along with shooting schedules so tight that production staffs had little or no freedom to make changes. Mostly they had to get it right the first time. And usually they did. The Anne Francis of "The After Hours" (6/60) also had a mole, but it cast no shadow. A *Twilight Zone* show about time travel enhanced by careful production values is Matheson's "Once Upon a Time" (12/61). The show's 1890 sequences relied upon many of the staples of the Mack Sennett two-reelers. Zicree has noted that these sequences only printed two out of every three frames the camera shot in order to give "a jerky look to every moment, similar to early, hand-cranked silent films" (260). From the silent films also come the conventions of the "wipe" between scenes and both the solo piano to build mood and the title cards to replace dialogue. The absence of dialogue dictates the show's abundance of sight gags, most of which, including a chase redolent of the Keystone Kops, feature Buster Keaton. Wearing his customary deadpan look, Keaton does his pratfalls with the same gawky grace he displayed in the silent comedies he had made 30 to 35 years before.

Even the sequences that unfold in 1962 rely more heavily upon sight gags than on verbal wit; to confirm his status as a misfit in 1962, Keaton will walk around in his shorts, whereas all the other men seen on camera have their legs fully covered. His harried antics lace the play's warnings about the dangers of time travel with both laughter and some pangs of nostalgia. By using bygone production modes, "Once Upon a Time" recreates some of the simple charm of an earlier day, a charm that might beguile and entice the viewer. Until Keaton's frustration shatters it; the intimacy and flair of "Time," finally, make us feel grateful that we can't move about as freely in time as we can in space.

8

Shades of Justice

Serling recommended in 1968 that "we properly put aside . . . our insatiable desire for pleasure, and with some modicum of courage begin to relate to the inequities and anguish of our fellow men" ("Challenge" 12). The compassion that Serling was calling for had already permeated *The Twilight Zone*. "Night Call" (2/64) describes the problems of lonely elders. Miss Elva Keene of rural Maine is isolated by both her age and her inability to walk. Other problems assail her. She has to disconnect her phone before bedtime in order to stop the late-night calls that have been breaking her sleep and frightening her. But, in a touchingly humanizing moment, she replaces the phone one night in its receiver. Perhaps for the lonely, the play's author Richard Matheson believes, being forgotten stings more sharply than being harassed. *The Twilight Zone* was always sensitive to the trials of age. Abusers of the elderly are punished in the two Serling scripts "What You Need" (12/59) and "A Short Drink From a Certain Fountain" (12/63) and also in the non-Serling "Spur of the Moment" (2/64) and "Come Wander with Me" (5/64).

Punishment for wrongdoing takes different forms in the zone. People in "Time Enough at Last" (11/59), "The Little People" (3/62), and "Last Night of a Jockey" (10/63) get so much of what they've been craving that they're crushed by it. "The Rip van Winkle Caper" (4/61) shows four men dying needlessly because their greed has misled them into flouting the constraints imposed by a self-regulating world that's also basically lawful and orderly. After stealing a million dollars worth of golden ingots, the thieves enter hibernation cabinets programmed to revive them in a hundred years. Literary tradition includes enough descriptions of the corrosiveness of greed to validate the downfall of the four. Serling's train robbers are driven more by mutual distrust than by the prospect of enjoying their bonanza. A helpful analogue comes in the passage in *War and Peace* in which Tolstoy compares the Napoleon who sacked Moscow to a monkey holding a nut in a paw trapped inside a bottle. In order to free his paw, the monkey would first have to open it and thus lose his precious nut. Serling's two surviving thieves in "The

Rip van Winkle Caper" are in a similar bind. After trudging with his fellow thief across a stretch of desert, the older Farwell discovers that he has forgotten his canteen. His partner De Cruz offers to share his water with Farwell, but at a price; each mouthful of water Farwell takes will cost him one gold bar, a figure De Cruz later doubles. Water now outstrips gold in value. By how much, the two wanderers will never learn. In a rage, Farwell brains De Cruz with one of the ingots that both men sacrificed so much for.

Retribution follow quickly. Like several other *Twilight Zone* characters (the main figures of "Perchance to Dream" and "Living Doll" come to mind), Farwell finds himself trapped between two devastating alternatives. Whatever he does will recoil on him. Obviously, he can't go on appeasing his sadistic partner. Yet killing De Cruz will isolate him in the baking desert, and isolation is life's greatest curse in the zone. Logically enough, he passes out from heat stroke and dies under his burden of gold. What he never learned was that the gold he violated reality for has lost all its value. The inhabitants of the year 2061 who find him in the sand wonder that he should waste his dying words on a substance that industrial changes have made worthless.

I

Broken eyeglasses in both "Time Enough" and "A Penny for Your Thoughts" (2/61) betoken failure of vision. To be fair, the heroes of both plays suddenly turn up in places where normal vision wouldn't help them, anyway, so swiftly does the commonplace lurch into the realm of the extraordinary for each of them. After the customary down-pan of the camera in "Penny," bank accountant Hector Poole is shown leaving a subway station and then buying a newspaper—acts he performs daily en route to work. But this time, the quarter he throws into the newsboy's box of coins lands on its edge—and sends him into the twilight zone.

"A Quality of Mercy" changes the pattern. For a broken eyeglass lens, it substitutes the broken lens on a pair of binoculars. The failure of perception dramatized in Serling's December 1961 script is that of being blind to the unity of the human family, a point important enough to justify restoring the binoculars to view during the running of the credits at play's end. "Mercy" makes good Serling's 1963 claim that *The Twilight Zone*, by adopting a strategy of indirection, could satirize a social or moral code without angering his show's sponsors: "The strength of 'Twilight Zone' is that through parable, through placing a social problem or controversial theme against a fantasy background you can make a point which, if more blatantly stated in a realistic frame, wouldn't be acceptable" ("The Gamma Interview" 70). "Mercy" argues that aggressiveness must be checked, even during war. At issue specifically is the inhumane belief that all enemy troops must be attacked and slaughtered, regardless of their health and battle readiness. Humanity pre-exists combat. Our shared humanity outweighs both the military and political considerations dictating any battle plan. The tie that soldiers share will outlast any war that pits them against each other.

The main subject of "Mercy" recalls that of "Judgment Night" (12/59). Though only a passenger aboard a British freighter, Karl Lanser pinpoints the exact moment when a torpedo from a German submarine will crash into the freighter's hull. He has this knowledge because he's also the officer in Hitler's *Kriegsmarine* responsible for firing the torpedo. These politics of identity take a multicultural twist in "Mercy." A lieutenant serving in the U.S. Army in the Philippines in 1945 suddenly becomes a Japanese lieutenant stationed in Corregidor in 1942. The speed with which he changes identities with his enemy shows him the humanity we all share, regardless of the causes we serve. He has seen the ugliness of war from the standpoint of opposing camps. Transported back to 1945, he feels both relieved and happy when the news of the dropping of the atomic bomb frees him from the dangerous and brutal chore of charging a cave in which some tired, hungry Japanese troops have been hiding. His reprieve also includes a lesson in conducting the arts of peace, a lesson both important and timely now that the war is ending.

The people in *The Twilight Zone* often need such lessons. When asked if he can be a good husband to the woman he has just proposed to, the eponym of "The Self-Improvement of Salvadore Ross" (1/64) answers, "I can buy her anything." Both the title and the denouement of an earlier script, "The Four of Us Are Dying" (1/60), infuse moral instruction into the interdependence motif that colors much of *Twilight Zone*. Like an existentialist hero, Serling's Arch Hammer learns that he has to accept the consequences of his deeds. But many of his deeds are vicious, so this "cheap man with . . . a cheapness of mind" is more villain than hero. His fantastic ability to change his face can't erase his guilt. It's incidental that he's wearing another man's face when he dies and that he's killed for committing a crime he was innocent of. Hammer didn't deserve to live. Director John Brahm addresses his guilt straight-away. "Four of Us" opens in a film noir environment. But the treatment is odd. The weather is clear; the neon tubes identifying the local night clubs all look neat and clean; the cheap grifter Hammer both dresses and acts like a hard-boiled movie detective. Only the sign in front of the Hotel Real, which Hammer books into, looks worn and tawdry. The evil-hearted will gravitate to what's shabby and ugly.

Likewise, even though the execution of the murderer Joe Caswell miscarries, justice is done. "Retribution is not subject to a calendar," Serling reminds us in the epilogue to "Execution" (4/60). The mousy, undersized crook Paul Johnson who meets Caswell in the office of the scientist who accidentally teleported Caswell to our century confronts the plains desperado with his banality. The ease with which this "minor-league criminal" bests Caswell in hand-to-hand combat also conveys the banality of evil itself. As if led by an unseen hand, Johnson activates the time machine that brought Caswell to Professor Manion's office. He and Caswell are interchangeable, a point made by his taking Caswell's place as a hanging victim on the Montana prairie 80 years before the New York sequences. That Johnson walked into the time machine voluntarily, having mistaken it for a safe, suggests that we create our own fate. Sometimes, the act of self-creation consists of making peace with the past, reclaiming or forgetting old memories. Both "Nightmare As a Child" (4/60) and "Spur of the Moment" (2/64) feature females 25 years apart in age who turn out to be the same person; in each case, the child has created the adult. This unity asserts its force elsewhere. In "One for the Angels" (10/59) and "In Praise of Pip" (9/63), men sacrifice their lives to save those of the dying children they love. As these men show, unselfishness brings rewards in the zone. Lew Bookman of "Angels" enters heaven "a man beloved by the children," and God accepts Max Phillips's offer to trade his life for that of his dying son. Granted, Max's offer is a lame one; he's already near death, and God can take him when-ever He wants, anyway. Yet life is Max's dearest possession; he has nothing better to offer, and God is impressed. Conversely, the apparent blessing or dream fulfillment sours when prompted by selfishness. Standing ten feet high stops Michael Grady of "Last Night of a Jockey" (10/63) from doing what he loves—riding horses for a living. Getting what one wants continues to carry stiff penalties in the zone. "The Silence" (4/61) and "A Kind of Stopwatch" (10/63) both show nonstop talkers getting their comeuppance by achieving aims that rob them of lis-teners.

"The Little People" (3/62) gives the motif political resonance. William Fletcher calls his power-hungry co-pilot "my wandering boy," an apt term since Peter Craig first appears to us reclining "on the floor of a canyon" rather than helping repair his and Fletcher's defective space-ship, as he was supposed to do. The end of the play finds him sprawled out again, buried under the rubble he dislodged when his corpse was dis-carded by his inadvertent killer. And just as Craig slighted his responsi-bility to both his colleague and the space mission the men were conduct-ing, so does he feel no duties to his subjects, saying of the mite-like inhabitants of the asteroid, "They're bright; they learn fast." The philosophy he has embraced of "discipline above all" has brought out the worst in this crypto-leader. He has already forfeited the warmth and companionability of friendship. Whereas Fletch calls him "Buddy" three times, Craig, preferring official over casual ties, addresses his superior officer as "Commander." (In "Sounds and Silences" [4/64], the arrogant Roswell Fleming always calls the wife who calls *him* by his first name "Madam.")

Fletch likes Craig well enough to ignore his faults. Craig, on the other hand, has no place in his heart for affection, which makes him "the victim of a delusion." During his last interview with Fletch, he's wearing the helmet that crowns the statue of him built by his subjects. His retreat into an image of power has bled his humanity. Confronting Fletch as an image rather than as a person, he has already whipped himself out of life. His literal death minutes later is more of a formality than a new development. It's certainly no surprise.

Charles Beaumont's "The Howling Man" (11/60) reminds us how overwhelming the truth can be. Specifically, nobody can outmatch the devil, particularly the person who thinks that the rules of the game favor him or her. *The Twilight Zone* endorses William Faulkner's belief that not only isn't the past dead; it isn't even past. And the series usually makes the point without resorting to the supernatural. The grip of the past chokes off the air supply of characters all over the zone. Nostalgia proves a destructive pastime in "Walking Distance" (10/59) and "A Stop at Willoughby" (5/60). Secret sins from the past gnaw at characters in the aeronautical dramas, "The Last Flight" (2/60), "King Nine Will Not Return" (9/60), and "The Arrival" (9/61). Peter Selden's inability to let go of a murder he committed 20 years before in "Nightmare as a Child" leads to his death; Chief Bell of "The Thirty-Fathom Grave" (1/63) can only silence his guilt by committing suicide. Perhaps because they can't forgive themselves, these men cling to what destroys them. They're not alone. Instructively, Jonathan West of "Caesar and Me" (4/64) says that his dummy, Caesar, isn't for sale when offered $25 for it by a pawnbroker. It doesn't matter to West that he needs the money. Still less material is it to him that getting rid of Caesar would help West, since he has empowered the dummy to destroy him.

Gunther Lutze of "Death's-Head Revisited" (11/61) is another whose private demon trips him up. This ex-Nazi officer got better than he deserved when he fled Germany at the end of World War II and found political asylum in South America. Haunted by the evil he performed as a death-camp commandant 17 years before, he has returned to his homeland to face his personal Nuremberg. His conscience, like that of most of us, is a stern taskmaster. The swagger and sadistic glee with which he enters Dachau, after checking into a nearby hotel, fade quickly. He wants to pay for his crimes. He becomes inseparable from the worst features of his captaincy. His atrocities are spelled out to him in what he calls a dream. During the dream, or trance, he invokes his sorriest victim, one Becker; he wants to have his sadism and his cruelty thrown back at him with utmost force. He's accommodated. Becker uses the phrase,"the misery you planted," while rehearsing Lutze's crimes; crimes so vile as these can't be buried and forgotten. The ensuing trial held by the ghosts of Dachau serves justice. During it, Becker equates this justice with retribution, denying any link to revenge or anger; life would be senseless if Lutze's crimes went unpunished. Lutze agrees. After the trial he calls himself Captain Gunther Lutze, an identity he had been suppressing all along. The doctor who examines him at the end calls him "a raving maniac." Facing up to his evil has wrecked his mind; no culprit could have walked away from an inventory of such crimes with sanity intact. He is last seen in a fetal coil. He has been reborn through justice into madness. The inner torment exacted by this madness can only be imagined. But we can assess some of its effects, Lutze having been told that the guilty verdict pronounced at his trial was "only the beginning" of his ordeals. It's also a logical outcome or consummation. As has been suggested, every part of Lutze is bound up with the guilt that drives him; he *is* that guilt. Scripts like "Death's-Head" and "Shadow Play" (5/61) show *The Twilight Zone* joining impulse to nonrealistic camera and acting techniques in order to probe beneath the secular pragmatism allegedly ruling most of our lives. "The Nick of Time" (11/60) invokes charms and omens to fight past the arbitrary formulas we have put in place to classify western culture. Another work that probes deeper levels of interaction is "The Jungle." Beaumont's December 1961 script develops the familiar idea that life is a seamless whole. It shows events happening in Africa menacing and ultimately destroying two New Yorkers. Hydraulic engineer Alan Richards has helped design a large dam that will displace an African tribe, and he is later attacked by a lion camped out on his bed. His wife, Doris, had wanted him to give up the dam project. The psychic distance between the witch doctor's oddments she displays and the upscale first-world luxury of the Richardses' apartment shrinks as the action progresses. For instance, at an executive board room meeting, Richards notes the similarity between the rabbit's foot carried for good luck by one of his colleagues and any number of charms used by primitive tribesmen everywhere. Finally, the primitive overtakes and then crushes the civilized. Just before the play's shocking finale, the cabdriver who takes Richards home at 3 A.M. dies at the wheel of his taxi. No explanation is given for his death, and none is sought.

As the suspense builds, the camera moves judiciously without straining for odd angles. Nor does director William Claxton betray anxiety in his use of special effects. Alan Richards's cosmopolitan good looks and bearing contrast brilliantly with the jungle mystique that finally consumes him. What's more, this clash is carefully foreshadowed by the jazzy urban riffs accompanying the opening shot of Manhattan's skyline that soon takes us into the Richardses' apartment. Yes, "Jungle," is flawed. Richards claims that anyone cursed by the witch doctors who lives near the proposed dam site in Africa will die slowly. Yet he, his wife, and the innocent cabdriver all die swiftly and violently. Next, Doris Richards conveniently keeps the charms she got from an African shaman in her jewelry box, presumably to help Alan find them more quickly and then burn them, an act of cynicism that helps bring him down.

Finally, after he abandons the dead cabbie, his homeward walk takes him through streets void of parked cars—a clear violation of probability; even in 1961, parking was a big problem in New York. Other strains on our credulity found in the script cause less worry. Yes, a dead goat can appear on a couple's doorstep, and a lion can show up in a bedroom in *The Twilight Zone*. In keeping with his size and mystique, the lion, through, invites larger questions than the goat. Zicree claims that it killed Doris (238). But is he right? Doris is certainly immobile in the play's last scene. But the bedroom in which she allegedly died shows no signs of struggle. Could she be sleeping the sleep of the sexually satisfied? Could the play's last frames, in which the once reclining lion springs out at Richards, initiate a rape scene rather than a killing? Invoking Yeats's "Leda and the Swan," the play's cross-cultural theme suggests the possibility. Raping both Doris and Alan and then letting their beastly offspring live would make perfect the revenge of any witch doctor who conjured the lion into the Manhattan bedroom. This wildness transcends facile animism. As sensitive as *The Twilight Zone* is to the fantastic and the bizarre, it also respects probability. In sexual ties, for instance, essences lie close to surfaces. Looks count, and physical attraction undergirds erotic love. "The Long Morrow" (1/64) makes the sensible point that a couple divided by 50 years doesn't belong together, mostly because the young feel more comfortable with people their own age. "The Trade-Ins" (4/62) portrays the same truth from the opposite standpoint. Appearances bespeak a reality that can't be talked away. A 22-year-old man, even a man of 79 with the face and body of a 22-year-old, can't love a woman of 74, even if she's his wife of 50 years. Long before John Holt will have saved the money for Marie's rejuvenating procedure, he'd have left her. An unsettling truth, but one that *The Twilight Zone* accepts; yet the Serling script in which it appears softens its bite. In our bleak, unforgiving world, in which a minute can sour 50 years of love, kindness will stem from an unlikely source. Farraday, the professional gambler, returns the $5,000 he had won from old John Holt in poker after Holt had gone to his den hoping to double his holdings so that he and Marie could be rejuvenated at the same time.

The free-floating eyeball in *The Twilight Zone*'s opening graphic during the show's final season reminds us that our eyes link us to the external world. The primacy of this link imples that reality is subjective. No passive recorders, we create while we perceive. Perhaps Miss Menlo, the Joan Crawford figure in "Eyes," a November 1969 entry in Rod Serling's *Night Gallery,* acts so ruthlessly because she's blind; her 54 years of darkness have convinced her that anybody can be bought because we all have something to hide. A few glimpses of our shared world of muddle and confusion might have shown her the difficulty of avoiding compromise, particularly with moral blackmailers like her poised to pounce as soon as we miscue.

II

When such meddlers are empowered by the state, individuality wilts. *The Twilight Zone* shows how ideologies menace life and how power politics crush the self. If beauty is used to promote conformity in "Number Twelve Looks Just Like You" (1/64), ugliness serves the same function in "Eye of the Beholder" (11/60). Ugliness in the police state of "Eye" isn't only tolerated; rather, it's encouraged, as is borne out by the words "glorious conformity," spoken by the state's deformed-looking leader during a TV speech. "Eye" depicts the dangers of leveling. Crime in the state where the play is set consists of being different. Anyone who looks different may also have different values, values that challenge the status quo. Again, looks have claimed an inner reality. The pig-snouted citizens of the state know they're ugly despite what their leader tells them. Thus they shrink from looking at themselves and, by extension, their motives. Introspection costs more than sloganeering. Besides, they already see more than enough of themselves in the twisted, rubbery faces of their fellow citizens. And what they see pains them. If they're not actively suffering, they're all sick at heart, a sign of which is the hospital where the action of "Eye" takes place. Everybody needs treatment for the disease of conformity. Even the doctor in charge of Janet Tyler's cosmetic surgery criticizes the state in an unguarded moment.

Clearly, one of the greatest dangers to the state is self-hatred. Having little to lose, the self-hater will take risks terrifying to the conformist. But these same risks and the benefits they might bring will lodge in the conformist's imagination. Thus it helps the state to make Janet Tyler look like everybody else. Though beautiful, she believes that she's ugly, a state of mind that could foment rebellion. The series of operations performed to change her face add up to shrewd statecraft. Besides honing her zeal for conformity, they also fuel the self-worth of those around her. But even *they* lack absolute value. The failure of the eleventh try to normalize her looks relegates her to a commune where she can live with others like her. This edict, cruel and despairing in a way, does suggest the triumph of nature over nurture and creed. Handsome Walter Smith has come to fetch Janet to her new home. Nearly immediately, the two feel a mutual affinity, if not an attraction. They leave the hospital hand in hand in response to the failure of every legal and surgical attempt to make them ugly.

Their beauty has survived not only political writ but also their belief that they're ugly. Perhaps their country now houses 30 or 40 people who look like them. In a century, the number may climb to 1,000. The play's artistry encourages this possibility. Serling says in his prologue that Janet's face will be displayed, and when it is, it will invite both moral and political issues we hadn't expected. The removal of Janet's facial bandages confronts the notion that the drive to equality bred by democracies can pound life down to its lowest common denominator, consigning all power to a state which becomes totalitarian in spite of itself.

But even here some hope survives, thanks to the decency that transcends politics. The hospital staffers who attend Janet are more than competent professionals. They also act with warmth and compassion. They explain patiently to Janet what they're doing and why. They even raise philosophical questions about beauty and ugliness, about difference and similarity. Rarely are they judgmental or patronizing, Janet's alleged freakishness disturbing them nearly as much as it does her at times. Finally, rather than exterminating misfits, their nation puts them in communes where they live in dignity. And dignity, as seen in works like "The Monsters Are Due on Maple Street" (3/60) and "The Shelter" (9/61), is difficult to attain, let alone preserve in the zone. "The Old Man in the Cave "(11/63) depicts one of the world's few communities that have survived a nuclear war. Recalling Hitler's policy of *Anschluss*, a Major French rides into town claiming to have brought with him the virtues of stability and order.

What he brings is chaos and death, supplanting a regiment of cooperation and faith with one of total license. All of the townsfolk except one give in to the gaudiness of his smash-and-grab policy of instant gratification. Goldsmith, the local leader, survives because of his restraint.

Now his powers of self-control will be tested anew. His ordeal of survival isn't unique in the canon. Though Serling withholds sympathy from the murderer Joe Caswell of "Execution" (4/60), he shows through Caswell's words and gestures the difficulty of condemning him. The civilized virtues come more easily to the well-fed lounging in comfortable, well-heated rooms than to the hungry pioneer on the prairie whose neighbor's crust of bread and jacket could spell out the difference between life and death. Temptation takes many forms in the zone. "You Drive" (1/64) by Earl Hamner, Jr., combines the motifs of the obsolete man and the guilty conscience (from "Nightmare as a Child" and "Deaths-Head") with the deistic belief, conveyed often in *The Twilight Zone*, that life regulates itself. Chubby, prosperous-looking Oliver Pope accidentally kills a 12-year-old newsboy in a hit-and-run driving accident. For a while, he's glad he abandoned his victim. The police identify the victim's killer as one of Pope's younger co-workers, whom Pope suspects of coveting his job. But Pope's security is thinner than he had believed. His car—a projection of both his conscience and his sense of the fitness of things—starts defying him. Its lights flash on and off, the horn blasts, and the engine dies in traffic. Then, after driving itself back home from the shop where it was taken for repairs, it throws a bumper. The suspense holds. Pope falls on the wet pavement after the car follows him down the street. At this point, it would have been easy for the driverless car to run him down. In fact, the car must stop quickly on wet road to avoid smashing into him. But stop it does. Then it opens its door on the passenger's side, admits Pope, and drives him to the police station, where, presumably, he exonerates his younger colleague.

Bartlett Finchley of Serling's "A Thing about Machines" (10/60) also gets his comeuppance through the medium of machinery. This "practicing sophisticate" who drives an English roadster, speaks BBC English, and lives in a mansion where he suffers from loneliness. Early in the play we're shown why. His calling his secretary an "empty-headed little female with a mechanical face" prompts her to stop working for him. He also accuses the repairman who fixed his television of overcharging him. Then he calls the repairman "an incompetent clod" and "the most forgettable person I ever met." The man has come to the Finchley mansion because the appliances in it often malfunction, rousing Finchley's wrath. Finchley has recently thrown a radio down the stairs and kicked in the front of his television. These acts have personal import for Serling, who wrote radio scripts before making it in television (Sander 65-78). Serling's image also appears on the screen of the recently fixed television in Finchley's living room. But his stake in mass communications goes beyond the personal. Acts of devastation like those committed by Finchley deny the technological advances that have been adopted to help us cope better with material reality. If houses have souls, as Virginia Woolf believed, then perhaps those appliances that ease our transit through life do, too. We should respect our physical surroundings as much as we do people. Because Finchley does neither, he's foiled everywhere. His typewriter, a dancer on his TV screen, and a telephone he yanks out of a wall all tell him, "Get out of here, Finchley." Then his electric razor chases him down the stairs and out of his house, after which his car pursues him around his neighborhood before maneuvering him into his swimming pool, where he drowns.

"The Brain Center at Whipple's" (5/64) shows in a different way how the abuse of machinery can cause havoc. If it's dangerous to mistreat machines, as in "Thing," it can also be downright criminal to rely on them too much. The havoc begins with the machine-obsessed person. By automating his factory, Wallace Whipple decries the human factor. Even the firm's board of directors, which will later replace him with a robot, tells him that spending too much time around machines has warped him. His replacing his workers with machines derides the intrinsic worth of people together with the virtues of pride, craftsmanship, and loyalty. His lonely, sterile-looking factory also bespeaks his ineptitude as a businessman. By creating wide-scale unemployment, he has destroyed the market for the product he makes; the ex-workers whose jobs he took away now lack the money to buy anything but the basic essentials.

The Twilight Zone often uses this kind of reversal to point a moral. A boor in "Sounds and Silences" (4/64) who once reveled in noise suddenly hears tiny sounds as if magnified many times, like the ticking of a clock or the drip from a shower head; ordinary traffic sounds, a squeaking shoe, or a pinging typewriter overpower him. Finally, a visit to a psychiatrist deafens him to any sound but that of his own voice. Matheson's "Night Call" (2/64) uses reversal more eerily. A storm collapses a telephone wire on the headstone of a young man dead 30 years. Now Brian Douglas is using the fallen wire to phone Elva Keene, his fiancée when he died. The teleplay's first apparition, an antique wheelchair seen during the late-night storm that felled the telephone pole near Brian's grave, focuses the plot. The car accident that both killed Brian and robbed Elva of the use of her legs happened because she talked him into letting her drive. He could never say no to her. Her discovery that he has been trying to reach her from his wire-draped grave elates her. The phone calls that she had been dreading, she now craves. Talking to Brian will end her loneliness. The play's final scene opens with her holding her phone in her lap waiting for its ring and then answering it. She's sitting upright, freshly coifed, in what might be her bridal bed. This image of a spinster crone who facies herself a young bride leads to a finale equally grotesque. Earlier, Elva had screamed into the phone, "Leave me alone!" But that was before Brian identified himself. Now she hears him telling her that he'll follow his usual practice of doing her bidding, in this case, leaving her alone. These are the last words she'll hear him say. The line goes dead, and she sees that she'll get no reprieve from loneliness.

Her willfulness has defeated her. Happiness in the zone comes to people who don't force their will on others. These fulfilled people can be humble and poor, like Henry Corwin of Serling's "Night of the Meek" (12/60), a jobless drunk. As downtrodden and despised as he is, Corwin proves that love in the heart can ennoble the ugly and the sordid. A bag of garbage he picks up turns out to contain Christmas presents that gladden the needy. As soon as he discovers the bag's contents, he heads straight for the place where he's most likely to find the depressed and the deprived—a mission house. His heart is right. Even though his lateness and his drinking cost him his Santa Claus job, he chose the job wisely. This down-and-outer has made giving, not getting, the meaning of Christmas. No wonder he's happy. The meekness that Serling equates with generosity is a neglected virtue in his confrontational society. Like the hero of "I Dream of Genie" (3/63), Corwin learns that happiness lies in serving others, not in arrogating things to oneself.

"Dust" (1/61) also shows that the degraded and the despised are redeemable. Salvation is at hand all the time, not only at Christmas. Even in its most squalid aspects, the world we inhabit is blessed. This argument reaches us largely through the pitchman Sykes, as scurvy a rogue as can be found in the zone. If Sykes's definition of himself as a businessman holds good, it only does so at the rankest level. The hangman of an ugly desert town buys a rope from him that will be used to hang a young man convicted for killing a local girl with his wagon. Then Sykes tells Luis's father that he has some magical dust. If old Gallegos buys this dust and sprinkles it around Luis's gibbet, he can save his son's life. Actually, the dust came from the desert floor; Sykes has cheated Gallegos. Or so he thinks. He stops gloating when, seconds after Gallegos performs his ritual with the dust, Luis's fall snaps the brand-new rope fitted to his neck.

Sykes's dust has borne healthy fruit. God can reveal Himself in the unlikeliest of places. He can also use a brute like Sykes to enact His will. That the loathsome Sykes wins redemption from the spiritual drama he helped engineer becomes clear immediately. Having already been rewarded by seeing Luis walk free, he can give the money he got from both the local hangman and old Gallegos to some local children. The comfort extended to Luis in front of the gibbet by Gallegos and the local sheriff symbolizes the watchfulness of God the father. Gallegos, naturally, does all he can to cheer his condemned son. The sheriff's kindness moves us more. It would have been easy for Sheriff Koch to cave in to the blood lust gripping many of the other locals. Instead, he shields Luis from the curiosity and the cruelty of the neighbors who have come to watch the hanging. What's particularly moving about his charity is that he extends it to a man sentenced to die for a crime he clearly committed. But we're not through with father figures. Though Luis has survived the springing of the trap beneath his gallows, should he be allowed to live? The decision is left to his victim's parents. Without hesitating, the girl's father decrees, "One killing is enough," and sets Luis free.

As the play's title suggests, the dry, powdery earth found all over the desert contains redemptive properties. This alchemy graces all transactions. A substance as common as dust can turn hatred to love, and it *is* worth a fortune, as Sykes had claimed without understanding how truly he spoke. As in "Night of the Meek," Serling rates charity and forgiveness above everything else in human affairs. What's more, nodding in the direction of the Whitman of "Song of Myself," he points out that these virtues are as accessible as the dirt we walk on. We live in blessedness all the time. And once in a while, God chooses a Sykes to remind us of it.

Serling's "Mr. Garrity and the Graves" (5/64) also includes, in its title character, an itinerant whose powers are greater than he knows. So blinded is Jared Garrity by the prospect of quick cash that he underrates his skill as a conjurer. But before blinding himself, he blinds others. He rides into the fictional town of Happiness, Arizona, walks into a bar, and, after tricking the locals once or twice, convinces them that he can restore to life their loved ones buried in a nearby graveyard. He's bombarded by requests—and dollars—to perform the resurrection. But the corpses who leave the graveyard and march toward town frighten their survivors. Their resurrection inconveniences the survivors' present arrangements, including those of the town drunk, whose 247-pound wife broke his arm six times during their marriage. Other resurrected corpses are coming to reunite with survivors who don't want them back but who claimed the opposite in order to sound loyal and respectable. The sight of the resurrected corpses marching toward town frightens their survivors into persuading Garrity to reverse his magic. Garrity welcomes their pleas. He knows that he can charge the locals much more to undo his fake magic than he did to enact it. What he doesn't know is that his magic wasn't fake. Having revived the corpses without knowing it has made him a fraudulent fraud. This "sad misjudger of his talents" implies, like Sykes before him, that we all possess powers we can neither compass nor control.

These powers lace the air we breathe. Granted, *The Twilight Zone* can perpetrate some confused theology. Contrary to what's claimed in Hamner's "The Hunt" (1/62), no living creature, including the devil, can damn any other to hell; the disposition of any soul belongs exclusively to the soul's possessor. Elsewhere, vision may run afoul of careless writing, as when the angel Cavender, in Serling's "Cavender Is Coming" (5/62), says that "you can't have your cake and also eat it. Somebody has to pay the fiddler." Yet the very presence of Cavender and also of his fellow angels in "A Nice Place to Visit" (4/60) and "Mr. Bevis" (6/60), not to mention their diabolic foils elsewhere, creates a unity of outlook. Like a great novel, *The Twilight Zone*, both mirror and pane glass, depicts how much and how little we mortals are vouchsafed to see. A work like "Static" (3/61) implies that each of us perceives the truth in his or her way and that this truth is largely unsharable. But it's still part of a larger truth we all share, one that the series invokes in its repetitions of plot, image, character type, and setting.

The laws of reality are intrinsic, not imposed. Walter Jameson (3/60) can't escape his past. Sooner or later, it will engulf him. Jason Foster's greedy relatives in "The Masks" (3/64) will come into a large inheritance that they won't be able to enjoy. The death of "grasping, compulsive" Fred Renard in "What You Need" (12/59) helps his victim. But so sour and desperate is Renard that he's better off dead. He was meant to die at 36; his death stems logically from a series of events he himself put in place. Sometimes this outcome, though not dramatized, can be intuited. "Number Twelve Looks Just Like You" (1/64), which Schumer calls "the most insistent of [Serling's] anticonformist diatribes" (151), reminds us that the most unjust societies are the ones whose chiefs decry injustice most passionately. Often, the accumulated tensions will find no release, as in "Young Man's Fancy." The title of Matheson's May 1962 teleplay adapts a famous line from Tennyson's "Locksley Hall." Having courted Virginia Lane for 12 years, Alex Walker is no longer youthful. And, though he has just married Virginia, his heart belongs to his dead mother. Clothing symbolizes this breach of the wedding bond. Whereas Virginia wears a short-sleeved, open-necked blouse, exposing a good deal of flesh, Alex keeps on his jacket and tie throughout. He's last seen as a little boy entering his bedroom with his mother. Still chastely clad in jacket and tie, he has only changed physically. He ignores the congratulations wish of the real-estate agent who has come to sell the house where the action unfolds and where Alex grew up. Meanwhile, Alex delays packing for his wedding trip. He resets his mother's hall clock. Advisedly, when the realtor, an outsider, entered the house, the clock stopped running. But Alex ignores this useful nudge. He tells the realtor that he's not ready to sell the house, after all; he reminisces about his mother; and after he goes upstairs to pack, he enters her room instead of his own, plays her favorite song on the old family phonograph, and rummages through the boyhood keepsakes she had stored. Toward the end of the play, he also starts calling his bride Virdge, or Verge; in fact, he uses the name seven times within two minutes. Her virginal status has pushed to the fore. What's more, she also lives on a verge, or margin, a state that sharpens her pain, for it's occupied only by those rare unfortunates who are both married and virginal. Lane, the maiden name she gave up to wed Alex, implies her permanent exile from the solidness and warmth of community life. She's a Walker condemned to walk a thin, solitary line.

III

Virginia has learned that the quick fix never helps anyone in the twilight zone. Marrying Alex Walker could never rid him of his mother complex; because we're unreasonable in our demands, the devices that could help us control reality bring us to grief. Serling says of the magical camera in the epilogue of his "Most Unusual Camera" (12/60), "it makes believe that it's an ally, but it isn't at all." He's right. The camera that photographs events five minutes before they take place causes the death of at least four people who try to make money with it. The four went wrong, to begin with, by electing total change. Such a surrender stems from a belief that all is lost; their lives are worthless and beyond redemption by normal standards. Most of the voluntary time travelers in *The Twilight Zone* also make this sad statement about themselves.

So does the title figure of "Jess-Belle" (2/63). First, this stunning play from *The Twilight Zone*'s fourth season depicts the centricity of the diabolic in human affairs. When Walter Bedeker of "Escape Clause" (11/59) asks the devil how he got into the Bedeker apartment, he's answered, "I've never been gone." The advisedly named witch in "Jess-Belle," Granny Hart, played with chilling insight by Jeanette Nolan, has always lived in the mountain village where the play unfolds. She's benign and maternal looking. And though her words are terrible, the back-country drawl with which she utters them soothes and comforts. Her sexual overture to the play's romantic lead, Billy-Ben Turner, on his wedding night, no less, has an outrageous, hideous appeal. Like Coeurville, presumably the idyllic childhood home of the robot Alan Talbot of "In His Image" (1/63), this appeal points to something familiar in all of us. Granny Hart's powers run deep. She has been suggesting throughout that a witch's love is wilder and sexier than that of an ordinary mortal. Her statement to Billy-Ben, made upon his arrival at her cottage, that she has been expecting him rivets us. We don't know what will happen. Jess-Belle Stone immediately regretted trading her soul to Granny for the love of Billy-Ben. Then she shocks herself by attacking Billy-Ben physically. And because she doesn't want to contaminate him, she tries to leave him. But she has bought him with her soul, and a vital part of her craves him, even if she needs black magic to keep him.

Unfortunately, black magic forbids half measures, violating the credo voiced by Pedott of "What You Need" in regard to his rare gift, "I must use it sparingly." This December 1959 play unfolds amid the grunge of film noir and *cinéma vérité*—race tracks, bars, cheap hotels, and dark, wet, lonely streets prowled by urban drifters. But Pedott redeems the grunge. His ability to read the future and his belief that "the things you need, you only need once," if too cheery, helps him reach out to the pinched and the straitened. But the same aid that's benign if used correctly becomes deathly when abused. "Undistinguished, meaningless" Fred Renard sees in Pedott a gold mine. Not satisfied that Pedott saved his life and then helped him win at the race track, he pressures the old street peddler for more favors. Pedott foresees a chain of demands that will end in his death. Thus he gives Renard a pair of shoes with soles too slick to help the thug avoid an oncoming car. These death shoes were what Pedott needed, not Renard. And had Renard been more sober in his demands, he'd have been wearing shoes that helped him dodge the car that killed him.

"A Most Unusual Camera" (12/60) also depicts the contagion of greed by reversing the conventions of a cinematic subgenre, in this case, the domestic comedy. The dapper, comfortable-looking middle-aged Chet and Paula Diedrich argue about Paula's brother, Woodward. But Woodward, who soon appears in their hotel room, and the Diedriches are criminals. Chet and Paula have, in fact, just robbed a curio shop. They find in their spoils, as has been seen, a camera that photographs events five minutes before their occurrence. Along with Woodward, they visit a local race track in order to identify the winners of races yet to be run. But they're not satisfied with the fortune they win. Their greed defies the adage about honor among thieves. When they learn that the fabulous camera contains only ten exposures, they quarrel about the subjects they will shoot with the remaining film. Serling's camera shows people being defeated by an object of great price because of their greed. Chet and Woodward fall out of their hotel window while trying to wrest the camera from each other. Then Paula and, finally, a hotel waiter who has discovered their racket die from a similar fall.

Beaumont's "The Prime Mover" (3/61) offers a more cheerful sermon on the same subject. Again, a bizarre way to get rich presents itself. But only one character grabs for it, and even he is redeemed. Jimbo Cobb has the rare ability to move objects with his mind. When Ace Larsen, his partner in a diner called the Happy Daze Cafe, discovers Jimbo's gift, he takes it to Las Vegas to get rich on. Like Franklin Gibbs of "The Fever" (1/60), he abuses gambling. (Some of the music used in "Fever," along with the play's Las Vegas setting, recurs in "Prime Mover.") Appropriately, the word "Daze," from the sign in front of the diner he co-owns, is the first man-made object seen at the play's outset. Larsen scolds the slot machine in the diner that gobbles his coins. But winning doesn't break his gambling trance. The more money he wins in Las Vegas, with Jimbo at his side concentrating his mind, the more reckless he gets. He throws his winnings around in a way that brings out the worst in others. He jokes about renaming Nevada "Aceville, USA." He cheats on his ladylove, Kitty. Ironically, he calls the day he shoots craps with the big Chicago gambler, Phil Nolan, his "lucky day." He had just hugged the cigarette girl he presumably slept with the night before. Then, risking the fortune he had just won from Nolan, he rolls a three.

These two events are really one. When Jimbo, a friend of Kitty Cavanaugh, sees Ace hugging another woman, he withdraws his power. The day of the dice game does benefit Ace. But he has to lose all his cash to win a life—and a wife. The play's last scene, like the first, takes place in the Happy Daze. And the play also ends as it began, with a coin flip. Perhaps life is a gamble. But it's wisest to bet on a person. Ace removes the slot machine that ate so much of his cash and proposes to Kitty. He sees that being rich corrupted him. He also realizes that he already had all he needed for happiness. Poverty can be endured if you have someone you love nearby. A difficult lesson? Probably. The Castles of "The Man in the Bottle" (10/60) and the Holts of "The Trade-Ins" (4/62) only learned it late in life. Ace Larsen is probably in his 30s, if not older. Perhaps most of the inhabitants of the zone have to put their misspent youth behind them before they can know happiness.

Age is also an issue in "A Short Drink from a Certain Fountain" (12/63). The work starts well. Blond, white-clad Flora Gordon is as brassy and bouncy as the jazz tune she's solo-dancing to, a wine glass in her hand, in the opening scene. The entrance of her aging husband into the apartment wearing dark clothes dampens her spirits. She tries to fend off gloom by bringing Harmon into her wild dance. But he tires quickly and stops dancing, confirming her sad realization that Harmon and, more specifically, his age, stand between her and the fun she craves. Her phrase, "jumping off a bridge," alludes to the failure of her and Harmon to bridge the 40-year gap dividing them. This "flashy little piece of baggage" merits our pity, even though, more weed than flower, she's destroying Harmon. Her white clothes invoke the innocence that first drew him to her. If anyone's to blame for the failure of the marriage, it's he. As in "Little Girl Lost" (3/62), though more guardedly, a scientist emerges as a savior figure. Harmon's brother, Raymond, is a doctor specializing in rejuvenation. Suppressing his misgivings, he injects Raymond with the youth serum he has been developing. Like other straitened *Twilight Zone* characters, Harmon can't be easily condemned, even though, by threatening suicide, he blackmailed Raymond into inoculating him. This "bright, charming, wealthy, discerning" elder loves Flora fanatically. He also knows, unfortunately, that he repels her at times. The truth that the young always leave the old deepens his woes. He stands more to lose by the break-up of the marriage than she. The loss of Flora could sink him, as his words about suicide show. On the other hand, Raymond's youth serum is untested on animals, let alone humans. No one can predict its effects on Harmon. He could lose everything regardless of where he turns.

At first, Raymond's quick fix augurs well. Flora, who lives for physical sensation, warms to the sight of a youthful-looking Raymond the morning after his injection. But the rejuvenation process continues. Her virile young husband keeps getting younger till he reverts to infancy. The answer to his marital problems has created new ones. Youth still calls the tune in the marriage. What has changed are the identities of junior and senior partners. Flora must babysit the ex-elder who used to bore and peeve her. The moral tone of "Drink" has taken on a medieval intensity and irrefutability. Flora has a larger helping of the youth she had craved than she can handle. Because her little boy husband has given her no grounds for divorce, she'll have to stay married to him—until he decides to leave her. But will he have this choice? Being reared by headstrong, childish Flora won't help him grow into a responsible adult. Yet how responsible was he to begin with? He judged badly in marrying Flora and again in blackmailing his brother into giving him the youth serum. Even a maternal Flora wouldn't have in him much to work with.

The "Old Man in the Cave" (11/63) portrays the devastation that comes from applying the quick fix to something that already works smoothly. A radioactive bomb that fell ten years before the plays's present-tense action has left only 500 survivors in the large area between Buffalo and Atlanta. In the village where the action unfolds, the blast contaminated most of the crops and canned goods. But Serling's villagers lead a satisfactory, though admittedly not a comfortable, life until interfering busybodies upset their routine. They have survived by heeding the advice of the old man in the cave. It doesn't matter that they've never seen the old man. They act on his advice as it's interpreted by one of their number, an elder named Goldsmith.

This circuit is snapped by the arrival of a group of soldiers wearing dark glasses who ride into town claiming that they've come to implement discipline and authority. Their brash leader, Major French, played with swift, hard competence by James Coburn, hits Goldsmith and threatens to hang him. Then French and his men muscle their way into the cave where the old man is kept. They find—a computer, which they also smash. Their frenzy brings wide-scale devastation. Without knowing it, French has cut the villagers' lifeline to the future. He opens the containers of forbidden food and wine and serves the contents to the villagers, who, having curbed their appetites for a decade, stuff themselves. Their binge kills them. Though they've identified the old man, their knowledge hasn't brought them freedom or power. The play's last scene shows the village's main street littered with corpses.

The only survivor is Goldsmith, whose last words are, "I'll never know." Knowledge and being exist inversely in "The Old Man." Like Goldsmith's last words, the corpses Goldsmith has to pick his way through remind us that faith sometimes helps us more than reason. Certain truths can be lived, but not analyzed. One character claims that he doesn't know what men live by. Ruled by the instinct to survive, he and his fellow villagers knew enough to avoid prying. Even Major French perceives the realities governing the village to be religious. He calls Goldsmith "Father," an accurate title, since Goldsmith performs the priest-like role of interceding between his flock and their lawgiver, or oracle. French strikes Goldsmith down because he knows that Goldsmith represents a level of spiritual attainment that he, French, can never reach, and he resents it. The words of one villager, spoken when the computer heretofore reverenced as the old man comes into view, "God, dear God," voice regret that the community has traded mystery for knowledge. The regret is well founded. Something that sustains life has given way to something that takes it, and the community will never recover.

The whole village suffers from impetuosity. Nor does it suffer alone. Elsewhere in *The Twilight Zone*, people concoct their own downfalls. Whipple in "The Brain Center" (5/64) eliminates 61,000 jobs and saves his firm $4 million in expenses for hospitalization, insurance, maternity leaves, and paid vacations. But in the process, he makes himself obsolete. A Soviet commissar in "The Jeopardy Room" (4/64) is blown up by a device he himself planted in a room occupied by an ex-comrade the commissar wants to stop from defecting to the West. "A Piano in the House" (2/62) also used the device of "the biter-bit" from

Renaissance drama. This tribute to the power of music shows one of *The Twilight Zone*'s vilest characters, drama critic Fitzgerald Fortune, caught in the trap he had baited for others. As a birthday present for his wife, Fortune buys a player piano the music of which brings out the hidden selves of its listeners. The rude, cranky shopkeeper who sells the piano to Fortune becomes poetic and expansive while listening to it. In the script's most poignant moment, another song inspires an overweight woman who imagines herself a graceful ballerina to pirouette around a drawing room.

Fortune has been prying into the hearts of others, including his wife's, in order to bare their innermost secrets. No less flagrant an abuse in the zone than in Nathaniel Hawthorne, this practice calls for punishment. And punished Fortune is. The joke he had prepared for others recoils on him. Within seconds, some music inserted into the piano reduces this sadist to a cringing, frightened little boy. He, too, was wearing a mask, a point foreshadowed by the masks that filled the store where he bought the piano. But he aches more than any of the others when his mask, or protective interface, is ripped away. Besides losing his professional standing, he sees his wife walk out on him with her long-time lover, a playwright whose last work Fortune savaged in the press.

"A self-righteous bigot with witch-hunting tendencies" (Parker 118), Oliver Crangle of "Four O'Clock" (4/62) will suffer still more than Fortune did from the slamming recoil of the trap he baited for others. This self-appointed scourge and avenger has vowed to punish all thieves, heavy drinkers, prostitutes, and communists. Fiendishly methodical, he backs his indictments with systematic records. *The Twilight Zone* has returned in spirit to Hawthorne's Salem; Crangle is the sin-obsessed puritan or "twisted fanatic" straining to unearth and then crush evil. And justice *is* done at four o'clock. The punishment that he claimed would crash down on all evildoers at 4 P.M. occurs exactly on cue, but on him. Instead of shrinking all of his accused malefactors to the height of two feet, he has shrunk himself.

He was first seen bent over his records. While inclining in the direction he'll later head, he has alongside him his parrot, Pete. But if Pete follows his usual practice of "parroting" his master, he'll inflict on Crangle one of the cruellest deaths imaginable. The biter will be bitten, or pecked, to death. As just as this retribution is, it repels us. The closing frames of "Four O'Clock" show Pete looking down on his tiny owner. That owner's last wild efforts consisted of reaching in vain for the jar of food sitting on his window ledge. Judging from the frequency with which Pete is fed, he'll soon start pecking at Crangle. And Crangle knows it. His fear grips us. The still shot of Pete accompanying the credits at play's end invests both his hooked beak and his glinting eye with menace. Crangle has good reason to panic. The survival of this would-be paragon who has always withheld kindness and charity from others now depends on kindness and charity, virtues usually not associated with parrots. We savor this bittersweet irony. We also understand that Crangle would welcome the justice of Pete's sharp beak were it directed to the flesh of the alleged wrongdoers he had targeted for punishment.

Everything has gone as Crangle planned it with one exception, the identity of the victim. Or so it seems. His plight revives our knowledge that residents of the zone damage themselves more than their enemies do (Elva Keene of "Night Call" [2/64] and Floyd Burney of "Come Wander with Me" [5/64] spring to mind). Perhaps, like that of Fitzgerald Fortune of "Piano," Crangle's downfall fulfills his dearest wish. Such an act of despair rests upon an acknowledgment that he can't end his destructive ways. The fear he has roused in his neighbors calls for a radical solution if tranquillity and moral health are to return to the community. And who better than Crangle can quiet the fear? That he dies because he plagues himself as much as he does others sheds shocking new light on the perils inherent in casting blame. His death also underscores the warning served by *The Twilight Zone* on the dangers of the quick fix. Though a social blessing, the retribution that makes Crangle a pygmy both challenges our moral priorities and leaves an acrid residue, most likely the smell of dread.

9

Edges and Twists

Serling has a sharp eye for the way people look, talk, and act. Works like "Nervous Man in a Four-Dollar Room" (10/60) and "The Long Morrow" (1/64) show him presenting ordinary people without condescension, sentimentality, or the impulse to poke fun. What interests him is the passion and intensity of life, his observational powers serving a dramatic, not a moral, function. Driving these gifts is the chance to make a story rather than a point. The people in *The Twilight Zone* are complex, ambiguous, and conflictive. They also come across as basically decent sorts who try to be honest and who mean well, but who miscue because of both personal limitations and the weight of external forces beyond their control. Their resemblance to us in this regard galvanizes our responses to them. Even though the moral outlook of *The Twilight Zone* is clear, even predictable, many of the plays in the series defy moral judgment. Speaking of the breadth of reference in the Serling-written *Twilight Zone* shows, Jeffrey Armstrong noted the danger of reducing dramatic action to ideology or message: "A central theme . . . was that there were universal mysteries and forces before which man, even modern scientific man, must inevitably humble himself. The general tone of many [of the Serling-written episodes] was cautionary: man can never be too sure of anything" (286).

The cautionary tone to which Armstrong refers is meant to foster dialogue. We're meant to debate what we've watched on the small screen after the show ends; if the show holds us spellbound while it's taking place, its finale rouses our activity. The creative source behind this alchemy is the show's auteur, or guiding spirit, Serling himself. A symbolic tribute to his alchemy occurs in Beaumont's "Printer's Devil," a February 1963 play about diabolism. A bonanza to any journal editor or publisher, the stranger known as Mr. Smith both reports the news and operates the Linotype machine at the Dansburg *Courier* on which the news is set. But not only does his wizardry with the Linotype put us in mind of a concert pianist; his strange ability to report events before their occurrence leads to the disclosure that he causes these events. That some of them create fatalities confirms our suspicions that he's the devil.

No fire-breathing dragon, Smith, played by Burgess Meredith, is a small man who's usually seen from above, a technique that diminishes him still more; he's almost always foreshortened while enacting his magic at the Linotype keyboard. And, like him, Serling, his creator at several removes, was a short, jaunty chain smoker who both womanized and enjoyed great media success. The speed with which Doug Winter, owner and publisher of the foundering *Courier*, trades his soul to Smith for a series of front-page scoops that brings the newspaper unprecedented sales proves Smith's power—along with his danger. The figure of the artist as an enchanter more determined to subvert than to enchant had appeared in Serling even before the debut of *The Twilight Zone*. What's more, this legacy of Schopenhauer, Freud, and Mann presented itself in terms consistent with those of "Printer's Devil." Going back five years in American history will help us see how.

"The Comedian" (2/57) featured undersized Mickey Rooney as Sammy Hogarth. Now at the peak of his fame as a TV comic, the 40-year-old Hogarth reveals his success to be bound up with nastiness and cruelty. Like several of Serling's other obsolete men, his chief writer, Al Preston, drinks too much. The echoes he sends out are familiar. Preston claims, "In the eye of the master, I'm long since over the hill." Perhaps Hogarth envies him his decency. Besides intuiting that Preston has become his unofficial conscience, he knows that he's always falling short of Preston's moral standards, and he resents it. Thus he grabs every chance to damage the writer.

His abuse of his brother is even more vile. To lower Lester's guard, Hogarth will buy him expensive gifts. He wants to savor the humiliation he inflicts on Lester. He'll slap him in the presence of others. He has made Lester's alleged worthlessness a major accent of his comedy act. He even propositioned Lester's bride, Julie, at their wedding dinner. "He killed me years ago," says Lester, the Mel Tormé figure, of his brother. And who wants to live with a corpse? Julie leaves Lester even though he loves her and needs her because she's fed up with his inability to stand up to Sammy. She might have a different reason. She finds Sammy attractive, as does Al Preston's fiancée. Serling has thrown in our faces the inconvenient truth that cruelty can ignite a sexual charge. And, just as inconveniently, Sammy may have spoken the truth when he called himself "the funniest thing on wheels." The Ernest Lehman story that Serling adapted for Playhouse 90 traffics in the truth that genius often defies our ethical programming. His treatment of Sammy also shows that Serling accepted this abrasive truth and that he had the intellectual honesty to explore it artistically, often to the joy of millions of attentive viewers.

I

The ambiguity that Serling saw in himself floods *The Twilight Zone*. In a cameo turn, "The Midnight Sun" (11/61) includes a housebreaker who, having lost both his wife and baby during childbirth, wins more of our pity than do his victims. Walter Jameson's fabulous longevity has become more of a curse than the blessing he intended it to be. It also frets others. Whereas Professor Sam Kittridge objects to his daughter's marrying a 2,000-year-old man, he also covets that man's imperishability. The 70-year-old Kittridge wants to live; his youthful-looking counterpart craves death. This yearning is familiar. Malcontents and nonconformists of different stripes people the zone, most of whom Serling tries to understand. Representative of those who trade their old lives for new ones and then want the old ones back is the title figure of "Mr. Bevis" (6/60). Serling enjoys the warmth and boyish charm of this loudly clad eccentric. But he also shows Bevis's eccentricity undermining the discipline and organization a firm needs to survive in a competitive market. Bevis is beautiful but, alas, damned, a truth conveyed by his having lost 11 jobs in the past 18 months. His record of unemployment is but one key disclosure.

As in Serling's later study of moral ambiguity, "Midnight Sun," many of the revelations in "Bevis" reach us visually, through scenic repetition. All this is carefully orchestrated. Certain repeated scenes will come before us exactly as before. Others will include small changes. This alternation shows, among other things, that appearances have their reality. Specifically, the way people dress and groom themselves influences their effect upon us. As the dapper Bevis wins the esteem of his neighbors and business colleagues, he forfeits some of their affection; the more they respect him, the less they enjoy him. Serling is thus asking through him whether discipline and dependability can coexist with a sense of fun and frolic in the same person. At a more important level, Bevis shows how and why those we love sometimes drive us crazy. Does the charmer who can't hold a job or pay his or her rent merit our serious attention? How much loss of inner peace is love worth?

Such questions may be soft-pedaled, combined, or recombined in the series. Yet the frequency with which they occur shows that they preoccupied Serling his whole career. Henry Corwin, the Art Carney role in "Night of the Meek" (12/60), finds that happiness stems from giving, not getting. His belief that Christmas "should come with patience and love, charity, compassion" inspired him to work as a department-store Santa Claus during the holidays. Yet, after reporting for work more than an hour late one evening, this paragon falls drunkenly from his "throne." How much irresponsibility can his boss overlook, even in the Christmas season? Corwin's travesty of Santa Claus frightens at least one child and angers several parents. Mr. Dundee, the store manager, acts correctly by firing him. Any business will drive away customers if its employees report for work both late and drunk. Though beyond blame, Corwin inspires little trust. And Serling wants us to know it. Before reporting to work, Corwin had tried to sneak a drink from a whisky bottle a bartender had turned his back on.

Moral ambiguity of a different sort permeates "Five Characters in Search of an Exit." Another Christmas play, "Five Characters" brings together a clown, a hobo, a ballet dancer, a bagpiper, and, most recently, an army major at the bottom of "an enormous, featureless cylinder" (Zicree 233). The five don't know if they're dead, in limbo, or in hell. Nor do they feel cold or heat, hunger or thirst. But they're active. In their self-division, they recall Vladimir and Estragon of Samuel Beckett's *Waiting for Godot*—both of whom twice resolve to leave their preordained meeting place with Godot but stay put. The five grudgingly enact Beckett's famous piece of advice about shrugging off failure: next time, fail better. Though they resent climbing on each other's shoulders so that one of them can scale the lip of their entrapping cylinder, they do make the effort. Their failure is qualified. Yes, the major finds himself back in the Christmas barrel he struggled to escape. He is also revealed to be a doll. And what kind of meaningful escape can a doll make, anyway? we ask.

Our dismissive question must account for the truth that the major's effort carried him further than any earlier attempt made by his four cohorts. Sisyphus-like, he has confirmed man's inventiveness, his refusal to quail before the difficult, and his urge for freedom. Even though these virtues don't always improve our lot, they invoke our greatness. And greatness carries rewards of its own, some of which defy accepted values. Redemption emerges subtly at the end of Serling's December 1961 play, validating his reference in the epilogue to an "added, hopeful note." The once hopeful dolls look flat and abandoned lying woodenly at the bottom of their donation barrel. But the teardrop in the corner of the eye of the ballerina, though unseen from above, conveys a poignancy that redeems their splayed-out indignity. Perhaps they will be adopted by a child who will love and care for them. And this devotion won't be one sided. The ballerina's tear implies in brilliant visual shorthand that the dolls would gladly repay it.

"The Grave" (10/61) begins where most plays end. Its first scene describes the shooting of a villain. But Pinto Sykes didn't die in a duel. Ambushed by eight gunmen while crossing a town square, he fell before he could draw his firearm. Montgomery Pittman's western deals with the effects of Sykes's death on Conny Miller, the gunman hired to kill him.

Miller may have defaulted on his contract by avoiding, rather than tracking, Sykes. His alleged cowardice withal, he acts guilty. The slightest suggestion that he avoided Sykes enrages him, and, to prove his bravery, he agrees to plunge his knife into the ground above Sykes's grave at midnight. He'd have fared better by forgiving himself for any misdeed he committed. Sykes's fey sister Ione (not Joan) deepens this tale of guilt. Other characters' names like Ira (which means anger or wrath in Latin), the Old English-sounding Mothershed, and also Steinhart (stoneheart) lend further resonance. The historical associations the names call forth invoke the implacability Miller is pushing against, but not very hard.

Ione, the only woman in the cast, finds the courage to visit her brother's grave late at night, an errand that both Sykes's assassins and his would-be assassin, Miller, shrink from. Miller only visits the grave because he's shamed into doing it. In this story of bogus male heroics, the woman literally has the last laugh. The male-driven vigilante justice ruling the Old West rings hollow. The discovery of Miller's dead body next to Sykes's fresh grave shows that the hired gun couldn't even fend off a corpse. His opposite number, Ione, though scorned as a lunatic by her neighbors, has much better survival skills. She can laugh at her detractors because she knows enough to avoid firearms. Like the characters' names, both the title and the family revenge theme of "The Grave" ask whether the dead can hurt the living. Ione can disregard the question (which *The Twilight Zone* brings back in "Uncle Simon"). She's the madwoman who has the truth. A reproach to all the others in this anti-western, she has learned to sidestep deathly values.

Male posturing causes havoc again in another 1961 *Twilight Zone* telescript. Rarely did Serling use reversal as cunningly as he does in "The Silence," a meditation on the injustice meted out to a wretch. The play is also a lesson in the art of misdirection. Rarely did Serling manipulate both our feelings and our moral sensibilities so deftly. The nonstop chatter of Jamie Tennyson offends all the other members of his staid men's club, particularly when he uses it as a stratagem to extort money. The disgust Colonel Archie Taylor feels toward this "shallow . . . ne'er-do-well" reflects that of the others. Taylor wins the acclaim of everyone in the room when he bets Tennyson half a million dollars that he can't remain silent for a year. These others will bask in whatever silence Tennyson can endure. But Tennyson's endurance shocks everybody, especially Taylor. The silence the colonel coveted so much begins to haunt him. He offers to buy Tennyson out of his bet. Quoting the poet Tennyson, he tries to trick his man into talking by taunting him with gossip he had allegedly heard about his wife.

This villainy shifts our sympathies. The artistocratic-sounding name of Jamie Tennyson that seemed so misapplied at the start fits better and better as its possessor rebuffs all of Taylor's attempts to lure him into speaking. The applause greeting his return to the club's library after a year of silence has our approval. The ugly tactics of his refined, well-bred oppressor give this April 1961 play an hour-glass structure. Taylor loses everything—his honor, decency, and social standing. The shock created by his disclosure that he can't pay Tennyson because he is broke confirms a surmise that has been brewing in us. The princely Taylor's ruin preceded his confession. Only a loser would have lashed out as cruelly as Taylor did during Tennyson's year of silence. Only a fool would have made a bet in front of 20 or 30 witnesses that he couldn't back with cash. Serling's "The Silence" punctures the myth of the old patrician family as neatly as "The Grave" did that of the brave frontiersman. Taylor is right to call the stalwart Tennyson his superior. He also acts correctly by resigning immediately from the club, declaring that an impostor like him doesn't belong among gentlemen.

This confession of fraudulence counts less to Tennyson than the cash he was swindled out of; without question, he'd prefer his half-million. In fact, he needs it so badly that he had his vocal chords cut the same day his ordeal of silence began because he knew that he couldn't remain speechless for a year on his own. But the surgery has also damned him to a lifetime of silence. Taylor may have judged well when he praised this ex-chatterbox and would-be extortionist. Accompanying Tennyson's loss of speech is a huge gain in self-knowledge. He identified his priorities and then acted on them. So great was his love for his wife that he sacrificed the ability to speak in order to provide for her. What's more, the silence he foisted on himself has created the ideal climate for mental and spiritual growth; talking is the worst way to learn. The growth in character that stems from his loss recalls the sacrifice of Mathilde in "The Necklace." But Mathilde's sacrifice and growth are both handled ironically by Maupassant. Coarsened and warped, Mathilde enjoys no clear victory. And neither does her American counterpart. The bittersweet satisfaction Tennyson gains from Taylor's disgrace costs him too much. He has deprived himself of his favorite pastime, talking. His long absence from his wife may have wrecked his marriage; his wife never visited him during his long ordeal. He misses out on the money Taylor owes him.

But did he earn this money? Marc Eliot says of him and Taylor that "neither one . . . kept the bet in good faith" (81). Eliot is right. Both men cheated. Taylor, played with imperious disdain by Franchot Tone, made a bet he couldn't back. Tennyson ensured his victory over Taylor through a deception of his own. If his victory is empty, perhaps he deserves no better. He has become Taylor's mirror image. Neither man has any money; neither will return to the club where they met; perhaps both have doomed themselves to solitude. Taylor, that remnant of a proud but obsolete social order, presumably has no wife; Tennyson may have lost his. No winner emerges from the bet. But our final impression is not that of two frauds removing each other from society so that ordinary, decent people can get on better with the tasks and occasional small joys that have been occupying them. Both men were marginal figures from the start. Their marginality gives us pause. It implies that life rests on a foundation of fraud and that only the vigilant exercise of self-control will save us from being engulfed by the fraudulence. Richard Matheson noted a kinship between *The Twilight Zone* and the time plays of J.B. Priestley (Zicree 379). But whereas Priestley's *Dangerous Corner* shows the upheavals that *could* take place if we spoke our hearts, "The Silence" portrays both the upheavals and their byproducts. If it threatens our safety more than does Priestley's 1932 play, it also stirs deeper questions about the appearance-reality dualism, a theme that has provoked playwrights and novelists for centuries.

Another Serling script that investigates degrees of guilt within the framework of the seem-be dualism, or spectrum, is the late "I Am the Night—Color Me Black" (3/64). The work opens on a harsh note. Though it's 7:30 in the morning, the sun hasn't risen over the "remote little Midwestern village" where a convicted murderer named Jagger is about to hang. This meteoric oddity counts as a protest. And the abuses that have occurred in Jagger's village are worth protesting. Sheriff Koch (who has the same name as his counterpart in "Dust," an earlier Serling play built around a public hanging) omitted crucial testimony during Jagger's trial because its inclusion could have hurt his chances for reelection. Koch isn't alone in having victimized Jagger in court. The local newspaper editor's worries about maintaining present levels of circulation kept him from noting Koch's omissions in the report of the trial. Afraid of risking unpopularity by taking a minority stand, the sheriff's deputy perjured himself to make Jagger look guilty. This malfeasance typifies the town. Jagger's neighbors howl and jeer at him as he approaches his scaffold. Jagger is indeed nasty. But perhaps the town that conspired to condemn him and that relishes his coming death is nastier still. The right-wing racist whom Jagger killed not only embodied its nastiness; he also laced it with an energy and a drive his neighbors lacked.

Neither cowardice nor hatred is redeemed when shared. Once released, these vices spread. Perhaps an injustice inflicted upon one person insults or disables us all. The bitterness surrounding Jagger's hanging may have extinguished light everywhere. Blackness has settled over Dallas, Budapest, and Shanghai. It symbolizes the fear and evil in our hearts that find an easy outlet in social conformity. It could also express the gulf between the law and the lawmen who enact it. But the play's chief spokesman for humane values is black, a reality that calls for a revision of the equation of blackness with fear and evil. And the surliness with which Jagger treats Mr. Anderson when the minister tries to comfort him is all too characteristic. A backer of unpopular causes, the caustic, friendless Jagger has always alienated his neighbors. And he never protests either his coming execution or the guilty verdict that brought it about. He claims that he enjoyed killing his victim, even if he did it in self-defense.

How to judge him? In the last analysis, his unpleasantness is irrelevant. The law is supposed to protect everybody. And the speed with which anger and spite overtake the villagers shows that we need to apply the law fairly to avoid sliding back into the primeval ooze whence we came. Minister Anderson appreciates this truth. And so does the play's other authority figure, Sheriff Koch. Koch makes sure that the doomed man is served a good hearty breakfast; he hopes that the hanging won't attract a big, noisy audience; he scolds his wife for calling the hanging a "necktie party." Is this withholder of evidence at Jagger's trial acting from guilt? His deceit did help condemn Jagger. But his ensuing remorse provides one of the few points of light in the darkness shrouding the earth. The severity of this judgment precludes our denying any brightness, regardless of its source.

A woman in Matheson's "Mute" (1/63) says of an orphan brought to grief by the misguided attentions of caring adults, "They all meant well. No one wanted anything but [to] help her." What the woman has overlooked is the truth that these adults chose ways to help Ilse Nielsen that would primarily benefit *them*. The play's opening scene in 1953 Düsseldorf harks back to Hitler's infamous Munich beer hall putsch 30 years earlier; perhaps the same number of Germans attended both events. A group of friends has gathered in a restaurant in order to help the cause of telepathic communication. When asked about the justice of forcing one's children to communicate telepathically, the group's leader shrills, "It's more than just. It's inevitable. Destiny demands it." He has made the same appeal to destiny and dogma that empowered the Nazis.

Because the telepathic Ilse never learned how to speak, she becomes a conduit through which the interference of other people's agendas rushes. This process also reverses itself; she fills a void in the lives of her elders, all of whom believe that because she's mute, she's also flawed, and thus needs their help. Representatives of institutions pledged to the welfare of children, like the family and the school, both misjudge and mishandle her. The teacher in whose class Ilse enrolls, for instance, sets out immediately to make her talk. This destructive meddling sends out political echoes. Ironically, Miss Frank has the same last name as one of Hitler's most notable victims, another female. Also, a picture of Lincoln, the great emancipator, adorns the wall of Miss Frank's classroom. Yet Miss Frank embodies more of the fascism of Hitler than she does the soulfulness of Lincoln. She will snap her fingers at an uncomprehending Ilse. She approaches Ilse during her first day in class holding a ruler, with which she'd like to whack the 12-year-old for her supposed defiance. On the day the play ends, Miss Frank tells Ilse to stand. And as soon as Ilse does rise to her feet, Miss Frank sits down, conveying her lack of sympathy. A Nazi-like precision asserts itself again when she tells her other pupils to think about Ilse's name "on the count of three."

She has read her own needs and longstanding frustrations into Ilse—specifically, the legacy of pain stemming from her father's attempts, many years before, to turn her into a medium. Better to make Ilse "exactly like everybody else," Miss Frank reasons, than to subject her to the mental rigors a medium must undergo. Cora Wheeler, the woman who cares for Ilse after her parents die, also allows an old hurt to galvanize her responses. The recent drowning death of her daughter, Sally, has taken away her sole outlet for maternal love. Resolved to avoid reliving this anguish, she clings to Ilse. She even destroys the letter her husband (another good *Twilight Zone* sheriff) writes to Ilse's parents' friends in Germany. This selfishness has blocked Ilse's best hopes for reintegration. Cora's angry cry, "Leave her alone!" directed to a crowd that flocks around Ilse, reveals *Twilight Zone* irony at its most potent. Cora's words apply more strictly to Cora herself. Having just burned her husband's letter, she has already hurt Ilse more than any crowd of curious neighbors could do, no matter how long they stare. It's Cora, too, the one whose designs on Ilse are the most selfish, who says, "The welfare of a child is everybody's business."

But the child in question would probably have drooped as badly under the watch of any of the other adult characters. Everything these others do to help Ilse hurts her. And for a good reason; their efforts are enacted less for Ilse's sake than their own. When the German telepathists who knew the Nielsens in Germany finally arrive at the Wheelers', they speak of their "responsibility to the project." Professor Werner particularly, cares more about telepathy than about Ilse. Afraid that explaining the girl's special powers to the Wheelers will threaten the project, he and his wife leave Pennsylvania without her. Symbolism lends this development impressive force. After the Germans arrive in town by bus, the camera cuts to the Wheelers' kitchen, where Cora is preparing an egg dish, symbolic of rebirth. But the Werners, those potential agents of rebirth, disregard Ilse's welfare, abandoning the girl to people they know are incapable of understanding her. And if this reversal of the symbolism usually evoked by eggs needs clarifying, Matheson reminds us that Cora was also cooking eggs when she heard of Sally's death.

"Mute" portrays a world gone wrong. A plea for patience and understanding, it describes individuality as both elusive and opaque. The closing scene reinstates this trickiness. Cora and Ilse are walking together down the Wheelers' comfortable suburban street. Yet their bond is smudged. Both characters' minds are racing; neither knows the other's thoughts. Ironically, Ilse, the play's only visionary, can't communicate her vision. And if she could, she'd be scorned and ostracized. Knowledge and power exist inversely in "Mute." Ilse's painful repetition of the words, "My name is Ilse," spoken to her classmates, conveys her apartness from the world of the Werners. The Coras and the Misses Frank have won. Little does it matter to them that they cheated to win their prize or that they never tried to discover that prize's value. The Wheelers, in fact, believe that Ilse's parents promoted her ignorance. They're wrong. The Nielsens interacted with Ilse at a level more refined than that of writing or speech. Ilse's early training helps the girl perceive truths that the Wheelers would never have disclosed themselves, like the death of Sally.

Ilse might feel tempted to follow Sally to the grave; nobody else in the play recovers from setback. The stridency heard on the soundtrack while her face fills the screen during the attempt of the Werners to reach her telepathically explains that she has lost the gift. But she hasn't adjusted to her new regimen, either. She fits nowhere. The play's bleak ending finds her abandoned to the tender mercies of people who would ignore her needs even if they could sort those needs out. "Mute" is one of *The Twilight Zone*'s darkest shows. Others like "Nightmare as a Child" (4/60) and "The Grave" (10/61) prove that there's nothing like secret guilt to fire a person up. Guilt asserts its power, too, in "The Encounter"; in his epilogue to this May 1964 work, Serling calls it a "disease all too prominent among men." But in "Mute" it's unknown. Walter Ryder, the unhappy young inventor in "In His Image" (1/63), says, "We're all potential murderers. But if we're normal, we're prevented by our inhibitions." Utterly selfish and predatory, the people in "Mute" decry inhibition. No scruple stands between them and their goals. What's worse, the family and the school, those social institutions that are supposed to bridle our selfishness, abet it in "Mute." Now that Ilse's link with her forebears has snapped, she awaits only grief from her school and adoptive home.

II

Another plea for tolerance comes in "The Fugitive" (3/62). Jenny isn't just the only girl in her group of playmates. She also wears a leg brace and she's mistreated by the aunt she lives with. But she finds more solace in the adult world than Ilse can. Most of it comes from an elderly neighbor. Old Ben recalls Arch Hammer of Serling's "The Four of Us Are Dying" (1/60). Instead of merely being able to change his face, though, Ben can become a mouse, a fly, or a monster—and not just for fun. The Beaumont script featuring him mingles the homey and the macabre. Gentle, soothing Ben gives signs of being on the run. But what wrong could this benign elder have committed to warrant the attention of the well-dressed, poker-faced strangers who have been asking questions about him? Hearing of the presence of these men in the neighborhood worries Ben. When asked by Jenny if he's a criminal, his answer, "In a way," raises more questions than it answers. Has J. Pat O'Malley, the Ben role, been cast against type? And, if he has, what kind of wrath do his pursuers intend to bring down on the sweet grandfatherly man he's playing?

These questions don't prod us for long. The goodness of the Prospero figure is reaffirmed as soon as his identity comes to the fore. Rather than being threatened or punished by his pursuers, he's called "Your Majesty." This honor reminds us that he has been displaying a kingly grandeur all along. Our surprise at hearing it yields quickly to the recognition that it tallies with his behavior. This double-whammy ending unifies the play's developing tensions without trivializing them. The two visitors have come to Earth to fetch home the king who left his throne because he wanted a vacation. Following the example of Mr. Death in Serling's "One for the Angels" (10/59), they ensnare Ben by endangering the life of a little girl he loves. Only by coming to the ailing Jenny's side can Ben save her life. But he has some tricks of his own in reserve. After promising his visitors that he'll return with them to his kingdom, he asks to spend some time alone with Jenny. Nor does he need much of it. On the brink of restoring their king to his throne, the visitors see two Jennies. Which one is their king? Afraid to pick the wrong one, they take them both to Ben's kingdom. Their decision proves wise. The king being restored to his palace is young and handsome. He has masqueraded as an elder to baffle his pursuers.

Now Jenny has won herself a handsome young lord, and the lord resumes his rightful office as his country's leader, an honor that might have fallen to a lesser man and thus compromised his subjects. This last development, an important issue in Shakespeare's *Tempest,* proves the allegiance of "Fugitive" to living values. Ben's subjects will serve a king under whose rule they enjoy their best chances for fulfillment; Jenny will fare better as Ben's consort than she did living under the thumb of a cruel aunt or sharing a baseball diamond with unfeeling playmates.

"Fugitive" is also notable for including the shock, or twist, ending that became *The Twilight Zone*'s most memorable feature. Although other *Twilight Zone* writers used the device, Serling introduced it to the series in his pilot script, "Where is Everybody?" (10/59) and then made it a staple of nearly every other script produced in *The Twilight Zone*'s first year. The device predates *The Twilight Zone.* Serling's "The Time Element" (11/58), for instance, uses it brilliantly. This inventive, challenging work, done for the Desilu Playhouse, centers on a recurring dream (as will Beaumont's "Shadow Play," aired on *The Twilight Zone* in May 1961). Pete Jensen keeps falling asleep in one town and waking up in another, several years earlier. Like one of many *Twilight Zone* truth-tellers scorned as eccentrics or madmen, Jensen tries in vain to prevent disaster, in his case repelling Japan's attack on Pearl Harbor. Going back in time has frustrated him. He explains his woes to a psychiatrist. Then he stops visiting Dr. Arnold Gillespie. But at play's end, it's revealed that he never visited the doctor at all. Having died years before at Pearl Harbor, he couldn't have. Gillespie imagined the whole incident into life, a disclosure that emits shock waves. Heretofore trusted as a therapist, the doctor needs therapy himself; his fantasies as well as those of Jensen must be analyzed and treated. His plight makes us wonder, as do the ordeals of the main figures of "The Silence," "Shadow Play," and "Mute," where we can safely invest our trust. Have ambiguity and inconsistency tainted everything? Is the smudge they have left so indelible that it warns us to withhold confidence from everybody?

Serling's shock endings can make us laugh as well as brood. "Witches' Feast," a five-minute tailpiece to an episode of *Night Gallery*, evokes *Macbeth* straightaway. In fact, this evocation accounts for the episode's fun. The witches whose roles are acted by Agnes Moorehead and Ruth Buzzi talk of covens and black masses. During their eerie conversation, they're concocting a brew that includes dainties like a rat's tail, a weasel's eye, viper's bane, and foam from a mad dog's lips. Then the macabre mood built from these details dissolves into laughter. The gruesome, hideous brew taking shape in the cauldron loses out to the only item eaten during the playlet—a ham sandwich on rye without lettuce.

Little more than a skit, "Feast" takes most of its virtue from what J. Michael Straczynski called in 1988 "that *Twilight Zone* twist that is so hard to accomplish without seeming artificial" (18). *The Twilight Zone*'s twist, or shock, ending resembles the last scene in a classic English country house mystery, in which the detective rehearses the evidence before the witnesses and suspects and then names the culprit. The closing moments of works like "The Sixteen-Millimeter Shrine" (10/59) and "Four O'Clock" (4/62) humble us. They reveal that the moral and emotional torques of the action preceding them were not where we had thought. Yes, we're dazzled by Serling's sleight-of-hand. But we're also rattled by discovering that the show we've been looking at has been moving toward a climax that surprises us, even though the climax was carefully foreshadowed. *The Twilight Zone* isn't for the timid or the stubborn; a typical episode gives the impression that the action that's developing differs from the one we've been watching. This deft misdirection of our attention brings the better episodes close to our favorite literary works. Only after viewing them are we in a position to view them intelligently, giving niceties of structure and characterization their proper due. In Serling's "The Arrival" (9/61), for instance, the searcher becomes the thing sought. The solver of mysteries embodies the mystery; he's the missing piece of the puzzle he's trying to solve. The safe landing of an airplane lacking pilot, crew, or passengers has flooded this investigator for the Federal Aviation Agency with memories. Fantasy overtakes reality for him. This scrambling of his sense of the time-space continuum also discloses the guilt that has been goading him for the past 17 years. His essence lies far afield from his assured self-image.

The endings of many *Twilight Zone* episodes leave us shocked, delighted, and a little abashed. Arlen Schumer calls "Eye of the Beholder" (11/60) "a classic Serling script capped by perhaps *Twilight Zone*'s most unforgettable shock ending" (*Visions* 21). Also worthy of admiration in this regard are "Third from the Sun" (1/60), "Obsolete Man" (6/61), and "To Serve Man" (3/62), all of which disclose in their final moments the significance of both their titles and plots. Now, plot structure determines whether most fictional writing fails or succeeds, particularly in a half-hour TV show, which leaves little room for character development. The shock ending associated in fiction with O. Henry, Maupassant, and Agatha Christie confirms in "The Long Morrow" (1/64) the jarring truth that the act that proves Doug Stansfield's love for Sandra Horn has also put her out of his reach. As has been seen, Doug disconnected himself from the hibernation system he was supposed to occupy during his 40-year space probe so that he could be Sandra's age when he returned to Earth, only to discover in Sandra, who hibernated herself soon after Doug's departure, a lass of 26.

But the irony springing from one of *The Twilight Zone*'s twist endings can disclose different strategies. The final effects of both "King Nine Will Not Return" (9/60) and Pittman's "Last Rites of Jeff Myrtlebank" (2/62) move away from what preceded them. This Brechtian touch adds to the artistic stature of *The Twilight Zone*. Perhaps we're supposed to solve the mystery ourselves and then debate its meaning. No matter that Brecht and O. Henry differ vastly as artists and sociologists. *The Twilight Zone* can borrow from both writers and then fit its borrowings snugly within its supple framework. One of *The Twilight Zone*'s most attractive features was its openness to developments in the world at large. The counterpoint between this flexibility and those elements we have come to prize as the hallmark conventions of *The Twilight Zone* induces much of the show's drive and fun. This counterpoint also helps make *The Twilight Zone* one of the greatest series in television history.

10

Under the Spotlights

Serling trusts his material to touch us emotionally. Particularly when repeated, his details clarify *The Twilight Zone*'s development and purpose without any need for explanation. The image of ruffians counting money at a table in both "In Praise of Pip" (9/63) and "Steel" (10/63) implies the hard, fighting world the heroes of these two shows must cope with every day simply to survive. That "Steel" was written by Richard Matheson drains none of the image's relevance. By the show's fifth (and last) season, when "Steel" ran, a set of tropes, attitudes, and techniques bearing the *Twilight Zone* stamp had entrenched itself. Like Serling's "Where Is Everybody?" (10/59) and "Execution" (4/60), Charles Beaumont's telescript "The Jungle" (12/61) uses a phone booth to convey anxiety, entrapment, or alienation in those who enter it, Alan Richards of "Jungle" hearing jungle noises over the phone when he tries to ring for a taxi at 3:00 A.M.

Another recurring motif that evokes the underside of loneliness is the bar or the tavern. Losers drink in bars in *The Twilight Zone*, particularly when they do it alone. Bevis of "Mr. Bevis" (6/60) and P.T. McNulty of "A Kind of Stopwatch" (10/63) both slouch into bars after losing their jobs, as does Doug Winter of "Printer's Devil" (2/63) after his newspaper business folds. Joey Crown, the Jack Klugman role in "A Passage for Trumpet" (5/60), gravitates to a bar after two setbacks—his selling his horn and his discovery that he could be dead. The main characters of "The Four of Us Are Dying" (1/60), "Execution," and "Dead Man's Shoes" (1/62) all die shortly after they leave bars, as might Alan Richards of "Jungle." Somewhat luckier is Henry Corwin of "Night of the Meek" (12/60), who only gets fired for reporting late for work. But, like him, the barflies in Happiness, Arizona, who get fleeced in Serling's "Mr. Garrity and the Graves" (5/64), enrich *The Twilight Zone*'s ongoing portrayal of bars as way stations for discards, drifters, and malcontents. Though Garrity's victims may have been losers before meeting him, their hours in a bar could have very well lowered their resistance to his wiles.

183

But *The Twilight Zone* can also challenge itself. Misfits in "What You Need" (12/59) gain both focus and direction in a bar. "He's Alive" (1/63), a study of "a quaking, whimpering boy" of 25 or so who's "a gift for the sewers," reverses expectations even more sharply. Peter Vollmer, the young neo-fascist, gives a Nazi salute to signal an oncoming police car. He repeats the gesture on his way out of the hall in which he makes his first successful public speech. It occurs again when he salutes Hitler, whom his imagination had conjured into life, just before he sets out to commit a murder. Yet he also uses a cigarette holder, a device associated with Franklin Roosevelt, Hitler's archfoe during World War II. What kind of statement was Serling trying to make with the cigarette holder? Vollmer resembles the main figures of "The Grave" (10/61), "A Piano in the House" (2/62), and "The Encounter" (5/64) in hiding his neurosis behind a facade of strength. To liken him casually to FDR after yoking him to Hitler is to shock the viewer. But the play was intended as a shocker. Serling warns us in the epilogue that hatred, prejudice, and bigotry, those ugly staples of the human condition, have kept the spirit of Hitler alive. And it can flare out at any time, even in the shadow of FDR's familiar cigarette holder. The Serling of "He's Alive" wants to stir us up. He has misled us and then made us feel foolish by falling into his trap. We're reminded to be watchful. Even the playwright who warns us against the snares of fascism can't be trusted.

I

Some of the other details slipped into the *Twilight Zone* episodes work less well. Either carelessness or mischief prompted Serling to have a soldier in "A Quality of Mercy" (12/61) ask his lieutenant if he has a yen for killing Japanese. Misjudged dialogue also mars "The Four of Us." When Arch Hammer, wearing the face of Johnny Foster, says to Foster's black-clad girlfriend, Maggie, "Mourning becomes you," he's answered, "Just like Elektra." The reference to both Sophocles and Eugene O'Neill lacks meaning. Neither Foster nor his impersonator is a father figure. Later in the play, a father does shoot to death a man he mistook for his son. But the shooting has nothing to do with Foster or Maggie. Other problems in dialogue stem from the way characters mangle their lines. The mispronunciation of names causes the biggest worries in this regard. Harold A. Stone, acting the role of an aviation inspector in "The Arrival" (9/61), calls a ramp attendant both Robbins and Robinson. Nor did any member of the production staff of "Cliffordville" (4/63) correct Albert B. Salmi when he called a fellow character Dietrick, Diedrich, and Diedrick. Carelessness with details hurts the play elsewhere. Unaccountably, the tic that helps both place and identify the character called Hecate changes. At first, Hecate twists a hank of hair growing behind his right ear. But during his next appearance, he fingers the ear itself. Details in costuming can also be flubbed. The astronauts who crash-land in the Nevada desert in "I Shot an Arrow" (1/60) complain justly about the blazing heat pummeling them. But they continue to wear the long-sleeved shirts and scarves they had on at the play's outset. What's more, they dress the same way at night as they do by day, even though desert temperatures dip sharply after dark. "Midnight Sun" (11/61) suffers from the same inattentiveness. Despite readings of 110° F, one man wears a long-sleeved shirt and a hat while another, though shirtless, walks onto the set in a jacket. Even Serling is wearing a jacket and tie during his narration, spoken on this "hottest day in history."

Other production flaws mar *The Twilight Zone*. Playing a Confederate soldier in "Still Valley" (11/61), Gary Merrill moves very slowly, stiff-gaitedly, and even at times apoplectically in scenes calling for foot speed. Moreover, a slight spurt of physical energy, like that required for a short run, seems to tire him. Whether a stunt man could have been used in the play's action scenes is doubtful, in view of the backwardness of camera and lighting technology of the time. This ignorance helps explain the dearth of highlights and definition given off by the flat pancake makeup in "A Short Drink from a Certain Fountain" (12/63), "The Long Morrow" (1/64), and "Spur of the Moment" (2/64). But only carelessness accounts for the oversight on the part of the show's production crew that allowed Diana Hyland, the star of "Spur," to wear the same finger bandage at age 43 that she had on as an 18-year-old. "Death Ship"(2/63) has a more serious problem. Though one of the top hour-long episodes in the show's fourth season, it suffers from imbalance. One of the play's three characters stands on the sidelines most of the time while his crewmates move the plot. The clash is the eternal one of the pragmatist and the idealist. Thoughtful, sensitive Lt. Ted Mason riles his commander, Capt. Paul Ross, a career officer without a family. Ross's determination to prevail over his more warmhearted junior officer has made him dogged and desperate. A victim of duty, he enters a time warp and interrupts a Mason family picnic in order to drag Ted back to the spaceship on which the men were serving, near the thirteenth planet of Star System 51. The third member of the space team, Lt. Mike Carter, is mostly left out.

Another wrenching of the time-space continuum occurs in Matheson's "Little Girl Lost" (3/62). Six-year-old Tina Miller falls through a hole in a heretofore solid wall and lands in another dimension. Her rescuer, the Millers' neighbor, Bill, is nurturing, supportive, and skilled.

While planning to rescue Tina, this scientist explains what he believes has happened to her and then how he can best restore her to her parents. But Bill's is an ex parte role; Tina isn't his daughter, and he had no hand in her disappearance. Also, Tina's disappearance wasn't caused by some moral failing, inherited curse, or divine directive. "Little Girl Lost" is more of a demonstration than a drama. The tension generated by the Millers' growing anxiety leaks away quickly, Tina's disappearance having neither a discernible cause or meaning.

Still, her return home brings relief—perhaps because it occurs in her bedroom. The presence of children in the rooms of adults in *The Twilight Zone*, on the other hand, brings trouble. "A little child will lead her by the hand and walk with her into a nightmare," says Serling in his prologue to "Nightmare As a Child" (4/60) of little Markie's visit to schoolteacher Helen Foley, an act that leads to Helen's near death at the hands of her mother's killer of 20 years before. "Caesar and Me" (4/64) reverses the pattern of intimidation. Susan, the little niece of Jonathan West's landlady, goes through West's belongings searching for evidence that will link him to a recent robbery and thus send him to jail. This fanaticism takes a different slant in "The Big Tall Wish" (4/60). As in "Caesar," the play's chief relationship joins an adult and a child; the pair live in the same building, they spend time alone together. But can "Wish" be called a healthy mirror image of "Caesar"? One of Serling's obsolete men, aging prizefighter Bolie Jackson scoops his downstairs neighbor's son Henry out of bed and then kisses him. No similar exchanges join Bolie to Henry's pretty mother, Frances, with whom Bolie spends much less on-camera time than with Henry, even though she's single and apparently available.

The pedophilia implied in "Wish" is emblazoned upon the action of "The Fugitive" (3/62). The closeness of Jenny's tie with her elderly neighbor would disturb most viewers today. Though identified in the play's credits as Old Ben (Zicree 247), the name by which he's known in his neighborhood, this benign elder has Jenny call him Ben. He encourages other responses in her, too. He quotes love poetry to her; he sits alongside her on a bed. The time she spends on his lap includes much touching and hugging. Nor do the sexual innuendoes end here. His nickname for her, "Little Monkey," carries an erotic charge. Perhaps more notably, her words to him, when he removes her leg brace, sound like what a virgin might say to her lover: "Will it hurt? Be careful." Advisedly, she's next seen lying on her back. And she's supine again when examined by a doctor, another older man.

The matter of age carries forward. As has been seen, the envoys from Ben's kingdom lure him back to his throne by inflicting a life-threatening illness on Jenny. This measure should have warned her to stay away from them. But during a brief off-camera exchange with Ben, she agrees to join him in his faraway kingdom. Her decision to migrate to another galaxy in the company of two men who nearly killed her is puzzling. After all, if the men brought her near death once to break Ben's resistance, they might do it again; her welfare means little to them. But Jenny obviously believes that the joy of being with Ben overrides the risk of dying. Perhaps she even welcomes the prospect of dying for love. It would be good to know how her enthusiasm for this fatal prospect is affected by the revelation that Ben is a handsome stripling rather than a drooping, gray-haired elder.

"Fugitive" turns on many contrasts—youth and age, male and female, the strange and the familiar, the official and the personal, the mask or disguise and the naked face. Whether or not the transgenerational eroticism the play invokes was planned, nobody can say. As he showed in "He's Alive," Serling likes to raise expectations in us that he'll deliberately dash in order to warn us against imposing stereotypes between ourselves and reality. His co-writers sometimes serve the same useful warning. A stereotype comes into view again in "Spur," only to be swept aside. Anne Henderson marries for love. By eloping with David Mitchell the night of her engagement party, she defies both her parents and the investment-banker fiancé they chose for her. Twenty-five years after her elopement, Anne sees that she should have listened to her parents, she and David having ruined themselves with drink. Their sad downfall makes us wonder if *The Twilight Zone* had grown rearguard. Or did Matheson give in to the surprise ending that had become *The Twilight Zone*'s hallmark? "Spur" certainly provokes such questions and cavils. But it also gives insight into the way people act in the privacy of their hearts. The script tempers its dramatic failings. By showing that parental approval of a prospective mate is no reason to jilt him, it also tries to distinguish between literary and real passion.

Banishing the smell of the studio can endow a teleplay with breadth, specificity, and density of detail. The scene in "Young Man's Fancy" (5/62) in which the mother-ridden Alex Walker changes into a little boy and sends his bride away balances absurdity and pathos. It also voices a refusal to let the viewer off easily. *The Twilight Zone* will sometimes use contrast to serve the same challenge. The opening image of "The Little People" (3/62), for instance, juxtaposes a gleaming, high-tech spaceship with the arid, rocky wasteland in which the ship has just made an emergency landing. This reminder of the brute reality that contrasts with our hopes and calculations took on a different weight and exactitude in "The Lateness of the Hour" (12/60). A bucketing rainstorm and the moans of joy coming from Mrs. Loren as she's being massaged contrast beautifully with both the symmetry of the richly appointed room occupied by the Lorens and, particularly, the immaculate self-possession of Dr. William Loren.

"Spur" also opens with a stark visual contrast. First, there are the elegant grounds and estate where white-clad Anne begins her ride on her white horse, and, next, the rough back country nearby where her black-caped pursuer appears. This contrast is more than a visual device. Following *The Twilight Zone*'s occasional practice of disconcerting the viewer, the Matheson script has the 18-year-old Anne restrain her mount on the brow of a hill, as if she's waiting for the "strange nightmarish figure in black" who soon starts chasing her on a black horse. Anne's would-be oppressor isn't unexpected. Perhaps in some mad sense she's even welcome. In her heart, Anne foresees the wreckage of her future life with David Mitchell. It's no wonder that her 43-year-old self seeks revenge for having been plunged into this wreckage. Equally plausible is the guilt that has stirred in Anne the recognition that she deserves to be punished.

Like Hitchcock, the early Roman Polanski, and David Lynch, *The Twilight Zone* will establish a normal setting and then shatter it with an abnormal terror. "The Jungle" (12/61), for instance, releases the carnivores from the cages of our imaginations and then shows them clawing the line between fantasy and reality. Actor John Dehner's Victorian face and voice, his manner and arrogance—he talks about the triumph of willpower over ignorance and superstition—induce a tension with the Africa he's despoiling in the name of science. To distance himself from the tuxedoed Dehner, Serling speaks his prologue without a necktie for the only time in the canon. "What You Need" induces a different kind of tension. Though strains of "God Rest Ye Merry, Gentlemen" run through the Christmas story (which played on Christmas night 1959), one character in the script is an ex-major-league pitcher, that is, a man of summer. This irony foreshadows a larger one—the script's reversal of the "corruption and despair" (Schrader 13) connected with film noir. The stark settings, long high-contrast camera shots, rapid intercuts, and shadows dominating "What You Need" all create a sense of foreboding characteristic of the genre. Yet this work that unfolds on dark, wet city streets, at a racetrack, and in a cramped rented room ends on a note of hope. The characters who saw themselves as losers and victims now enjoy hopeful outlooks. Thus they transcend the genre in which their stories were framed. Analogously, we too can shrug off depression. By creating ironic distance between plot and mood, Serling is reminding us that nothing is fixed; we're creative beings, and we're free to try to create for ourselves the lives we would be happiest living.

The Twilight Zone will use the same kind of irony to let us know that the changeable often fights change. Her addiction to romantic stereotypes relegates Anne Henderson Mitchell to a pit of drunkenness, poverty, and self-loathing. The prosaically named Hi-way Cafe in "Will the Real Martian Please Stand Up" (5/61) (the title of which comes from the TV quiz show *To Tell the Truth*) sets up expectations that will be subverted. "Martian," in fact, subverts the expectations set up by its title. After immersing us in the commonplace, in the form of the bus driver and passengers forced by heavy snows to take refuge in a road-side diner, it identifies, among the castaways, the Martian who intends to colonize our planet. But aesthetically apt as this plot point is, it yields to one more apt and satisfying—the revelation that the "big, good-natured counterman who handles a spatula as if he'd been born with one in his mouth" is a Venusian whose imperial ambitions include wiping out all other extraterrestrial rivals, like the Martian sitting across from him.

A highly original detail in "Long-Distance Call" depicts in a different vein the hurdles we must overcome to achieve both freedom and fullness of being. There's something ridiculous about a grown man talking into a toy telephone. But the dramatic context in which the act occurs in William Idelson and Charles Beaumont's March 1961 *Twilight Zone* telescript gives this potential sight gag a poignant—and thoroughly convincing—twist. The script treats two disturbing ideas familiar to *Twilight Zone* fans—the strange power exerted on youth by the elderly and the selfishness of love. Grandma Bayles has an unnaturally close tie with her grandson. For his fifth birthday, she gives him a toy telephone. Within days she dies. Billy is crushed. But he soon recovers his high spirits because of the conversations he claims to be having with her on the toy phone. Grandma Bayles, though, wants more from him than talk. His parents disbelieve Billy when told by him that Grandma is lonely and that she wants him to join her. A suicide attempt makes them rethink their disbelief. And it's a second, apparently successful, try at suicide that drives Billy's father to the toy phone. Though unsure of a listener, Chris Bayles pleads with his mother for Billy's life. The phone into which he has been pleading remains a toy. But Bayles's desperation, conveyed thrillingly by his gripping words, his urgent tone, and the haunting music accompanying his pleas turn it into something else—a conduit to the twilight zone.

II

Such moments make the watching of a *Twilight Zone* episode a transmuted experience. At their worst, these episodes are contraptions or cleverly elaborated ideas that can look fake, rehearsed, and sentimental. Though the series slumped artistically after its second season (1960-61), some of its most inventive scripts belong to the three seasons that followed. George Clayton Johnson's "A Game of Pool" (10/61) reveals early on that pocket billiards means little in itself. It acquires value in direct ratio to the energy the player pours into it. The same argument applies to any endeavor, be it swimming, music, or acrobatics. Anything worth doing is worth doing badly because the longer we do it and the harder we focus on it, the more we'll improve. And our improvement matters. Besides building our confidence, it also enlarges both our understanding of the discipline in which we're working and our admiration for the discipline's rare giants.

Bunny Blake, the eponym of "Ring-a-Ding-Girl" (12/63) is no giant. She's merely popular—and powerful. The vapidness of the title of the play by Earl Hamner, Jr., mirrors that of Bunny most of the way through. Among this film star's many baubles and trinkets is a ring sent her by her home town fan club. Though the ring reveals to her faces and scenes from Howardville, any other gewgaw would have served as well. It does give her a few chances to say "Ring-a-ding," a phrase made popular by Frank Sinatra's version of Jerome Kern's "I Won't Dance." When Bunny's not ring-a-dinging, she's calling herself a star, prating about the prizes she has won, or complaining about autograph hunters. This vanity seems to dictate her stop in Howardville en route to Rome, where she's shooting a film. So what if the stop will delay production? She asks her ex-townsfolk to arrange a gala for her. But she also wants the gala to coincide with the annual Founder's Day Picnic. Anyone who wants to see her perform at the local high school auditorium will have to forgo the picnic. Why has she forced such a decision on her ex-neighbors? Does her timetable for her one-woman show reflect the brattiness she has been displaying all along?

As soon as the play takes a dark turn, it drains these questions of meaning. Bunny Blake's best performance was one she never gave. She couldn't have; she vanished from Howardville minutes before curtain. She was riding in a jet bound from Los Angeles to New York, the same jet, revealingly, that crashed on the picnic grounds near Howardville and killed many of the Founder's Day celebrants. Those who flocked to the high school auditorium lived. And Bunny saved them, in perhaps the only way she could. Had she warned her ex-townsfolk of the disaster she foresaw, she'd have been ignored, like her counterparts in "No Time Like the Past" (3/63), "Nightmare at 20,000 Feet" (10/63), and "Black Leather Jackets" (1/64). Instead, she traded on her image as a spoiled Hollywood starlet. The loss of local esteem her tactic brings her means little alongside her magnanimity. This magnanimity may never be appreciated, though. The people of Howardville will ignore it in favor of wondering how Bunny was spotted several times locally when she was also an airplane passenger hundreds of miles away. Their confusion skirts the play's real issue—that someone doomed to die had the presence of mind to devise a plan intended to save as many other lives as possible. Her actions make "Ring-a-Ding-Girl" one of network TV's sole attempts to blend Hollywood glitz with Emersonian self-reliance.

"The 7th Is Made Up of Phantoms" also discloses a sharp sense of incongruity. Though Serling's December 1963 play suffers from many flaws, including the depiction of a National Guard lieutenant who neglects to return the salute of a sergeant, it provides some offsetting virtues. The dynamics joining three of the Guardsmen have much of the incalcuability of life. The lowest ranker has most of the ideas about the maneuvers the men are conducting. And the most intelligent member of the patrol is a poor soldier, a sign of which is his inability to read a map. Perhaps Serling thought he could halt *The Twilight Zone*'s artistic skid by modifying a tactic he had used in "Third from the Sun" (1/60), a play whose major idea is voiced by its scurviest character. "Two" (9/61) had used the military to depict humankind as a baffling mix of the angelic and the beastly. Two survivors who fought on opposite sides in a recently concluded war meet while foraging for food. The man makes overtures of peace. But he's also a slob. He gobbles his food like an animal, and he scatters the remains of his meal, as he does the old newspapers he chances upon. His female foil, though more fastidious and more mindful of the environment, is also violence prone, as she demonstrates by firing several unprovoked bullets at the man.

Nearly every *Twilight Zone* show has at least one shining insight. Allegedly by accident, Harmon Gordon's much younger wife in "A Short Drink" (12/63) smashes an "aged eyesore" that came from Harmon's mother. Though the broken object is probably a figurine, it's kept discreetly vague. Serling wants to focus instead on Flora's outburst. If the eyesore came from Harmon's mother, so did Harmon. Flora has vented her frustration over being trapped in a May-December marriage in one of the few ways she can. "Perchance to Dream" (11/59) grips us straightaway. Thirty-five-year-old draftsman Edward Hall calls himself "the tiredest man in the world." His weariness includes a more serious problem. He has stayed awake for 87 straight hours because he'll never wake up if he lets himself sleep. Once asleep, he'll redream a dream so terrible that it will stop his weak heart. Yet that same weak heart can't survive many more hours of sleeplessness. Nan Adams of "The Hitch-Hiker" (1/60) also feels menaced. But dramatic tension in the *Twilight*

Zone episode built around her moves slowly. Designed more conventionally than "Perchance," it places its denouement nearer the end. Nan
believes that a hitchhiker has been following her during her cross-country drive. She's frightened. Her fears intensify. The sailor to whom she
offers a lift to quiet them seems more threatening than protective. He
ogles her; his speech bristles with sexual innuendoes; he sits closer to
her than is appropriate. And what brought him to a deserted stretch of
New Mexico road at 11 P.M. the night he thumbed Nan?

The play's figure of menace turns out to be Nan; the sailor has
much more to fear from her than she does from him. She nearly smashes
the car when the hitchhiker materializes again. Naturally, the sailor never
saw the hitchhiker, who was only visible to Nan. But he wants to live,
and he'll improve his chances for survival by leaving a car whose driver
has lost control. He does leave, rejecting Nan's offer to drive him to San
Diego, which she sweetens with a sexual overture. The departure of the
shaken sailor, her last link to normal life, shifts the mood of the play. She
belongs on a par with the hitchhiker she tried in vain to kill. We understand before she does that death can't be killed because it's already dead;
no sense in trying to ram the hitchhiker with her speeding car. Her discovery that she herself has been dead for some time, by joining the
play's various plot lines, works more like a resolution than a new development. The shock caused by her discovery distances her from us, since
her death had already been made clear to us. Ironically, the moment in
the action when she most needs our compassion and support is the
moment when we have withdrawn ourselves from her.

No distance divides us from the grimy desperation of Michael
Grady, the banned jockey in Serling's "Last Night of a Jockey" (10/63).
Grady hates himself for having wrecked his life. This self-contempt
comes across painfully in his slapping himself in the head at close
camera range. Close-ups capture his pain throughout. The pain persists
when framed less conventionally, as in the shot taken of him from below
floor level as he smashes a fragment of mirror bearing his image. His not
being able to see himself while looking down at the floor of his room
doesn't stop us from seeing him. And what we see is relentless anger that
recoils on itself and poisons all it touches; each shard of broken glass
bears Grady's full image. Another inventive camera shot, in "Caesar and
Me" (4/64), shows a little girl firing a toy gun at the back of the play's
main figure, who's next seen falling face down on a bed in the next
room, as if the toy gun fired real bullets. Though not literal, Susan's act
of hostility does symbolize her betrayal of Jonathan West. As has been
seen, she spies on West and then takes her finds to the police so that she
can put him in jail.

Expertise with the camera also distinguishes "Jess-Belle," a work that any extended look at *The Twilight Zone* should single out for praise. Warm and tender, yet imbued with a dark power, this February 1963 Hamner script deals with one of the rare love triangles in *The Twilight Zone*. The motif works well. Even for an hour-long work, it covers a broad range. "Jess-Belle" is an intimate character study, a survey of the social dynamics of the Blue Ridge Mountains, where it takes place, and a study of the contagion of evil. Opting unwisely for a quick fix, Jess-Belle Stone trades her soul to a local witch in order to regain the love of ex-beau Billy-Ben Turner, who has just celebrated his engagement to another villager. Jess-Belle has been duped. Lacking a soul, she can't enjoy the prize she has won. What's more, having been bewitched herself, she can't avoid frightening her neighbors. Or performing acts of evil; the play only moves into high gear with Billy-Ben's wedding to Ellwyn Glover, a sign of which is the spider that lights upon Ellwyn's bridal dress. Despite her wickedness, Jess is the play's most pathetic figure.

Another backwoods *Twilight Zone* episode that uses James Best as its male lead is "The Last Rites of Jeff Myrtlebank." Though less stunning than "Jess-Belle," Pittman's February 1962 work carries its age well. It does this by defying normal guidelines and controls. Jeff was pronounced dead two days before his funeral, i.e., the celebration of his last rites. He had no pulse; his heart had stopped; he was no longer breathing. In a striking inversion of the well-known *Twilight Zone* shock ending, Jeff climbs out of his coffin during his funeral service. Visual irony helps regulate the following action. James Best's Jeff is the tallest, handsomest, and most upright man in town. But the locals suspect that he's bewitched. Everyone is afraid of him. The only person who welcomes his return is his small sister. Even his fianceé won't kiss him.

How is he to be judged? Pittman drapes a traditional frame around "Last Rites." The work starts with a death and ends with a renewal. The two main characters marry, and their future offspring is mentioned, a resurgence prefigured by the youngsters watching Jeff's funeral through the window of the makeshift church where it was being held. This pattern of comic renewal, though, provides no soothing affirmations to the wary; earlier *Twilight Zone* installments having dismantled the guidelines fostering their growth. Our wariness is well judged. Some fresh roses die right after Jeff picks them, and, years later, his only son becomes a United States Senator "who's noted as an uncommonly shrewd politician." But is the word, shrewd, meant to sugarcoat a quality more sinister and dangerous? Whereas the tongue-in-cheek humor implied in Serling's epilogue fits the trendy political cynicism of post-

1950s liberal America, it also invites the possibility that at least one devil has a Senate seat. Perhaps we should be pleased to find the number so low. Yet both the flow of the play's plot and the issues the plot evokes stifle the laughter intended by the little joke.

The reversal that concludes "Stopover in a Quiet Town" (4/64) also jars the viewer. The camera fixes on Bob and Millie Frazier walking hand-in-hand during their last attempt to flee Centerville. Then after the shadow of their owner's hand drives them apart, the hand itself descends upon them and picks them up. The helping hand has yielded to that of control. Part of *The Twilight Zone*'s impact stems from the show's ability to jar the viewer's complacency. As "Stopover" proves, the impact is most impressive when it declares itself within the context of a motif already in place. "The Sixteen-Millimeter Shrine" (10/59) uses an impressionistic camera to register the shock caused by Barbara Jean Trenton's defection to the silver screen of her acting heyday. Before depicting Barbara on the screen of her private studio, the camera shows the horror of both her agent and her housemaid as the reflected images from the screen flit across their appalled faces. This impressionistic device will recur in both "Person or Persons Unknown" (3/62) and "A Short Drink" (12/63). In each play, the camera records the reactions to shock before revealing the surprise, or horror, that caused the shock. The plausibility of a fantastic image like elderly Harmon Gordon appearing on screen as an infant shows how even a mediocre work can include a moment of distinction that evokes both the special slant and the ambience of the series itself.

III

As with cinema, words matter less than the camera in television; video drama has to rely first on image and movement and only secondarily on dialogue. Television is thus more of a director's art than an actor's or a writer's. The camera has both a freedom and a vividness that can capture an emotion like terror and touch in background with an authority beyond that of the stage play. But television doesn't tell a story in images as well as cinema does. During the years from 1959 to 1964, the screen on which most viewers watched *The Twilight Zone* for the first time measured about 16 or 19 inches on the diagonal. The characters enacting the teleplays thus had to move inside a small fixed rectangle, undermining the illusion of reality. The format furnished by this black-and-white frame made it difficult to maintain high standards of plotting, characterization, and credibility. Capturing surreal visual effects was next to impossible. Expressionistic techniques like the dissolve, the distorted camera lens, and the jump cut to record abnormal states of mind had been in use for decades in film. They adapt less well to the small screen. Ambitious directors of teledrama felt stymied. Because they wanted to avoid congestion on the screen, they were accused of wielding cameras that were honest, earnest, and dull. A show like "Little Girl Lost," though, demonstrates the gains accruing from a camera happy to stay in one place. To convey the fourth dimension, into which little Tina Miller falls, director Paul Stewart distorted the video and the audio portions of the show while infusing the screen with drifts of fog. The ominous grids of slanted light in "The Dummy" (5/62) create a mood of desperation and entrapment. Suitably, most of these grids appear near the end, in the vicinity of alleys and dark streets, when the main character is going mad.

Editing with the camera combines with innovative lighting in the dream sequences that enrich "Perchance to Dream" (11/59). Sometimes shot at unexpected angles, the images comprising these sequences look soft and cottony at the edges. This fuzziness is augmented by both Van Cleave's haunting, otherworldly sound track and the use of dissolves, rather than jump cuts, between some of the scenes. During one of these dissolves, in fact, the camera spins. This movement captures the main figure's fear of wheeling out of control. There's a fast-spinning carousel in the same sequence that shows a high-contrast gorilla head. Freakishly tight head shots, evocative of the graphics of Chuck Close, dominate the carnival sequence that ends the play. By darkening the grooves and ridges on his people's faces with bright light and then shooting the people against a black field, director of photography George T. Clemens creates a frightening sense of alienation. Light and image divide characters rather than joining them. The division holds. The self is isolated in "Perchance." The wild roller-coaster ride at the end equates death with the sexual abandon that Edward Hall's weak heart has been denying him. The wildness of his deathly passion comes to us as an amalgam of the racketing wheels of his car, his stricken, helpless look, and the shrieking laughter of the siren sitting alongside him during his thundering ride.

"In Praise of Pip" (9/63) starts conventionally. A soldier wounded in Vietnam looks clean and peaceful while being treated for battle injuries that could kill him. Light years in appearance from the grimy grunts in Oliver Stone's *Platoon* (1986), this sanitized combat casualty turns out to be the play's title character. His father shares his unrealistic look. Max Phillips is too tidy and well-kept for an alcoholic grifter living in a cheap furnished room. Then the camera gets bold and creative. The sharp, remote outlines of the buildings in the American city where Phillips lives makes him seem small, hemmed in, and threatened. Sustaining the claustral mood created by the black-and-white clothes Serling wore during his prologue, high-contrast images prevail over easygoing grays. The occasional long-range shot will augment the anxiety, projecting small, dark, stick-like characters against an encompassing glare mighty enough to gulp them whole.

By finding the best positions from which to shoot his scenes, G. T. Clemens rivets us. His highly active camera will pan and then focus upon a figure or an object. It will distort certain physical features and then dwell on others, creating a rhythm expressive of director Joseph M. Newman's imaginative intent. Using camera angles to gain psychological depth, Clemens will include sitting, standing, and prone figures in the same shot. The sequence that unfolds at a local amusement park, a visit to a hall of mirrors, shows Max together with the little boy version of Pip he conjured into life during his dying moments. The panic roused in Max by his inability to distinguish between the real Pip and the many mirror images of him inspires Max's bargain with God; ordinary perception will no longer help him. Help does come. Because Max had already risked his life for a surrogate son, the dazed young man who lost a great deal of money to Max's gambler-boss, he wins God's favor. God agrees to spare Pip's life in Vietnam in exchange for Max's.

Max's dying revelation that his offer has been accepted creates one of *The Twilight Zone*'s most poignant moments. This poignancy must have gladdened Serling. He held strong hopes for "Pip," the opening play of the series' fifth season. *The Twilight Zone* had already been threatened with cancellations several times, and deservedly so. Even Serling knew of its sad artistic comedown (Zicree 362). To launch the series' fifth season, he poured a great deal of himself into the writing of "Pip." A sign of his ambitions comes in the work's bloodlines. Two motifs from his most personal work, "Walking Distance"(10/59), recur in "Pip," the carousel and the boy who flees forever a man with love in his heart. These allusions fit smoothly into the design of "Pip," a work of taste and sensibility whose narrative and pictorial strengths do full justice to Serling's ambitions.

"Pip," though, is a stylistic anomaly in the *Twilight Zone* canon. Usually the material being videoed for one of the episodes calls for a more foursquare camera. The standard editing sequence of a *Twilight Zone* show aims for immediacy rather than lyricism or rhythm. The downpan following the opening graphics will resolve in a wide-angle cover shot that establishes setting and mood. Next comes the medium range shot, which is close enough for intimacy yet also far enough from the people to maintain the distance needed for critical perspective. The final step in the viewer's orientation consists of a close-up shot, which features a specific image or feeling related to the work's theme, like the

TV set in Ed Lindsay's rooming house in "Static" (3/61) or the coin that lands on its edge in a newsboy's collection box in "A Penny for Your Thoughts" (2/61).

J.E. Parker explains how canted camera angles "express disorientation, vertigo, paranoia, and other extreme conditions" (310) in the *Twilight Zone* episodes influenced by film noir. Yet the blunt primitivism of the stationary eye-level camera, with its abruptness and formality of movement may suit the theme and tone of a show better than a series of angle shots. By cutting from speaker to speaker, the anecdotal ("he said, she said") camera of "Judgment Night" (12/59) divides characters instead of joining them, creating a sense of alienation that deepens the mystery put forth by the action. Each scene begins with an establishing shot before moving between speakers. The basic two-camera set-up rules out the development of visual interest within the individual shot.

But it promotes interest of a different kind. "Judgment Night" has the feel of a photographed stage play. The characters move toward the microphone, which can be heard echoing off the back of the sound stage. While the distraction precludes richness and depth, it also has its source in the TV studio technology of the day. It can't be blamed on the show's production crew. The making of "Judgment Night" does show more diligence than imagination. But it's always competent and professional. Close-ups are used discreetly to show emotion, and both lighting and sound help establish the play's nautical setting quickly and economically. The static camera also evokes the black-and-white naval battle films of World War II, with their dimly lit ships, carefully selected casts, and mood of solidarity. "Judgment Night" is straightforward in the same way that its older cinematic cousins were. Occasionally, a loud noise on the sound track and a sudden blast of bright light will record the jolt of a torpedo tearing into the flank of the passenger ship on which most of the plot unfolds. But these techniques were also staples of the World War II maritime genre to which "Judgment Night" belongs, an echo that creates a sense of nostalgia and, with it, the joy of recognizing both a genre and an era in which we had invested perhaps more emotion than we had thought.

In the main, *The Twilight Zone* plays it safe with the camera. The small screen on which it took life, its highly imaginative subject matter, and its wrenchings of everyday causality all argued against using effects that could be construed as ornate and fanciful. Its more innovative moments usually invoked a genre familiar to the viewer, for instance the surreally menacing alleys and grubby interiors from film noir that darken the mood of works like "Nervous Man in a Four-Dollar Room" (10/60) and "Dead Man's Shoes" (1/62). The flashbacks instrumental to films like *Rebecca* (1940), *Citizen Kane* (1941), and *Casablanca* (1942) return in several *Twilight Zone* episodes. As indeed they might: the series' major script writers discovered the excitement of cinema before the advent of commercial televison in the mid-1940s; they came to television from the cinema.

They and their colleagues in the show's production department kept their eyes on the big screen. *The Twilight Zone* will sometimes photograph a character with a distorting lens. For example, the camera in "What's in the Box" creates a useful psychological perspective for the issues the work develops. Joan Blondell plays an attentive, loving wife in Martin M. Goldsmith's March 1964 script. But the tight Fellini-like fish-tank view of her managed by Clemens's alert camera, along with the shrillness of her voice, portrays the strain she puts on her husband. The young owner of the model village in "Stopover" is probably average and ordinary. She's certainly not fiendish. But seen from below in full-face close-up, she looks sinister. We share the Fraziers' fear of her. Robert W. Pittack's impressionistic camera has convinced us that this huge child whose face consists of shadows and puffs of flesh might have accidentally killed her human pets had her mother not stepped in.

Her laughter raises questions that transcend Bob and Millie Frazier's safety. The authenticity of the details comprising the model village in which the Fraziers are trapped—a church with a ringing bell, a furnished home, a running train—show the child to belong to an advanced culture. Like the little people in "The Little People" (3/62), she invites the question of scale. She's so much larger than her pets that she needn't act maliciously to destroy them; a child's sense of fun would suffice. And how safe would the Fraziers be if their owner found herself captive to a member of a still larger race? The headless mannequin that tumbles from a car at Bob's feet sheds dark light on the question. It also reminds us that Bob and Millie's owner roused false hopes in her pets when she set into motion the train she knew would return them to the Centerville station where they boarded it. Imagery continues to describe their entrapment. After leaving the train that took them in a circle, they're next seen through the spokes of a wheel. Then they shout for help through the bars of an empty ticket office. Apparently, the most they can hope for is to continue wheeling in circles. But how long can they keep it up? The jail-like bars of the empty ticket office, their owner's innocent laughter, and that owner's having neglected to feed her pets after enticing them with fake food hold our attention till the end. "Stopover" is nobody's favorite *Twilight Zone* episode. But its photography director R.W. Pittack has shown how an agile, opportunistic camera can temper and sometimes even redeem a labored, overshrill telescript. This alchemy is standard practice in *The Twilight Zone*. In its often quiet, workmanly way, the camera editing and lighting effects of nearly every *Twilight Zone* show add vibrancy and depth to the treatment.

Conclusion

In 1988, Stephen Farber and Marc Green said of the Serling of *The Twilight Zone*, "At no time before or since was a single screenwriter given such freedom" (56). Most of us would agree that Serling used this freedom well. *The Twilight Zone* explores the possibilities of the ordinary in a chain of progressive revelations, each of which clamors for our attention long after the last surprise has been sprung. Conveying both the texture and the mood of experienced life, *The Twilight Zone* portrays human strength and weakness, evil and good, dream and crunchy reality. Serling's sensibility is formidable, and so is his video technique, even at its most pared down. An episode can move us by being poignant and intimate, rambunctious or thought-provoking. It can also be orchestrated as a set of intertwined plot developments or as a serial progression. But regardless of whether it takes place on an asteroid, in a city pool room, or in the backwoods, it will usually convey both a folklorist's eye for detail and the born raconteur's sense of pace. What's more, these gifts look unforced and natural, Serling knowing instinctively how heavy a burden he can place on his rhetorical and dramatic gifts. Much of *The Twilight Zone* is discreetly underscaled. Rather than cluttering the screen with high-tech gear, the show achieves most of its effects through nuance, body language, and dialogue that sounds simple, considered, and precise.

The makers of *The Twilight Zone* understood what could be gained from rhythm, understatement, and teamwork on a shooting set with actors playing their roles straight and suppressing avant-garde stylization. *The Twilight Zone* will be remembered deservedly for its exuberance and expansiveness. But what has lodged most in our imagination is the aptness, directness, and emotional justice of the series' twist endings. Even the events that don't move that plot have poetic authority that can both disclose and deepen the mystery. The nimble wit and buoyant spirit of a Serling, a Charles Beaumont, or a Richard Matheson serve a set of values that imbue the twist endings with sting and resonance. These men write swift, clean prose; they have an eye for significance in places where others would see none; they're gifted with a keen sense of the ridiculous. More surprisingly, the intensity they generate is tempered by understanding that leads to forgiveness, particularly of the self.

Serling, the show's guiding spirit, allowed a few simple ideas to galvanize his oeuvre. Although these ideas don't make him a philosopher or a social reformer, they suffice him as an artist. He pursues them show after show, creating stylistic and thematic interactions that express his inner world; scripts as different as "Walking Distance" (10/59) and "The Old Man in the Cave" (11/63) can give insights into that world that are equally trenchant, equally valuable. Thanks to his gift for making the abstract visible, he draws us quickly into the vortex of his characters' disorders. These disorders set forth an intensified version of reality. The characters seek stability while wavering between the seen and the unseen, sleep and wake, light and dark. Comparing *The Twilight Zone* to the narrative art of Henry James, Andrew Sarris notes the thematic link in the zone between character and revelation: "A motley array of loners, losers, misfits, wanderers, aliens, ghosts, malcontents, and victims of every description is let loose . . . and though the 'problem' is seldom, if ever, 'solved,' some insight or other is gained as a consolation" (48). Works like "The Eye of the Beholder" (11/60) or "A Hundred Yards over the Rim" (4/61) will portray both what happened and how it affected their people. Then, while showing why the transforming event happened as it did, the works attain that flametip of vision after which no character feels, believes, or acts as he/she once did. The episodes are packed with sharp insights, poetic images, and intriguing scenes often crowned by cunning reversals. No other TV anthology misdirects our attention so deftly; none succeeds better at puncturing our complacency.

The wheel, that medieval symbol of recurrence, retribution, and unity, flickers over the anthology. A vortex dominated the opening graphics of *The Twilight Zone*'s 1961-62 season, and both a clock and an eye appeared on screen when Serling introduced ("You're traveling through another dimension . . .") the 18 hour-long scripts comprising *The Twilight Zone*'s shortened 1963-64 season. The show's fifth season also features the wheel. As has been seen, Bob and Millie Frazier of "Stopover" (4/64) appear to us through the spokes of a wheel while intuiting their entrapment. The symbol voiced the same irrevocability in "You Drive" (1/64). The spinning wheel on the bicycle of the newsboy that Oliver Pope accidentally killed, and later, the clock in Pope's home both convey the might of the moral justice he's violating by trying to blame the newsboy's death on someone else. Before he can enjoy a second chance at happiness, he must confess his crime.

The exercise of the ensuing operation of moral justice occurs out of view, if it occurs at all. By testing our imagination, *The Twilight Zone* heightens our apprehension of reality. If the pig-snouted citizens of the police state of "Eye of the Beholder" are as beautiful as Janet Tyler is ugly, they're applying some aesthetic standard unknown to us, a standard we lack the information to evaluate. Analogously, the frozen people in "Elegy" (2/60) could be moving, just as the hour hand of a clock moves. Such possibilities bring us to a standstill. *The Twilight Zone* challenges our skepticism. Observing laws of its own, the series disallows both conclusive judgments and the cognitive habits they rest on. This scrambling of guidelines can be therapeutic. If a show like "Miniature" (2/63) persuades us that reason can miss the truth, then it has refreshed our awareness of our surroundings.

Showing us how to see the world anew is an extraordinary achievement, and *The Twilight Zone* deserves acclaim for managing this feat. On the other hand, the series earns no plaudits for artistic consistency. After its second season, *The Twilight Zone* dropped so far in quality that Serling left the show both to teach (at Antioch College) and to recharge his imagination. Nor would any discriminating viewer call the 65 scripts aired on CBS-TV during *The Twilight Zone*'s first two seasons uniformly topnotch. But so what? An Ibsen couldn't turn out an inspired script every week, even a half-hour one. Then there's the vexed question of the show's incompatibility with the hour format that CBS decreed for *The Twilight Zone*'s fourth season. Yet exploratory masterpieces like "Jess-Belle" (2/63) and "On Thursday We Leave for Home" (5/63) both belong to this mostly ill-judged season. These two works stand with 20 or 25 others from *The Twilight Zone* that are both dramatically compact and emotionally riveting. Such works remind viewers how much television can matter. The show's stumbles should be dismissed as minor. Much more noteworthy are its successes. The passion with which a Walter Jameson or a Horace Ford pursues his goals transcends the social atmosphere he helped define.

In the end, *The Twilight Zone*'s feats are both impressive and worthy; its failings minor. At its best, the show works handsomely. It was a brave original series that rarely missed an important detail. The odd pang of regret caused by one of its blemishes pales before the breakthrough it made in video art. This achievement has been duly noted. Ed Naha calls *The Twilight Zone* "the most important SF series ever televised" (35). According to Gary Gerani and Paul H. Schulman's wider frame of reference, it's "perhaps the brightest series ever on American television" (37); Schumer deems it "a legacy that continues to teach, entertain, and inspire" (22). All these critics are right. *The Twilight Zone* crowned television's golden age. Its vision and its craftsmanship assure it as honored a place in the history of teledrama as Ibsen enjoys in that of the modern stage. The show's influence on television is incalculable. And now that television has become our main connection to the public world, this influence could spread in ways we're maybe just starting to imagine.

Works Cited

Material by Rod Serling

Serling, Rod. "About Writing for Television." *Patterns*. 1-42.

——. "The Challenge of the Mass Media to the 20th Century Writer." *Journal of the Producers Guild of America* 10 Dec. 1968: 9-13.

——. "The Gamma Interview." *Gamma* 1963: 69-75.

——. *Into the Twilight Zone: A New Collection of Startling Explorations into the Realm of the Supernatural*. 1964. Mattituck, NY: Rivercity, 1976.

——. "A Machine to Answer the Question." *Rod Serling's Twilight Zone Magazine* Sept. 1982: 93-100.

——. *Patterns: Four Television Plays with the Author's Personal Commentaries*. New York: Simon and Schuster, 1957.

——. *Stories from the Twilight Zone*. Introduction T.E.D. Klein. Toronto: Bantam, 1986.

Other Material

Armstrong, F. Jeffrey. "Rod Serling (25 December 1924-28 June 1975)." *Dictionary of Literary Biography 26: American Screenwriters*. Ed. Robert E. Morsburger et al. Detroit: Gale: Bruccoli Clark, 1984: 285-88.

Barnouw, Erik. *Tube of Plenty: The Evolution of American Television*. Rev. ed. New York: Oxford UP, 1990.

Barron, James. "Rod Serling's Hometown Basks in His Twilight." *New York Times* 30 Jan. 1989: 13-14.

Breville, Linda. "Rod Serling's Last Interview." *Writer's Yearbook* 1976: 64-69.

Burrows, Thomas D., Donald N. Wood, and Lynne Schafer Gross. *Television Production: Disciplines and Techniques*. 5th ed. Dubuque: Brown, 1992.

"Education: Those Who Can." *Newsweek* 5 Nov. 1962: 108.

Eliot, Marc. *American Television: The Official Art of the Artificial*. Garden City: Doubleday, 1981.

Emshwiller, Peter R. "The Twilight Zone Review 1988: Television." *Rod Serling's Twilight Zone Magazine* Apr. 1989: 50-51.

Engel, Joel. Rod Serling: *The Dreams and Nightmares of Life in the Twilight Zone*. Chicago: Contemporary, 1989.

Farber, Stephen, and Marc Green. *Outrageous Conduct: Art, Ego, and The Twilight Zone Case*. New York: Morrow-Arbor House, 1988.

205

Fox, Richard Wightman. "The Reality Box." Rev. of *Unsilent Revolution: Television News and American Public Life, 1948-1991,* by Robert J. Donovan and Ray Scherer. *New York Times Book Review* 3 May 1992: 7.

Gerani, Gary, with Paul H. Schulman. *Fantastic Television.* New York: Harmony, 1977.

Greene, Bob. "Serling Was Trapped in a Real Twilight Zone." *St. Louis Post-Dispatch* 22 Oct. 1989: 16c.

Jonas, Gerald. "Science Fiction." *New York Times Book Review* 27 Oct. 1991: 30.

Joshi, S.T. "The Life and Work of Rod Serling." *Studies in Weird Fiction* 7 (Spring 1990): 22-28.

Kerbel, Michael. "The Golden Age of TV Drama" *Television: The Critical View.* 3rd ed. Ed. Horace Newcomb. New York: Oxford UP, 1982. 47-63.

Le Guin, Ursula K. Introduction. *The Norton Book of Science Fiction: North American Science Fiction, 1960-1990.* Ed. Ursula K. Le Guin and Brian Attebery. New York: Norton, 1993. 3-28.

Lofficier, Jean-Marc, and Randy Lofficier. *Into the Twilight Zone: The Rod Serling Programme Guide.* London: Virgin, 1995.

Mack, John E. *Abduction: Human Encounters with Aliens.* New York: Scribner, 1994.

Naha, Ed. "Rod Serling's Dream." *Starlog* Oct. 1978: 35-39.

Olshaker, Mark. "Requiem for a Heavyweight: Final Tribute." *New Times* 25 July 1974: 68.

Parker, James Edward. "Rod Serling's 'The Twilight Zone': A Critical Examination of Religious and Moralistic Themes and Motifs Presented in the Film Noir Style." Diss. Ohio U, 1987.

Quinn, Robert Samuel. "A Study of the Selected Teleplays of Rod Serling." Diss. U of Wisconsin, 1966.

Rabkin, Eric S. Introduction. *Science Fiction: A Historical Anthology.* Ed. Eric S. Rabkin. New York: Oxford UP, 1983.

Reach, James. *Patterns: A Drama in Three Acts.* Adapted from the Television Play by Rod Serling. New York: French, 1959.

Rosenbaum, Bob. "Life with Rod: A Conversation with Carol Serling." *Rod Serling's Twilight Zone Magazine* Apr. 1987: 46-50.

Sander, Gordon F. *Serling: The Rise and Twilight of Television's Last Angry Man.* New York: Dutton, 1992.

Sarris, Andrew. "Rod Serling: Viewed from Beyond 'The Twilight Zone.'" *Rod Serling's Twilight Zone Magazine* Apr. 1985: 45-49.

Schrader, Paul. "Notes on Film Noir." *Film Comment* 8 (Spring 1972): 8-13.

Schumer, Arlen, "The Museum of Radio Broadcast Communications [Chicago] Presents an Afternoon with Arlen Schumer." Speech given to the Rod Serling Memorial Foundation. Unpublished VCR cassette, 27 June 1991.

——. *Visions from The Twilight Zone.* San Francisco: Chronicle, 1990.

"Serling, (Edward) Rod(man) 1924-1975." *Contemporary Authors, 65-68.* Ed. Jane A. Bowden. Detroit: Gale, 1977. 533-34.

"Serling, Rod (1924-1975)." *The Encyclopedia of Science Fiction.* Ed. John Clute and Peter Nicholls. New York: St. Martin's, 1993. 1086-87.

Stein, Ellin. "Inside the National Box." Rev. of *Serling,* by Gordon F. Sander. *New York Times Book Review* 18 Jan. 1993: 20.

Straczynski, J. Michael. "Scripts: Adventures in *The Twilight Zone.*" *Writer's Digest* Dec. 1988: 7-21.

——, and Kathryn M. Drennan. "A Show-By-Show Guide to Rod Serling's Night Gallery." *Rod Serling's Twilight Zone Magazine* Oct. 1985: 74-80.

"Tale of a Script." *Time* 30 June 1958: 36.

Updike, John. "Books: The Flaming Chalice." *New Yorker* 26 Feb. 1990: 126-30.

Venuti, Lawrence. "Rod Serling, Television Censorship, 'The Twilight Zone.'" *Western Humanities Review* 35 (Winter 1981): 354-66.

Wallace, Mike. "What TV Censors Won't Let You See." *True* Mar. 1961: 286.

Williams, Raymond. *Television: Technology and Cultural Form.* New York: Schocken, 1975.

Wolcott, James. "On Television: X' Factor." *New Yorker* 18 Apr. 1994: 98-99.

Zicree, Marc Scott. *The Twilight Zone Companion.* Toronto: Bantam, 1982.

Ziegler, Robert E. "Moving Out of Sight: Fantastic Vision in *The Twilight Zone.*" *Lamar Journal of the Humanities* 13 (Fall 1987): 33-40.

Index

209

Schmitt